woman in hiding

A True Tale of Backdoor Abuse, Dark Secrets & Other Evil Deeds

Kathleen Hoy Foley

Published in the United States by Women in Hiding Press.
www.womeninhidingpress.org

Artwork by Kathleen Hoy Foley
Artwork Photographed by Bryan M.S. Minnix
Back Cover Photograph by Philip Foley
Copy edit by Dina Forbes
Composition by Bob Bovasso and Liz Geary

Cataloging-in-Publication Data is on file with the Library of Congress.
Library of Congress Control Number: 2010940740
Foley, Kathleen Hoy
  Woman in Hiding / A True Tale of Backdoor Abuse, Dark Secrets & Other Evil Deeds
    p. cm.

ISBN-13: 978-0-9828558-0-5 (print)
ISBN-13: 978-0-9828558-1-2 (ebook)

PRINTED IN THE UNITED STATES OF AMERICA
10 9 8 7 6 5 4 3 2 1

FIRST EDITION

This work is dedicated to

Phil

I never understood. Now I do. You saved my life.

to

Jackie, *my brother....*

to

every victim of sexual abuse ~ past and present

Your story is vitally important.

Your voice of truth is beautiful.

Each time you speak you grow stronger.
Each time you speak you chase away more of the darkness
where broken girls, dispirited women, and terrified children hide.
Each time you speak you ease the burden and illuminate the way
for another victim.
Each time you speak, the shame of sexual violation is lessened.
Each time you speak you help another abuse victim find her voice.

to

every single person of courage and compassion

who chooses to stand fearlessly in the fire with a victim as she
struggles to confront and understand her ordeal...bless you.
Truly, you are helping to save her life.

FIRST WORDS

I will speak
I will speak
I will speak
I will speak
I will speak
I will speak
I will speak
I will speak
I will speak
I will speak
I will speak
I will speak
I will speak
I will speak
I will speak
I will speak
I will speak
I will speak
I will speak
I will speak
I will speak
I will speak
I will speak
I will speak
I will speak

I will speak
I will speak

I will speak
I will speak

I will speak
I will speak
I will speak

I. will. SPEAK.
OUT LOUD.

ouch. ouch. ouch.

step by step

KATHLEEN HOY FOLEY

My hands cease belonging to me as they tremble, bowing to a will that is not mine. I do not want to move for fear the moment will vaporize and I will wake up and flatten beneath the understanding that all along I have been bobbing on a dream, and the font of joy sitting in my lap will drift into the night, out of reach of my grasping fingers. I dip my hand into the pile. And as if I am opening my mouth for the first taste of fudge, I begin to salivate.

I draw an envelope away from the rest. I hold my mother, the mystery of who she was as a girl, in my hands. And the gift of such a privilege — to cradle a wingless bird — makes me feel like a gentle giant, and I caution myself to be extra careful, to treat this creature with reverence, because I am about to get an extraordinary, one-time-only peek into the so very well hidden past. But I am also about to sin; I can feel its bulk prodding my delight, because in my family, only the briefest, most cursory of nods to personal history are tolerated.

Exploring the past is equivalent to spitting on God; I know that. And what I am about to do is punishable. But I close my eyes against the threat of getting caught, because the yearning to touch my mother, to experience her so closely that it seems an embrace against the soothing beat of her heart, is much stronger than any punishment I can visualize. At night as I lie in bed in my room where screams sweep beneath the closed door, I will now be able to lull myself to sleep with my images and imaginations of her stirred by the letters I hold.

Close by, the clock with its pit-pat, pit-pat sounds a bit like rain dropping against a window. The first envelope has Nellie Weaver of Fieldsboro printed neatly in the return address: Aunt Nellie, the once-striking ingénue left at the altar by her prettier fiancé. Perking my ears to any sounds of the car pulling up in the driveway, I remove the letter and unfold it and begin reading, barely blinking my eyes. At first I don't understand. Then I feel the color drain from my face as a rush of confusion dives to the pit of my stomach and crouches there, quivering like a knot of rubber bands. I read and reread the words that have no attachment to any meaning I can comprehend — just a dizzying swoop and plunge of unspooling symbols, stripped of sense.

Adopt. Jack will adopt Kathleen. He looks like her father anyway — they have the same nose. No one will ever question it.

Aunt Nellie's words, written in rounded, childlike script, keep sliding off the lined paper as if they are oiled. I don't understand. I can't understand. I grab another envelope, yank out the yellowing paper. Then another. Love letters. To Jack from Pat, dated long after my birth. To Buzz, my father's first pet name for my mother, professing his unwavering love for her and for little Kathleen. They would simply shift the date of their official wedding back a couple of years to include enough time for a baby to make an appearance — for Kathleen's birth.

A sandstorm of panic whips and pelts me, biting me from every side, blistering my skin, singeing my eyes. What does it mean? What does it mean? As surely as if the Communists had goose-stepped to 14 Beaumont Road and lobbed a live shell into the center of the house, the structure of my life as I understand it explodes. How can this be? How can my father not be my father?

The panic of that fact, the sheer hopelessness of being adrift with no solid ground underneath my feet, even though what is beneath me is ugly and stained, the anguish of John J. Allen not being my father, boils over into wheezing, hulking gasps; tears and snot flood thick and sticky, unstoppable, down my cheeks, into my mouth, clogging my throat, choking me.

Maybe I'm wrong. Maybe I misunderstood. Yes, I am a reader, devouring library books by the dozens during summers. But even I can make a mistake. Misunderstand the meanings of words I don't know.

I read the letters over and over, wiping my face on my sleeves, until my tears dry up, leaving my eyes waterless and gritty, and all that remains are dry sobs, something like the dry heaves — what's left after all the vomit has spewed from your stomach. No, there is no mistake. And there is no way back to innocence. John J. Allen is not my father.

~ ~ ~

I paid the price for pretending I did not see what I saw, and I fell early into bed exhausted, my eyes smarting from tears shed and tears strangled right at the brink of falling. With my knees drawn in tight, I pulled the thin blanket up until it covered everything except my eyes and stared at the pink and yellow flowers fading into the night. Tomorrow. I would return to the closet tomorrow. Maybe I didn't read what I thought I'd read. Maybe, in a swirl of girlish musing, I had invented the letters speaking of my adoption. Tomorrow I would make sure. Tomorrow I would read all the letters; surely there were explanations. Maybe Aunt Nellie was merely a good storyteller, her script an outline for a romance she fancied in her head. Maybe adoption did not apply to me after all. Maybe I'd misread the dates in my mother and father's love letters. Maybe I had actually discovered the true romantic stories from my mother's past I'd always longed for, sentimental chronicles that would bolster me and lull me to sleep in the bedroom that had become a hiding place.

I would have to make sure. Tomorrow I would make things right. That was my hope; it was not what I believed. I knew darkness when I came upon it. And I knew beyond doubt that what ambushed me in the shadows of that closet was the truth. A harsh and dirty truth. I hated my father for stealing my mother from me, and that night I roamed inside that hate that glowed like an ember refusing to die. I wrapped myself in its comfort, in its shelter; luxuriating in its veil of soft, downy plushness, hoarding it as I would fine jewels, polishing it like a rare stone. And retrieved an incident and played and replayed it until I fell into a fitful sleep.

~ ~ ~

Though I know I can't get away with it, I open the rear door and start to climb into the backseat. "I'm not your chauffer," he says, his tone heavy already with anger. "Get in the front." It's a command. I steal a glance at my mother standing on the front steps ready to wave good-bye, pointlessly begging her with my eyes to rescue me, and slide into the passenger's seat, huddling as close to my window as I can get. John J. Allen, bow tie in place, pipe clenched between his teeth, drops behind the steering wheel, waves to my mother, and before the station wagon reaches the end of the driveway, begins his tirade. I've heard it all before. I hear it every time I am trapped alone in this seat beside him. It is how I come to know who I am — disgraceful and ugly.

"You want to know something?" He always begins this way, as if I have been waiting, wanting to hear from him. "You're nothing but a snob." I can't look away because that would signify disrespect, which would cost me a privilege. "I don't ever want to see you ignore a neighbor again." I nod. I don't remember ever ignoring anyone, but somehow he's seen me withhold a wave, I guess. Sometimes I walk down the street lost in a fog of daydreams; maybe that's when I missed someone's greeting. I will have to do better, pay more mind to the wants of others. "I won't have everybody around here thinking my daughter is stuck-up. Do you hear me?" I nod. "Then say something, damn it." "Yes," I reply, looking toward him. "And you better help around the house more. You're the laziest thing I've ever seen. You don't do one damn thing around the house. Don't you think your mother deserves some help?"

I know now to speak so he can hear. "Yes," I say, squeezing my hands colorless, pressing closer into the door that I wish would fling open and hurl me onto South Broad Street. "I've never seen anybody with such a miserable sense of humor, you know that? I'm sick of seeing your sour puss moping around the house." I don't know what to say anymore; I try nodding. My jaw aches from gritting my teeth, my head is pounding. I wonder if being imprisoned and tortured by Communists could be any worse than being locked in this car beside John J. Allen as he rants on about my failures and worthlessness. Yes, I decide it could be worse; being hacked to death must be agony beyond description. Being gnawed away bite by bite is something you grow used to.

"And I don't want to hear any more of your lip," he snarls. My body is as heavy as wet sand, my arm hardly lifts as I direct my hand to wipe away the sweat collecting on my upper lip. "Do you hear me? Do you hear me?" I mutter, "Yes." "I didn't hear what you said," he replies, jerking his head toward me, then back to the road, then back to me. "What did you say?" "Yes, I hear you," I say, louder this time. He goes on, "You don't appreciate a damn thing your mother and I do for you. None of you kids do."

I am very, very close to tears; they are stinging my eyes. "Yes I do, Daddy." I cry. "I appreciate what you do." But I don't know what he's talking about. Is he talking about food? The three meals plus snacks I consume every day? Is he talking about my having my own bedroom? Or does he mean the dreaded, endless Sunday drives through miles and miles of parched pine trees where the wind licks the melting tar and blows its hotness into the car windows, making all the kids ornery? "No you don't," he says. "All you do is gripe!"

On and on it goes — the recitation of my despicable behavior, a list of my sins it seems he compiles daily — for the entire ride to Trenton, to his office, where as the daughter of John J. Allen I will be expected to be gracious and friendly. And as he spits out his venom, I gather up his loathing for me and pull it over my head and wear it as I would a winter sweater whose weight slumps my shoulders and tugs my bones downward. And as always, I join forces against myself and abandon the young girl locked in the car beside a man gone angry.

~ ~ ~

In my rush to leave the closet before getting caught, maybe I bumped the tidy row of high heels and sent them toppling like dominos one after the other. Or despite my best efforts to place the envelopes back in the box just so with hands I couldn't control, maybe I left them out of order. I knew that Aunt Nellie's was on top. But what about the others? The love letters with their professions of passion and angst? I had snatched them out so quickly that I forgot to study how they were arranged. When I shoved the shoebox back into the dark, did I not take enough time to place it exactly as I had found it?

Somehow I had left a trail, a telltale sign that I had been where I was not supposed to be and had seen what was never meant for my eyes. Because the next day, when the house was once again quiet and I was alone, I tiptoed to the closet to read the letters once more, this time slowly, calmly. But they were gone. Vanished as if they never existed. The closet was neat, orderly as before, only this time no secrets lurked in the shadows. There was no proof — no confirmation of the words that had burned and blurred my eyes. I knelt down, reached to the back, again and again. Stood up, stretched my arm onto the top shelf, patting and patting where I couldn't see, searching for the shoebox. I hunted behind clothes draped on hangers. Dug around the castoffs, pushing my hands under every worn blouse and faded pair of pedal pushers folded carefully in the corner.

Nothing. No hint of the ambush, as shocking as slabs of cement dropping from a tranquil sky that only yesterday had demolished the structure that was my life. No clue of the blow that had left me staggering with shock, dangling in confusion high above a house that now looked make-believe, ready to cave in from the impact. I had to see the letters again. I had to. I kept searching, searching, thrusting my hands into the dark. They were there; they had to be. Somehow I'd missed them. Where were they? I needed to hold them, touch them just once more. That was all. I needed to concentrate, study the words until I understood what they meant. I needed to figure everything out.

But they were gone as if they had never sat in the dark waiting to tattle. As if they were just an illusion fashioned from cobwebs and fog and the silly wonderings of a child. How could that be, though, because they were real. I'd held paper in my hands, saw the handwriting — the loops and swirls, the exclamation points, all of it. I know I did. Now if only I could see them again just to make sure I had read what I thought I'd read. Because maybe I was mistaken. Maybe I had made it all up, just like the stories I scribbled onto lined paper.

No, that couldn't be it. I'd felt my life crumble in those words. I knew what I knew. I just had to be positive, check one more time. But the shoebox had spooked. Reared up and escaped just as sure as if it had mighty legs attached. It wouldn't matter if I ripped everything out of the closet piece by piece; I wasn't going to find it.

I ran back to my bedroom and threw myself on top of my bed, rocking and rocking, eyes closed to all that was familiar — the flowers splashed across my walls, pictures of Elvis and Ricky Nelson thumbtacked amongst them — rocking, sobbing into my pillow. Every kid ever born wonders if they are adopted. And I, cocky at the laughable impossibility and long before the discovery in her closet, had asked my own mother, "Mommy, am I adopted?" — giggling when I posed the question because it was so absurd. And she confirmed my certainty, effortlessly, without hesitation. As easily as if I had asked if we were having grilled cheese sandwiches and tomato soup for dinner on Friday, a question I already knew the answer to. Not for a second did she change her expression or grasp for words. Just, "Of course you're not adopted." Back then, finding out you were adopted was a kid's worst nightmare. There weren't a whole lot of families in suburbia breaking up because of divorce, and drug-addled teenagers had yet to storm the schools, so adoption and Communists were the big threats.

And there I was, adopted — halfway or all the way didn't matter. I was adopted, and I couldn't find a way for it to make sense. Buzzing insects took up residence inside my skull, drowning out the quiet I needed so that I could peel apart the nightmare. I had to figure out how one day I was an average girl with a father and mother and four younger brothers, then the next day a fatherless stranger untethered in family now so altered.

I don't have a father. I rolled that statement around and around inside my head. Said it out loud. Sobbed it into the silence of my room. Tried to make it untrue, but I couldn't erase it. Whether or not I ever saw the letters again, I knew it to be real, and I hated the deadweight of it. The way the gravity of this new truth pressed me into the mattress made even opening my eyes a chore that I could not manage as I curled tighter into my bed. The letters that held in them understanding, perhaps solace, words that could have helped me to somehow reorder my new life, had been snatched away, thrown into the land of secrets and silence.

How would I put together a puzzle with most of the pieces missing? Wade through a pile of debris and try to organize it? Where would I start when even my bedroom with my triple-mirrored vanity, where each night I sat and brushed my hair 100 times, seemed as alien as the freshly washed clothes folded neatly in my bureau and the *Photoplay* magazines stashed under my bed? The image of my life now seemed a berserk kite whirling out of control, pulling away from my grasp. Refusing command, no matter how hard I tugged the line. Diving and twisting in crazy spirals toward the ground, swooping up toward the sky, plunging again.

Even as I lay there wallowing in a lake of sorrow, I knew that shortly the station wagon would roll into the driveway, and before chaos invaded the quiet, I would have to pull myself off my bed, swipe at my eyes, and go downstairs where I was expected. I couldn't let anyone see that I'd been crying; the swollen redness of my eyes would give my father something to play with and I might not be able to distract him from his game that could grow serious very quickly, falling into accusations as he sensed guilt lurking beneath my flush.

If I allowed panic to overtake me when I saw them, if I melted into the realization of what this shock meant and I snapped, if I screamed my fool head off because I didn't know how else to cope, it would be like getting caught with my face in the closet. I could deny the truth all I wanted, but they would know. Even if I didn't confess in actual words, by the clairvoyance of parenthood, they would see through my lies and I'd be snared in a trap I would never be able to spring. Snooping around where I didn't belong was no different from spying on my parents as they shared the bathroom, ogling them as they stood together stark naked.

No, I could never admit to my visit to the closet or cast even the tiniest whiff of what I now knew. Not to my mother, not to anyone. If my parents discovered what I had done, punishment would be certain and severe, and without question would include humiliation of the type I could not even conceive, born loud and vicious out of John J. Allen's disgust of me, now justified by my sneakiness. He would slam me with a fresh list of my failures until he could at last get me to admit what a poor excuse for a daughter I was.

Nor could I risk my mother's wrath, laser-aimed at me — a snap of cold in the middle of summer, quiet, frozen, and immobilizing. Her stare as empty as a mannequin's, never again to be warmed over, no matter how much I begged. I would be banished from her good graces, placed on her list with all the others who had dared raise her molten ire, forever expelled from her affection. And forever with my mother meant forever. There was no way back. Nothing you could do to right your grievous error. No apologies accepted. No absolution granted. When she was finished with you, that was the end of it. You might as well pack your bags and leave.

From just above my left shoulder I watched myself suck in a deep breath, stand up, straighten my clothes, and wipe the sorrow from my face. I was pleased with such a simple, complete action on my own behalf. By the magic of *poof and it's gone*, the secret that seconds ago felt like a death pulsing with life, burrowed into the dark — a burial ground of sorts where I suspected it would shrivel up and waste away, just another day's dust.

Suddenly, my life fell back into right. Well, not exactly, but close enough. Me, my parents, my brothers, all back in place, but listing slightly sideways. Even though my feet felt the floor beneath them and my room looked recognizable, everything had the spongy feel of a fruit past prime.

They were home. The racket of feet thumped across wooden floors, and the rise of voices in need echoed up the few stairs into my room. I plastered a broad smile on my face, a smile I was sure would overcome any lingering signs of tears. From the peaceful, comfortable space above my shoulder, I watched myself descend the stairs — floating, it seemed, in gauze — and into the mess that signified life in a large family. It was odd, that newborn business of cloud-walking, but I liked the tranquility of poking along behind myself, watching the show play out in front of my eyes. Everyone was there — my mother, my father, all the boys: Jackie, Bobby, Paul, and Tommy. And me, moseying a few beats behind the commotion, my life now on five-second delay.

CHAPTER 3

Jackie

Most people don't know this, but my brother Jackie was the cause of the Cuban missile crisis, the unrest in China, and, in family legend, all my father's heart attacks. If you have enough patience and the intelligence to back it up, you can also trace the cause of cancer back to the person of John J. Allen, Jr. — Jackie, for short. Never to be confused with senior.

What's more, in your research you will find that I, his sister, was a true hero because I did my part, though unsuccessfully, to foil all those worldly and familial disasters, following the examples set by the adults on 14 Beaumont Road. You need to know that I took it very seriously, this responsibility to beat back this scourge undermining our society and the Allen family. So seriously, in fact, that if good fortune had cast its glowing light on me and I had actually killed my brother Jackie, wrung the life from him with my very own hands, beaten him senseless about the head until blood spurted from his ears and he finally ceased to breathe, I would have stood up, glared at him, given him one last punch in the face for good measure, and turned and walked away — most likely back to my room, where I'd flop on my bed, grab a *Photoplay*, and revel in my status as a hero.

It never occurred to me to love my brothers. Nor did it cross my mind that my parents did either, since I measured love by affection and kindness, and that seemed to vanish after babyhood stretched into gangly limbs and exasperating attitudes that couldn't be amused away with a rattle. The boys were nuisances, unruly and noisy. Jackie, worst of all, was branded with an acute, sneaky hostility and the keen ability to work his wrath beneath my skin. When I was eleven years old, my parents started leaving me in charge of the four of them. Nobody asked, but I would have preferred to be chained to a wheelbarrow full of boulders and forced to push it uphill.

While my parents aimed for strikes and settled for spares at the White Horse Bowling Alley, laughing, pulling in long drags of smoke — my mother from Raleigh cigarettes, my father from well-gnawed pipes — and faked freedom, I was seething, floundering in a whirlpool of chaos. Maybe their nights fled by in a riot of wooden pins scattering across waxed alleys and spirited camaraderie and ended too soon, leaving them hungry for more. Maybe slapping down royal flushes in noisy penny ante games or sharing popcorn at the movies felt like ingesting illicit drugs, igniting a rush of ecstasy they hadn't felt since falling in love. Maybe those leisurely dinners taken at the diner in Bordentown or the shows they cheered at the Latin Casino, where Liberace or Snooky Lanson camped and crooned for well-dressed patrons, made them feel young, sexy. Unburdened.

My nights, though, did not speed by in a blur of careless celebration. My hours inched and clawed along through squabbles and tears. Threats. *I'm telling!* Punishing blows. Breaking up fights. And my anger was so ripe, so visible, that no parents in their right minds would have left me in charge of their children.

I just wanted the boys to leave me alone. Let me be with my fantasies and daydreams and romantic notions of being an only child or at least one of just two kids in a neat and tidy family. A family that didn't stir up snide glances of disapproval for its brood-like size or gawking stares when John J. Allen decided to disregard public scrutiny and reduce a child to tears or stunned silence with the back of his hand or words meant to scald and degrade. But what did little boys know or care about the emotional well-being of their sister? They acted crazy wild, creatures sprung from their cages, spinning with liberty, shouting, fighting.

Jackie was always the instigator, but all of them refused any reason. Until I got the belt. Not just any belt, but the belt that would bite and sting and hurt the most. The one that would shut them up, settle them down. The plastic number with the blue stripe down the center. It had heft and balance. I imagined it to be a whip used to corral renegades. And I would swing that strap hard, snapping it across their young bodies with crisp licks. I can still picture Tommy standing beside his bed upstairs in the attic room that resembled an orphanage dormitory, wearing powder-blue pajamas patterned with tiny cowboys sporting Stetsons and fringed chaps. I swatted him. He laughed at me, taunting, daring me with his little-boy bravado. Brave. Foolish. Because my rage was nothing to toy with.

He could not know, nor could I, that my wrath was a fire provoked by more than bratty rowdiness. The more he laughed, the harder I swung, cracking that belt like a bullwhip, landing blow after stinging blow until he dissolved in tears. Until the four of them dissolved into tears. Powerful tears. That's what I was after: the sobs that convinced me that they understood that they had to stop fighting and shut up — and most of all, *leave...me ... alone.* I never got in trouble for beating them. It was my job, third in line behind my parents; that's just how they were kept in lockstep.

But when I wasn't in charge, I stood aloof from my brothers, outside of their noise and activities. Uninterested in them. Preferring the quiet of my room, latched onto a book or drifting through romance magazines and spinning my dreams. Detached on family day trips, I sat in the front seat next to my mother, peacefully encased in my imagination, staring out the window, hypnotized by the barren countryside snaking past sun-baked shacks and crops lying crisped in farmer's fields, inhaling earthy scents and exhaust fumes swelling up from the road, completely indifferent to the ruckus escalating in the back. I did not even flinch or bother to pull my attention from the passing landscape when the station wagon weaved and lurched as my father yelled and swung his right arm into the backseat brawl, attempting to restore order while trying to hold the car on course with his left, as we barreled down the road toward fun.

Only Jackie broke through my off-duty trances, and the desire to kill him lived in my fists until the day I was married at nineteen years old. A few weeks before my wedding, when Jackie was more than half a foot taller than my five feet two inches, I took a bicycle pump to his head. On the morning of my actual wedding day, just after the bouquets of yellow roses and pink carnations were delivered, in the presence of the bridesmaids dressed in their sapphire-blue gowns, I raged at Jackie until I was hoarse and sweaty and seconds from going for his throat. Did I mention that he started it? That he always started it? Always. And I always finished it. Always. Because I took the bait every time.

Jackie's rage did not boil over in a splatter of foot stomps and defiant stares. That would have been simple, "march right up to your room" manageable. No, his fury was low and fierce. Sly, as he discharged taunt after taunt until he happened upon a sensitive spot to target, and with a smirk would pound and pound until it exploded back in his face. Not unlike our father.

John J. Allen liked to snatch my diary out of my hands and hold it up over my head, laughing and waving it out of my reach. My little red book was a chronicle of my deepest secrets. My crushes. My true loves. In its pastel pages, I swooned over cute boys and untouchable rock-and-roll heartthrobs — Fabian, Frankie Avalon, Elvis — pouring out my angst and what lived deep inside my soul. I drew swirls and hearts and intertwined my name with boys I swore I would love forever.

As John J. Allen brandished my mourning scribblings and aching desires far out of my reach, I clawed at his chest, jumping up, trying to grasp it, screaming, crying. He'd laugh and keep waving the book above my head. "Say please," he'd say. I'd say anything just to get it back before he read it. "Please," I would beg, sobbing. "Pretty please," he'd demand. "Say pretty please." "Pretty please," I'd shriek, lurching and grabbing at air. "What's so secret in here that you don't want me to see?" he'd tease, then make a grand gesture of opening and reading it. "No! No!" I'd howl. "Say please with sugar on top," he'd say, riffling through the pages. "Please with sugar on top," I'd wail at the top of my lungs, crying, sobbing. "Say uncle," he'd say. "Uncle!" I'd scream.

And it would go on until he tired of the game or my mother said, "Jack," in a calm tone that had a kind of warning hidden in it. "Here," he'd say. "Crybaby." I'd clutch my diary in my hands, tight against my heart, unable to unwind my hysteria, and slink away like a kicked animal hoarding a tattered piece of soiled meat.

Jackie used the same technique of goading as John J. Allen. Only Jackie, the hated kid, was powerless, and I wasn't. Remember, I had rank as third-in-command disciplinarian. Eleven years old and I could wield a belt as ferociously as my father, my swing fueled by a force beyond myself. It made me a hero and granted me status in a family so crowded with needs and out-of-control emotions. Beating up Jackie only enhanced the one success I could claim alongside my infinite list of failures.

Like John J. Allen, Jackie constantly crashed through the crystal bubble of my daydreams, wrenching me from enchanted ballerina fantasies where, bathed in petal-pink tulle, I flawlessly executed pirouettes and elongated leaps that would have me soaring free over trees and great bodies of water. He jerked me into his world of crackling hisses and lightning strikes of spite, no different from John J. Allen's startling, thundering crashes through my bedroom door. Suddenly I would be surrounded with the blast and racket of Jackie's anger, pushing and prodding, tormenting me with a laugh that had nothing to do with humor but emerged full-blown, raw with antagonism, from some frightening place inside his bones.

I never circled him. There was no cat-and-mouse testing of strength. I was not interested in playing games. I wanted to kill him. I paraded punch after punch into the cackling that would not cease. Beating pulpy, hairless flesh with my fists, each hit harder than the last, slamming him in the face, in the neck, whatever exposed skin I could reach. Pinching soft tissue between my fingers until I could feel the bones of my thumb and forefinger fusing in agreement to hurt, and hurt bad. Pounding him with fury that seemed God-given, bottomless. And still he laughed. Spurring me into hitting harder and harder until my breath jammed in my throat, exploding my lungs, and spittle foamed at the corners of my mouth. Screeching until all that remained were guttural barks. Until I was an animal baring its teeth in rage. Slapping, hitting.

And still he laughed, collapsing onto his back, whipping his legs and feet in the air, kicking. And still I went after him, immune to his cheap, imitation Converse high-tops flailing like propellers, his hands and arms crossed over his head, trying to keep me away but at the same time issuing invitation after invitation with his laugh. I wanted to kill him. Bash the life right out of his body. And in the monumental frustration that had boiled and solidified into the hate that feasted on my flesh in that house on Beaumont Road, I would have, had I not run out of fight.

Long before he gulped down LSD and injected heroin into every vein that wasn't collapsed, Jackie was a skinny kid with big ears and a lazy eye that rolled in toward his nose and had him wearing a patch for a while. As I did, he lived in a house where harsh responses, the spitting-mad anger, the heavy-handed striking out, seemed reserved for missteps in protocol, violations of arbitrary rules. Like too much fooling around. The rule on that one was murky, liable to change daily. Or the "two pieces of toilet paper per visit to the bathroom" law. Though I can't be sure how this was calculated by John J. Allen, but he was a numbers man, so maybe there was a ledger with red and black ink entries stashed somewhere out of sight. Two sheets per visit. That was the rule. And the three-minute phone call decree, enforced by John J. Allen with minute-by-minute, increasingly loud warnings. At exactly three minutes, he would march over, and even if you were in the middle of listening to your friend crying about the death of her mother, he would push the button, disconnecting you. No amount of begging or tears could get him to relent.

But the truly disturbing situations, the ones that should gouge your heart and have you sweating blood — like when neighborhood bullies tied Jackie to a tree in the woods near Gropp's Lake and beat him mercilessly, leaving him hanging there for who knows how long — seemed to float along in a fuzzy state of suspended animation. No shroud of shocked disbelief hovered over the family. No circling of wagons to embrace him, offer him protection or healing. No tiptoeing about, speaking in hushed, gentle tones because one of us had been hurt, as even babies do instinctively when they sense the suffering of someone they love.

There was just a vague sense of shoulders being shrugged, a sensation that maybe he got what he deserved. Maybe it was no different from the beatings John J. Allen frequently administered, which Jackie brought on himself anyway. There was nothing but an eerie, encompassing impression of empty. Of nonchalance. Surely a horrifying incident to witness or read about on paper, but in our family, it was an ordeal that left no permanent footprint, except on the spirit of an unimportant young boy.

So there we were, Jackie and I, locked in a torrid feud, acting out anger as pure as glacier ice, unsullied by posturing and hollow accusations. Me going straight for the kill. Him daring me to do it. Trapped in a bizarre, mystical rite of flying fists and saliva. Were we merely venting? Two combustible kids, tapping into our own separate reservoirs of fury? Or were we warriors for hire, our role in the group to absorb all the turbulent emotions and grievances of seven people? Enacting everyone's turmoil?

I don't know. But we bare-knuckle brawled, battling until all that was left for us was sweat-lathered exhaustion. And for the listeners, sequestered and unseen with ears perked, it was a crude, makeshift orgasm, leaving them with a sense of release as peace settled over drying beads of perspiration. The younger boys exhilarated with relief. The grown-ups with the urge to light a cigarette. The combatants driven back to their respective corners until next time.

For sure our fights were matches of good versus evil. Jackie, always the instigator, was the villain. I, the responder, was hailed as the hero. Though not in words. There were no actual cheering sections cordoned off, no shouts of encouragement as I ripped hair from his scalp. Only afterwards, when I basked in the glow of coded, satisfied glances and tight-lipped nods, did I glimpse the "she showed *him*" attitude that made me feel as if I'd conquered the evil I believed I was fighting.

Jackie never stood a chance. Nobody cared about the little boy who devoured stacks of superhero comic books. Or the artist who drew intricate, complicated pictures. Who could even take notice of such sweetness for all his incessant, antagonizing anger? Even a Sunday morning, with everybody spit and polished, trailing our gussied-up mother, prayer books and rosary beads in hand, all set to leave for Mass, seemed as good a time as any for Jackie to turn it into an occasion for a thrashing. Who can remember what he did? His defiance was constant, always fierce enough to draw nasty ass-chewings chased by thudding, cracking body blows.

One day, in less time than it would take to make the sign of the cross, as mellow rays of early-morning light streamed in past the ruffled café curtains and glanced off the gleaming porcelain sink, spilling into a spotlight onto the speckled tile, Jackie was down on the kitchen floor, his feet whipping the air, his arms crisscrossed over his face. The rumpus of my mother's threats and curses bounced off the stove and the refrigerator and the toaster that produced only burnt leavings. It invaded the cabinets stashed with dishes and cookware and rattled her collection of goofy salt and pepper shakers lining open shelves. And beneath the din of thumping and smacking and my mother's hollering, "Don't you dare kick me, damn it," an undercurrent — the swish, swish of starched-stiff crinoline whisking against crisp cotton and seamed nylon stockings. And, oh, was her dress beautiful: a swing and sway of vines and flowers, its hues — ruby and black — intensified in the beam of light. The grand circle skirt was a dancing garden as she straddled my brother and clobbered him, balancing on peek-a-boo high heels, spinning her arms like a windmill come loose. Looking like a world-class lady wrestler, only better dressed.

And what witness could forget the hat? A black velvet, cut-out little thing with a dramatic fishnet mini veil that angled and dropped halfway down her forehead, making for mystery if you were starring in a grade B whodunit. A half hat, actually, the type that all suburban ladies in the fifties and sixties tacked to their scalps with black bobby pins and wore to church and funerals, and other occasions calling for a bit of over-the-top dress-up. That hat was having its own party on top of my mother's head, bobbing and flapping, hanging onto those lacquered curls for dear life. And could my mother, as little as she was, lay down a string of cuss words. And land a good solid punch or two during a licking, as well.

My brother, you had to give it to him, never stopped laughing. Though he never pulled that stunt with John J. Allen: Jackie understood that provoking a tyrant could mean something even he didn't have the stomach to contemplate. No, he only employed the laughing bit with my mother and me, and it kept her going until she couldn't lift her arms anymore. After spending her anger, my mother stood up, stepped over Jackie, smoothed down her dress, and wiggled that hat back into place. Then off we went, in silence, to eight o'clock Mass at St. Raphael's, Jackie baring scarlet welts and fevered handprints.

Every Sunday my mother and the five of us filed into the same pew: second row back, directly in front of Sister Thomas Marie and her posse of saintly cohorts. It was my mother's way of maintaining order. If any one of the kids got out of line — whining, fidgeting, or whispering were the big offenses — a nun would wallop him on top of the head with her missal. I never got hit. Not so for the boys. It wouldn't surprise me at all if Jackie ended up with a permanent knot on top of his skull.

~ ~ ~

It didn't take long for Jackie to start running away. A lanky kid, somewhere on the cusp of adolescence, he had fantasies of escape that never took him anywhere but back where he started. The family was aghast, ashamed, unable to control him. Unhinged with confusion and disbelief, as truant officers and policemen started showing up at the door. Eventually, worn-out social workers joined the procession, and the not-so-surprising finale, before he was kicked out for good, featured a couple of white-coated men rushing into the house carting a straightjacket.

In those years, only his juvenile status and John J. Allen's government contacts, who thought they were extending goodwill, kept Jackie out of doing really serious time. Jackie had turned himself into something we did not understand, worse than anything we had ever seen firsthand — a familiar stranger with a growing list of crimes. Truancy, robbery, assault, drug possession, destruction of property — whatever, it appeared, came to his mind that he thought he could get away with. He was counseled, incarcerated in one juvenile detention center after the other, and when he returned home from those stabs at hammering him into a well-mannered, good-behaving boy, he would be put on severe restriction, only to climb out his window and run away into the night. The person snuggled under the blankets, sleeping peacefully at bed check, turned out to be pillows, master-crafted into a body double.

Annandale Juvenile Hall stood against a backdrop of rolling hills and lush greens, and if it weren't for the heavy metal grates on the windows and the uniformed guards standing watch, it could have been mistaken for a health resort. Once I went there with my parents to visit my brother. Sitting across from him at a picnic table as the sun dissolved into melon-pink splashes that pulled fireflies out from hiding, I listened to him weave brand new promises of how he was going to change, declared with such conviction that it truly seemed possible that he had learned his lessons. His Annandale stay was somewhere toward the beginning, and Jackie had not yet formed the hardened crust of a weathered criminal.

On that evening with the bloom of nature all about us, he looked thin and sad. Alone. Vulnerable in a way I did not know him, sounding as if he actually believed his own strange words. That he really could straighten up — could stop *it*, all of *it*. Only, I thought, where would he begin? Because it was everything he was, the whole of what he became after the first swing of the leather strap, minus the present, delicate pledges. How would a boy deconstruct the bad and fashion himself into good? With his fingers? With the clammy breath of his hopeful promises? Could he possibly grit his teeth through the beatings, holding out for the higher good?

Back then, I believed in promises, even Jackie's. And during those times of his hope and professions, something would begin stirring inside me — an unexpected sense of caring, a fluttering of faith — and for those moments, I couldn't hate him. Stripped of his hostility, he seemed just a boy with big ears and a few paltry dreams. But there was something else. Something I would detect on those occasions of his quiet charm with his defenses lowered. Something massive and unseen, unheard, kept pushing and pushing into me. Pulsing shockwaves from a far-off explosion riding low on the wind seemed caught in the space between us, and the energy of that invisible undertone kept pressing against me.

What was it I was sensing? Soft cries of despair leaking out from the raw underside of his words? Hopelessness? An enormous lode of unvoiced words sheathed in such tender pain that he dared not speak them, dared not reveal them even to himself for fear of shattering? If that's what I was sensing, who could expect Jackie to muster the courage to dismember himself before us, beneath the burden and glare of John J. Allen's disgusted anger? Sorrow — mine or his, I couldn't tell — would jolt and prod me with its potent silence and burrow beneath the armor of my self-protection, and the force of that grief, both subtle and overwhelming, weighed heavy in my chest like the first rumblings of a nasty cold.

I would shift and wiggle, trying to dislodge its presence while I searched Jackie's eyes to catch sight of this vast something I could only sense. What was it hiding beneath his lavish promises that set fire to the tips of my nerves? That had me wanting to slice through the cryptic silence with my own shriek? What lingered in the veil behind his eyes, perceptible only in the fleeting quiver of a lash? Was he begging us to hear what he could not say? Pleading for a touch he could not bear to ask for? Did he want reassurance? Help? I didn't know. I didn't know. So many times I cried out to my mother with my own eyes, imploring her to interpret what I could not voice, frantic for her to pull me into the shelter of her protection. But she never heard those coded prayers.

~ ~ ~

I have to get into the car, but panic is inching its fingers around my throat and begging my legs to break out in a crazy, mad dash back to the porch where my mother is standing, ready to wave good-bye. I'm holding the passenger-side door open, staring back at her, pleading with my eyes, begging for her rescue. "Please," I want to scream, "please call me back. Let me stay with you today. I will do anything, anything." "Get in," John J. Allen commands. My mother just stands there, gazing into the day, waiting for the car to back down the driveway so she can send us on our way. She does not notice my growing panic that has blossomed into beads of dampness rolling down my cheeks like tears. Or maybe she does and is just too exhausted to deal with any more kid emotions this morning. I swallow back the urge to cry out — who, except John J. Allen, will hear me now — and I slump into the seat beside him, trapped beside my father and his long list of my failings.

~ ~ ~

I kept staring at Jackie, poking imaginary fingers into the air, trying to seize discordant notes. Knowing he was saying something I was missing, but not knowing what. I couldn't, though, capture anything to hold on to. Not then, not ever. Yet, during those times enmeshed in his private darkness while he still had the inner resources to pour out assurances, there were glimpses, promises that seemed polished for the occasion of dream-sharing; times when belief flickered in his eyes, hope in mine. Sometimes I hugged him, pulling in tight against his gauntness, my embrace arising straight from the softest part of me that knew and understood and wished for him. But Jackie's oaths never lasted long, dissolving quickly under all that was

Beaumont Road, a perfect storm of turmoil and uneasy rest. As I watched Jackie plunge deeper and deeper into his personal torment, I did not know that my own inevitable fall from grace was barreling toward me. That my parents would be visiting me in a stark, institutional setting. And I would be alone, wracked with despair that no one would hear either.

There was no redemption for Jackie. Any family concern dried up and grew into calloused hate, stone cold and as unforgiving as the drugs he pumped into his body. Pills — yellow, black, blue, red, whatever he could get hold of — that would send him somewhere other than where he was. Glue, the stench always persisting in the bathroom long after he squeezed it into a plastic bag and stuck his face into it, sniffing that high into his brain. LSD that launched him into wild, uncontrollable psychotic hallucinations that left him screaming and writhing on the floor. Then heroin, intravenous and deadly, came around and never left. And all the attendant behavior that trails someone so totally out of control.

Other than absolute mental decay, what would possess him to drill peepholes from his bedroom into the family bathroom? Fights with John J. Allen escalated, only Jackie started returning the blows. When my mother jumped on his back screaming, "You're going to kill him!" after he answered John J. Allen's open-handed strikes with a volley of his own, I wanted to scream at Jackie to just back down, goddamnit! Just stop it, and sit down and eat the goddamn meat loaf and mashed potatoes like everybody else. Home became a scarred battleground, the ugliness uncontainable as it leached out into the community via glaring newspaper headlines featuring his sloe-eyed mug shot. "Local Teenager Gunned Down by Trenton Police." "Hamilton Youth Attempts Child Abduction." Charges of kidnapping. Rape. Child endangerment.

He was hauled from his bedroom late one night, strapped tight into a straightjacket, and taken to the Trenton Psychiatric Hospital, only to escape days later. Each disaster fed on itself, and the tragedy that was Jackie's life increased, worsening until he was exiled from the family. Banished. Gone as if he had never existed. Struck from history. No smiles offered when his name was uttered. We were, after all, his victims. All his talk of straightening up, becoming a Buddhist — pure lies, made up just to torture us with hope so he could wiggle his way back into the fold, contaminated as it was with disgust for him.

How many times did we have to sit in silence at the kitchen table, staring down at our laps while he sweet-talked his way to forgiveness, only to stroll out of the house and plunge a fix into his arm, then roam the streets until he found a way into the next morning's headlines? There wasn't a day in his life that he hadn't been bad, was there? A more contemptible human being did not exist. He needed to see that. There was not an ounce of remorse or dignity in him. He never cared about the agony he inflicted on the family. All of us had tried to teach him a lesson. Many, many lessons. No-holds-barred lessons where he would get the point. How many beatings would it take for him to see, at last, how despicable he was? That he was the reason for every ounce of grief in the family?

I never did kill Jackie. In the end, he killed himself. An overdose of heroin, the same drug he'd been pumping into his veins since he was a teenager. Accidentally? With purpose? I will never know. Disowned from the family, he died in his early forties as alone as one soul can get. Found dead in a squalid motel room somewhere in Virginia, surely ragged and pale, skinny beyond measure — his body, for certain, black and blue from needlesticks. There were no treasures amid his belongings, no fine collections from a lifetime, no hints of any personal accomplishments. No records of a wife or children, or even a close friend to notify. No names of family to contact in case of emergency. Anyway, why contact the family that held him in such contempt? What point in making one final attempt to reach beyond what he had become and try to touch the hearts in the circle he once played in?

He could not appeal for forgiveness. Even in his drug-induced haze, Jackie had to understand that the process of forgiving him for the misery he imposed in his life was a vast and enormous task that none of us would want, or even know how, to begin. In his last hours, though, did he battle the instinctive, purest pull of love that lives within all of us, alive still beneath the noise of his anguish, that mystifying urge to reach back home to try to touch the innocence of *before*? Before he was hated? Before he was discarded? When home meant a safe embrace?

He was, in reality, my mother and father's firstborn. A son, a namesake. Somewhere back in time, they had cuddled him, nestled in a baby-blue blanket, warm from a bath. They must have marveled at what their love had created. Made silly faces at him, trying to get him to coo and smile. He was loved then. In his final descent, did Jackie ever want to desperately plead with us to acknowledge the brief speck of time when his face lit up someone's eyes and just his name called forth a smile? Did he pray for us to remember? Remember that he was loved once? He would know, of course, that we couldn't. He would understand that his death would do nothing to soften our hearts.

Dead of an overdose of heroin, we were told. *Well, what did you expect?* we said to each other. Despite chiding by a Virginia police officer, in the wisdom of people who believe in crime and punishment, none of the family would claim his body. We had our reasons. Hadn't he forced our father into an early grave? Hadn't he caused this family enough grief? Though by the time of Jackie's death, we really weren't much of a family any longer, each holed up in our own separate lives, ignoring the past or rewriting it, as necessary. Whenever an unavoidable occasion called for a gathering, some of us would paste on a smile and attend, only to suffer awkward, meaningless small talk; others would either make excuses or just not respond.

Jackie's death did not get us dusting off the old wagons and circling them as once we did during The Terrible Jackie Years. Years I feared my mother would slice her wrists and kill herself. Years I watched my father slur his prized dignity with sloppy, frightened tears all because of the trauma of Jackie's monstrous shenanigans. All his death did was reignite the old flashes of helpless anger. "I can't afford to bury him," my mother said. "Flush him down the toilet," my brother Tom said. I agreed; he wasn't our problem. So John J. Allen, Jr. was cremated by the State of Virginia, and in a ceremony reserved for the destitute, his ashes scattered on the waters of the Chesapeake Bay by some government officials who may or may not have offered a final prayer. Back in our disconnected lives, it was business as usual, the day just another date on the calendar, each of us shaking our heads in disgust at our brother who never did learn his lesson.

But now, I'm thinking that he did.

CHAPTER 4

College — The Forbidden Dream

"You're not going to college and that's final!"

Another decree handed down by John J. Allen. Outside of *Looney Toons*, was it possible for a man to blow his face clear off his head in anger, showering a girl with veins and headcheese just to make a point she might otherwise miss in the fixed, steely eyes, flaming cheeks, and tone that possibly might not sound furious enough? He wouldn't have to explode through his skin for me — I got the message; I just chose to ignore it, wrapped up as I was in the bliss of possibility, pumped high with excitement and hope. That day I employed my version of standing up to the giant. Not that it worked, but at least I tried.

I'd spent the afternoon with my best friend, Margaretta, and her mother. Mrs. Smith was astoundingly beautiful and wore the kind of clothes that made men drool and that only the likes of Marilyn Monroe and Jane Mansfield could pull off effectively — pointed bras and skintight sweaters and Capris glued to her bottom. At work she wore nurse's whites, including a stiff cap perched on top of her bleached hair. But at home she ditty-bopped around in movie-star getups or paraded her stunning figure about in the nude — imagine that tricky conflict for her adolescent sons. I never saw her naked in real life, only in a few 8x10 glossies, posed and lewd, and she was astonishing in her beauty and in what she was willing to do for the camera.

Usually Mrs. Smith simply tolerated me. I didn't have the panache or status of a kid she wanted Margaretta to associate with. It wasn't as if Margaretta attended a snooty private school or the Smith family lived in Princeton. We were Beaumont Road neighbors separated by only a few houses, trekked to the same ordinary schools, and were even in the same grade. But at fourteen, Margaretta was keenly intelligent, hitting the honor roll with every report card. And to add to her superiority, she was named after a Swedish screen goddess, as she often bragged. Nothing in my life was so pedigreed. I was named after my grandmother, who died when I was still a baby and lived in my heart as a patron saint. But I wondered if the splendor of that notion was canceled out by my middle name given to honor my mother's sister, who wore men's clothes and beat her up as a little girl. Then there was the messy business of my father not being my father, which led into all sorts of personal stigmas I didn't dare contemplate.

Unlike her mother, Margaretta's father didn't walk around putting on airs in spite of the fact that he was an important person at Sears downtown with a private office on the upper floor. Even if I was afraid of him, Mr. Smith was a kind man: not once did he sneer or roll his eyes the time I showed him the five dollars John J. Allen had given me to buy a new winter coat at his store. He never cast even the tiniest smirk while he tried to come up with suggestions as to where I could actually get a coat with sleeves and buttons for my five dollars.

Where Margaretta was academically gifted, I was perplexed and foggy, lost in a daze of disinterest and overwhelming struggle in my attempts to comprehend anything but English, where I could lose myself in a world of words. The two things I had over Margaretta were that I was cuter and not quite as chubby.

And away from the Allen house I had this penchant for high spirits — I grabbed joy wherever I could get it. Margaretta was too serious with her bent toward the highbrow and her persistent crowing about the Swedish movie-star thing. None of that won her any status with the kids at school. Not that she didn't have a lot to brag about. Look, her family had money to spend, she wore nice clothes, and her grandma owned a house in Cape May.

Weighed down as she was with brains and a floozy for a mother, who could blame her for lacking a funny bone? Mine was enough for both of us. It took nothing for me to pull her into my crazy, fearless antics stoked by my jubilance at being away from the Allen house. So, adding it all together, Margaretta and I made sort of an even pair — though in the end, she won. Intellect and confidence and a vague tie to stardom trumped silliness and my victories in our obsessive, flat-stomach competitions every time.

While I could kick it up with my friends, I fell nearly mute around adults, suffering as I did from mental amputation of the tongue. The Communists would have been pleased. And I had this uncanny ability to disappear into the surroundings like a reptile cloaking itself in its favored color of dingy cement. I would have been right at home in a burka. From the safety of my silence, I offered up John J. Allen-style smiles — wide and fake — and the ever-protective shield of unwavering politeness. Maybe Mrs. Smith sensed something disquieting about me, something she couldn't quite put her finger on — reading my crippling shyness as a disguise for malice that might sway her daughter into corruption. Maybe she thought the smiles I offered too easily, too quickly, were counterfeit, concealed something devious.

How could she know that for me, smiling was a trained response forged by John J. Allen? *You better put a smile on that face* was a John J. Allen demand that I had worked into an art form, fashioning my grins into useful barriers of defense against my father's anger and the disapproving Mrs. Smiths of my world or any other dominant mortals sporting an aura of danger. The politeness hammered into me by John J. Allen that she may have eyed with suspicion was simply my version of spiked body armor, another tool to keep me safe. Surely Mrs. Smith had spied me whispering secretively to Margaretta only to clam up when she walked into the room. Probably Mrs. Smith just plain didn't trust a girl who wouldn't speak openly around adults. Then there was that incident in Woolworths. I am quite sure I didn't win any points with her after that escapade.

Margaretta and I spent the day in downtown Trenton going to the movies and darting in and out of the department stores, testing perfume and riding the elevators, ending up in Woolworths just a little while before we were to catch the bus for home. There we were, racing down the deserted stairwell to the basement restrooms, when the bare walls sliding by suddenly jumped out and called my attention. Whoa! A blank canvas. Fresh, crisp paper, but gigantic. Teeming with possibilities. Words! Doodles! Playing right into the thwarted artist in me; I could not possibly resist. Dim lights and lipstick — all I needed for added inspiration — and soon Margaretta and I were drawing gigantic frosted-pink hearts and huge cupid arrows, entwining our names with current heartthrobs in fancy loops and curls right onto the lumpy plaster. Not graffiti: art. Forerunner to urban murals, but happy.

Lost in our giggles, we never heard the footsteps raging down toward us, and when the fat clerk in a tent-sized dress grabbed us by the necks yelling for security, we threw down our lipsticks as if the county sheriff himself had warned us to drop our weapons. Margaretta froze, but since I'd had lots of fight training, I broke the hold, ducked under that flabby arm, and tore out of there so fast, I thought I'd borrowed somebody else's feet for the occasion. Margaretta didn't follow, and I didn't go back.

I've already confessed that I would not die for Jesus, and I was not about to be captured in the execution of a crime if I could help it, even if it was just a lipstick misdemeanor. Can you imagine what John J. Allen would do to me? There were no minor missteps in his universe. Worse, his office was only two doors up from Woolworths. What if the fat lady marched me right up to his desk in handcuffs? Punishment wouldn't be a few glorious days spent in my room. I could be stripped naked and placed on public display right there in the Division Of Pensions and Benefits. Margaretta had a normal father and would never understand the lengths my father might go to just to prove a point.

It was a lousy thing to do, abandoning my best friend like that, but it was molten terror that propelled my legs as I bolted out of the store, raced to the bus stop, and caught the 4:12 to Yardville. And it was frozen terror that, less than an hour later, led me to stroll into my house right on time for dinner, smiling as if nothing had ever happened. No doubt, Mrs. Smith caught wind of my little exploit and my utter failure as a friend and was disgusted with me. I couldn't blame her or Margaretta, though neither of them ever questioned me about it.

But things always sort of evened out. Like the time when Margaretta's parents forgot about Christmas. In the early hours of December 25 one year, when the three Smith children wandered into the living room only to discover the leavings of the day before — dirty dishes, old newspapers, and rifled magazines strewn about with no sign of a tree or presents — I shared Margaretta's misery and outrage, and cried along with her. When her little brothers scoured the neighborhood and lugged home a spindly evergreen, and her parents finally stumbled into the late morning half dressed and carrying stale drinks from the night before, and the family laughed and decorated the tree with a few baubles, I understood that for Margaretta the magic was gone and no amount of festive, forgiving laughter could bring it back. That would never have happened in my house. My parents stayed up long into the night every Christmas Eve, wrapping, assembling, decorating, my father placing tinsel on the branches one strand at a time until the tree shimmered silver. Like I said, things evened out every now and again.

Mrs. Smith believed in Margaretta. That day, as the three of us drank Coca-Colas in the Smiths' cramped dinette, she believed in me, too. Sitting at the table wedged alongside ambling philodendron and thirsting English ivy, the FM radio playing quietly in the background, I leaned forward and listened to her talk to me. With her eyes zeroed in holding my gaze, I searched for the telltale flicker or breaking smirk that might signal ridicule when she told me I was smart enough to go to college, just like Margaretta.

It was stuffy in that little room with barely a breeze drifting through the window and all that heat parked right on my face and burrowed under my arms. I ignored the urge to wipe and scratch and stared right into Mrs. Smith's eyes. I didn't want to breathe or move for fear I'd break the spell and she'd chuckle in awkwardness when she saw excitement mistakenly glowing in my eyes and have to confess, "Oh, I wasn't talking about you. Did you think I was talking about you? No, I was talking about my niece Kathy." Or the next-door neighbor, or the daughter of friends, all with the same name. "Sorry," she'd say, screwing her face into a big grimace that would be masking pity.

Then she'd be compelled to make up some kind of line for me, because now she was embarrassed that I was embarrassed, so she'd have to throw me a bone in the form of, "Well, OK, yes, maybe you could go to college too. You never know." And I'd have to mumble, "Oh, I knew you didn't mean me." But we would both know that wasn't true. And there I would be with the ache and truth of my longings revealed, the utter rawness of my begging and pleading private yearnings disclosed — that I dreamed of being a star in my own eyes. That was my disgraceful, arrogant truth, and just by allowing my eyes to light up, I exposed myself to the sting of ridicule, the snap of criticism. Confessing to anyone that buried beneath everything that was dark inside me was my belief that I was more than just useful, more than mediocre, was the same as posing a knife at my own throat and thrusting. Because revealing what I held so close to my heart meant handing over the weapon to destroy it.

The secret no one was ever to know or have the opportunity to batter was that I knew that hidden within me lived something exceptional. Its loyal presence stalked me with insatiable, unidentifiable cravings, worse than the gnawings of midnight hunger that I could at least satisfy with cookies and milk. Maybe it was an undiscovered, innate talent. Maybe it was a seemingly impossible task I was to perform. I don't know, maybe I was supposed to martyr myself on a flaming sword. Or maybe I was simply crazy. But I was positive it was there, like a ghost with a prickly attitude, always poking me, nudging me toward something, but I didn't know what. One thing was certain: other than my faults, which did seem pretty outstanding, nothing special about me was ever hinted at until now, as Mrs. Smith talked of my latent abilities, my camouflaged intelligence.

I was terrified to believe her, because what if I was wrong and the exceptional quality I sensed was just teenage voodoo playing tricks — a deception dug up straight from the gloomy land of adolescent angst, where even chubby girls believed they truly had a chance with Elvis? What if she was mistaken about my potential and I really was dense and impenetrable, learning-disabled? Incapable of performing all but the most basic tasks? Trainable but not teachable? I was horrified that she would see all these things, know with the authority vested in all adults that I was stupid and my fantasy of being extraordinary in some way was the pathetic, shake-your-head, wishful musings of a girl who was never going anywhere.

But there she was, chatting with me like she was talking to her own daughter, promising me that if I studied hard, got my grades up, and took college prep courses, I could do it. There was no reason I couldn't. "You just have to apply yourself," Mrs. Smith said in that breathy tone I'd heard her use with Mr. Smith. "You have what it takes." *You have what it takes.* Those words clustered like dancing stars in front of my eyes while somewhere far and away, a dream beckoned and pitter-pattered its shaky fingers against my doubt, prying, working it loose until the alien sensation of hope surged into all the cheerless spaces and infused me with such ecstasy that I could have jumped up and boogied several rounds of the hokey-pokey and thrown in a jig or two with the leftover energy.

Suddenly, what *if*s barraged me. What if I could be proud of myself? Do something real that had meaning and value? What if I could actually climb out of my brain fog at school and understand the teachers? My gosh, raise my hand and ask questions, possibly answer some, too? What if I weren't afraid? Of the teachers, of the principal, of textbooks that spouted theories I didn't understand? Afraid of Big Alice, who roamed the schoolyard and selected one girl a week to bully? Suppose I didn't have to cringe in my seat every time a test was returned, knowing it would be slashed with red checkmarks? What if I didn't have to carry the shame of failure everywhere? Not always hide behind my smile? What if I could endure slights and challenges because I was going somewhere — somewhere that counted?

I looked hard into their eyes, Mrs. Smith's and Margaretta's, and a pall settled over my enthusiasm. What if they really were only ridiculing me? Reeling me in, plying me with kind words just to see my eyes spark with naïve trust? Waiting for the perfect time to point their fingers and laugh hysterically at my gullibility, my absolute stupidity at thinking that even just the word *college* could be applied to me? But no, they weren't; I could see that; I could feel the truth in the way they were talking. They were making enthusiastic plans, bolstering me with flesh-and-blood possibilities, offering me a path through the tangle of the impossible. I allowed myself to slide down into genuine hope with all its newborn tenderness, and suddenly I was cuddled in my grandmother's lap, listening to her whisper praise and encouragement in my ear. With my head leaning against her imaginary heart, faith began to lay down its timid roots.

But I was jumpy and excited, and lunged at those *could be*s like the starving failure I felt like and began to clutch at my mission, imagining myself succeeding, understanding now what I must do. Buckling down and working hard were the ground rules. But I'd proven I could do that. Look at how I'd tamed my brothers and was teaching myself to finesse my way around John J. Allen. If I could accomplish all that, surely I could plow through math problems; force myself to learn how x equaled y, how chromosomes worked; discover the hidden meaning in poetry. I could do it. I *would* do it. I'd trade my daydreams for serious study. Devour textbooks instead of movie-star magazines. Sit up straight at my desk rather than disappearing into the chalk dust. I would hold my head up. Carry my books proudly, because suddenly they meant something other than drudgery: they would be my passport to a world where a person wouldn't have to walk with her head down, afraid always of being laughed at.

All of this seemed feasible in that little dinette as, wide-eyed, I watched boundless possibilities tumbling toward me. Me, Kathy Allen, going to college. Imagine. *Me*, going to college. I could barely make sense of it, dizzy at the image of myself packing my hand-me-downs and stepping off the front steps into a world of wonder and mystery, the world reserved for girls in Bass Weejun loafers and pastel twinsets and strings of pearls. I'd been injected with the wonder drug of hope, and I was instantly addicted. I imagined myself confident. My smile sincere. I visualized myself magnanimous and selfless, extending my help to others because I would never forget where I came from, and they would benefit from my experience and ultimate success.

Oh, for those few moments I lived an entire life in the fantasy world created by Mrs. Smith and Margaretta, fully believing in its truth. Trusted it as I floated home six inches above the sidewalk and soared into the living room and stood before John J. Allen, still in his shirt and tie from work. Believed in it even as I spoke the words and stood my shaky ground. Believed in it for a good minute and a half, as long as it took me to understand that it was all just a filthy lie.

"I want to go to college," I announce, spit-staring John J. Allen straight in the eye. Right now I am somebody. I feel its rise in my blood like a fat gurgle and I am ready to pop into laughter. My dream tastes like the syrup from a sun-warmed peach flowering on my tongue, and I know the pure force of my delight will transform my father and I will win his approval. I just know it. He will see this newfound belief in myself that I have discovered, and the magic of it will be contagious, and I will hear him say, "Yes. That's a terrific idea. I'm going to help you."

I believe this in the seconds it takes me to deliver my announcement. Fear has not yet begun its curl up the nether side of my chest, and I am convinced I can weave my way into my father's good graces. Bliss allows me to ignore the annoyance flattening his eyes. Nor do I smell the pot roast I know is simmering on the stove. The boys' bickering somewhere off to the left of my shoulder and my mother's rustling about in the kitchen, all barely noticed background song. *I am going to college.*

His anger, primed as always, spitfires right back. "You're not going to college and that's final." He roars these words as if we've been locked in a stalemate for hours and he has, at long last, had enough and his frustration explodes. No. One statement. One response. I look up at him, unsure. Did I hear correctly? Maybe I missed it. Maybe when I blinked he wrenched his head to the right and bellowed a warning to my brothers and I misunderstood his words. No. There was no misinterpretation; I'd heard what he said.

"But I want to go," I plead. I am determined not to abandon my confidence and now call up the encouragement in Mrs. Smith's eyes, the sparkle in Margaretta's, to bolster me. But when I mumble about what Mrs. Smith said, this only invigorates John J. Allen and tugs further on his anger. "I don't give a damn what Mrs. Smith said. If she told you to jump off a bridge, would you?" I bobble, unsure of how to respond to this familiar attack, made original each time simply by inserting a different name.

There are at least a dozen bridges I would like to jump off, I'd like to say, but of course, I don't. "Well, would you?" he demands. I shake my head and whisper, "No." John J. Allen has a way of cutting me off at the knees, and bloody stumps are so very hard to stand on. "You're not going to college. You keep this up and you're not going anywhere." Where else I wasn't going I could only imagine; for certain, it involved the movies and anything to do with friends. And, as if I didn't know it was bound to happen, those stumps of mine begin quivering, and that fair-weather sidekick, hope, makes a mad dash and hightails it out the front door, leaving me marooned in the middle of the living room, staring down John J. Allen.

A soggy mass of disappointment fattens into a bruise and clogs the hollows abandoned so quickly by my wistful thinking, and I know now, as I have always known, that it does not take a well-aimed belt to yank me back in line. I always make it easy for John J. Allen—he brags this to me often enough, that I'm not even a challenge. We both know that all it takes is a booming voice and an unblinking stare. Now, I crack even before the punctuation mark lands at the end of his sentence.

Soon my mother will call us to supper, and he has already settled the direction of my life with minutes to spare. I smell the pot roast now and its scent is both comforting and infuriating, because it's almost ready, but not yet. And I need for my mother to call us to supper right now! If I don't get away, somehow break the hold of this conversation that ruptured before it ever got started, it will turn into one of John J. Allen's rants, fueled not only by my stupidity but by his grumbling stomach, as well. Except in the kitchen my mother is engrossed in decimating all potato lumps, whipping them into milky gruel, and the clatter and grind of the electric mixer against metal buys John J. Allen extra time. I am caught in the mental minefield of John J. Allen's anger, and I know what is coming. I have yet to hone the high art of distraction, and it doesn't look like my father is going to clasp his chest and collapse at my feet anytime soon—say, by the time I take my next breath. Outside of fainting dead away or Petey, our diseased parakeet, breaking loose from his cage and landing on top of my father's pipe and shitting into the tobacco this very second, I cannot escape.

"I know what happens to girls every month," he says. On my best and brightest day, I could not have predicted this. My jaw drops, I feel it unfasten, and soon I will be dripping spit if I don't jerk it back into position. He is talking about my period, the awful bleed that humiliates me with its odor and clots and refusal to be tamed. My mother has never spoken to me about my monthly. It first came upon me at my aunt and uncle's house in a deluge of sticky hemorrhage and mortification that had me wadding up all the toilet paper and tissues I could find while straining to keep up my smile and good humor and, most of all, keep the bloody shame hidden. Shortly after, a box of Kotex and a skinny sanitary belt materialized in my bedroom, along with a booklet, courtesy of my gossiping aunt and her comical tale to my mother of my running back and forth to the bathroom every five minutes. That was it.

Now my father is using the disgrace of my bleeding between the legs to stain me further. He didn't have to say that. He didn't have to make me any uglier. He could have said the truth — that I am too dumb to go to college. Doesn't he think I know that? I know I would never be able to work my way around an SAT, or to grasp algebra and calculus, whose language of numbers and symbols would only free-float around my head, refusing to land. Memorize historical dates that never do merge with corresponding events in my brain. Conquer the maze of a foreign language, when just the thought of trying to wade through the babble makes me feel like an idiot.

Was I dumb enough to believe him even if he said yes, I could go? Don't I know that I would be clutching my suitcase full of cheap clothes, a *wow-I'm-doin'-it* grin lighting up my face, and just as my toe tipped the steps outside the front door and I inhaled the first whirlwinds of freedom rushing toward me, John J. Allen would pipe up and announce, "You're not going anywhere." Don't I know him? Don't I remember? Yes. Yes, I do remember.

~ ~ ~

There was that day at the cusp of summer when John J. Allen came to me all smiles and promises, reaching out and offering me a deal. Unfailingly kind and considerate to strangers and friends, and to relatives as well — even the in-laws — he never extended that sensitivity to us, his kids. Except there he was with a plan, and there I was, all goo-goo eyed, sopping it up. However much money I saved from babysitting neighborhood kids for the summer, he told me, he would match. Dollar for dollar. Did my cloudy brain deceive me? Could this be true? My father would give me a dollar for every dollar I saved? No limit? Just free money? Was the world at this moment imploding and Beaumont Road about to be swallowed up in a quake of asphalt and rebar? *Dollar for dollar,* he repeated. *Whatever you save is what I'll match.* Good grief, I was going to be rich. I'd fallen into a pirate's treasure chest and all I had to do was scoop! And he wasn't kidding. John J. Allen was serious.

There I was, slain by the Spirit just like those Holy Rollers at the revival meetings right outside of town, because I wanted to throw my hands in the air and scream, "Thank you, Jesus. Thank you, Jesus." Only I'd shout, "Thank you, Daddy. Thank you, Daddy." There was no time to waste.

I'd scarf up every babysitting job I could and squirrel away every cent. Not spend a dime of it. Not even for Gropp's double dips or six-packs of Nestlé Crunches. I was on a mission, and I was getting double the money for it. Who cared if I hated babysitting so much that I'd rather puncture my eyeballs with thick needles than be stuck for endless hours in strange, smelly houses with whining, pasty-looking kids? Who cared if I had to plunge my fingers into cold, grease-slicked dishwater and scrub mysterious wet cysts from dinner plates and peel unidentifiable crusty scabs from burnt pots and pans to earn my twenty-five cents an hour? I didn't.

All would be rewarded, because in the days before school started again, I'd be haunting the downtown department stores —Yard's, Nevius-Voorhees, Dunham's, Lit Brothers— my pockets stuffed with money to buy whatever I wanted. Let's see, did I want Bass Weejuns in Oxblood or Burgundy Brush Off? Visions straight from heaven flooded my daydreams. I pictured myself, all dressed up, admiring and selecting from items that regular girls bought, withdrawing money from my wallet, politely handing it over to the refined salesclerk, walking away with a shopping bag embossed with a first-class trade name. The stuff of fantasies soon to be realized. So I thought.

By the end of the season, I'd managed to stash away twenty-five dollars, earned a quarter at a time with an occasional tip thrown in. A huge amount for me. I'd have fifty dollars to spend any way I wanted. The day came. I pulled my stash out of my underwear drawer and recounted it just to make sure. Heart flip-flopping in my chest, I presented John J. Allen with twenty-five dollars in bills and change. I'd done it, and I was proud of myself. He was proud of me, too. He said so as he handed me twenty-five dollars in Two Guys coupons. Two Guys was a warehouse-type discount store planted in the weeds along a highway in the middle of nowhere that sold the likes of motor oil and fishing line and, somewhere toward the back, bloodworms. And, oh yeah, shoes and clothes that nobody without severe arm twisting would wear, especially to junior high.

"This isn't money!" I practically screamed, glaring down at the bogus bills scorching my hand. "These are coupons for Two Guys."

"They're Two Guys dollars," John J. Allen said. He was calm, almost mellow, ignoring my rising hysteria. "You'll get more for your money."

"I don't want Two Guys dollars. You promised me money." I was nearly screeching. "You said I would get money."

"I said I'd match your dollars with dollars. I'm giving you dollars, Two Guys dollars."

I'd never seen him this calm in a confrontation. Then I understood. This was his plan all along. There never were real dollars in play. No matter how many quarters and fifty-cent pieces I amassed, no matter how often I rhapsodized in his presence about my upcoming shopping spree downtown, the entire time my payout was going to be cut-rate coupons to a bargain basement. My grandiose dreams were no more than air bubbles fostered by a *nudge nudge, wink wink* game he played without a flinch.

Then there was President Kennedy's challenge to all the kids in America to join in his physical fitness campaign. Inspired, I'd arranged a bike ride with my girlfriends to Bowman's Tower, an observation lookout perched high on a summit surrounded by views of the Delaware River and the patchwork of pastoral countryside where General George Washington's troops actually scouted the advancing British army. Every kid I ever knew, including the Allens, had been on day trips or school outings to Washington Crossing State Park dozens of times. We'd all toughed out the panting climb up those dizzying, winding stairs so often that most of us could do it with our eyes closed. Not me, of course; eyes bugged, I crept along, hugging the damp stone walls for fear I'd trip and pitch over the rail to my demise.

A good 25-mile stint from Beaumont Road, my friends and I would log 50 miles for the day on our one-speeds. The President would be proud. I'd gotten permission from John J. Allen, mapped the route, and dressed for the day in baggy jeans and an ironed blouse. My frayed sneakers would peddle me through the miles. With a bagged lunch tied to the fender and my bike chain in good order, I was leaning against the garage door waiting for my girlfriends — they were due any second — when John J. Allen came out of the house on his way to Saturday-morning overtime at the office. "You're not going on that bike ride today," he said. He ambushed without warning, inflicting wounds with the casualness of clipping on a bow tie.

By that time I should have learned to be alert when John J. Allen was nearby, paid attention to his cues, instead of always mooning about in my head. Been prepared for the unexpected sucker punch of his meanness. Gauge his moods, watch for a peculiar gait, the certain set of his mouth, judge how tightly he clenched the pipe in his teeth. But I never was a great student.

"Get back in the house. I said you're not going," he repeated. Next to hate, hysteria was my second trusty companion, and it burst out in a gush of tears and wails that left me gasping and sputtering, furious not only with him but with myself because I couldn't jerk my words in line and organize them into intelligible sounds that might persuade him to change his mind. All I did was scream, "No! No! That's not fair! That's not fair!" I wanted to tear at my hair, pull it out in gory clumps, scream loud enough to explode the veins in my neck. A bomb detonated inside my body and each jellied mass pulsed its own outrage and utter helplessness.

I ran back into the house, tripping over my feet and my fury. "Mom! Mom!" I bellowed. "Daddy said I can't go! Mom!" I don't remember how my mother calmed me down or how I managed to string all my fractured parts back together. She did concoct some sort of story, a protective lie that would explain my absence if John J. Allen returned before I got home from the ride. Her warning that I had to keep it a secret from him was unnecessary. John J. Allen would never be able to pry a confession out of me. I would ride my bike to Bowman's Tower with my girlfriends and act as if I'd spent the day doing homework.

That would have been easy except for the cops showing up just as we were leaving the park for home, threatening to throw the gang of us in jail. We'd littered—tossed our Coke bottles in the grass—and had gotten caught. When that squad car with its official emblem and red beacons and two uniformed officers rolled right up to my bike and I was face-to-face with the terror of authority and its massive onrush of power, I burst again into those pieces that I had barely managed to glue together earlier. No soothing mother on hand for protection—just an officer and his untempered anger, low-slung and snarling, curling out of the rolled-down window and clawing at my breath while I sobbed and gasped for air, just as I had done earlier with John J. Allen.

It didn't matter that behind me my friends were giggling, not taking the exchange seriously. The cop threatened us with jail, and in my universe, there were no empty threats; I took all authority seriously. I don't suppose we were ever in real danger of landing behind bars, but the likelihood was absolute truth to me. We cleaned up our mess and the police finally let us go, but fear and worry and liquid panic rode my bike home with me and tucked me into bed that night.

~ ~ ~

Standing before my father, I remember these incidents quickly and fret that it does not matter what form a male takes. It does not matter whether it's John J. Allen, the cops, my brothers, or the boys in the schoolyard who pinch me until I bleed and pin my arms behind my back and race their filthy hands across my chest. I see that age or clothing makes no difference. Men pounce out of shadowy recesses, looking to destroy, and there is nothing to be done about it.

Yes, I do know my father. He will use anything to degrade me, including my menstrual blood. I am shaking inside, chewing down hard on the doughy wall of my cheek, trying to stall the tears that are welling up and chafing my eyes with grit, thinking that soon I will taste blood. That ever-present festering hate boils now, sweating onto the surface of my skin, and I strain to keep from huffing my breath into little white clouds like in the comic strips.

I lower my eyes and stare at the rug. Instantly it appears one of the ugliest things I have ever seen. It is like straw, and scratches my feet when I cross it barefooted. I want to whine about yearning to sink my feet into thick, soft carpet, and I resent, suddenly, that this rug is not really a rug anyway, but a woven mat that feels like a hay bale and belongs in a tarpaper shack. And the color, muddy sea foam, reminds me of a slimy lake bottom, and it unnerves me to look at it. I am so sick of myself and my stupid dreams and my mouth that blathers on and on about them. The pot roast no longer wraps me in comfort. Now the thought of the stringy meat and shriveled peas that I will swallow one by one makes my stomach curdle.

"Look at me when I'm talking to you," he says. It takes effort culled straight from my anger to drag my eyes up from the floor, to lug my thoughts away from the rug and from the fat and gristle about to be served for dinner. I want to nail him with a death glare, level him with one clout from my steely eyes as he does me. I want him to be done with me, to let me go. He knows that I know a girl like me could never go to college. Despite my lofty excitement, I was never fooled by Mrs. Smith and Margaretta. I know my thoughts about packing my suitcase and heading off to such a grand adventure are complete flights of fancy. That he would never release me into that delight and wonder. All I wanted was the damn dream. Now I want to grab him by the shirt and shake until his teeth rattle, screaming, "I just want the dream. Just the dream. Can't you even let me have that?"

But he is beginning to sputter, and maybe his face will blow up as he is building up to a tirade that I have stupidly made myself the brunt of. I am so overwhelmed by the anger that crashes and erupts in this house. By my mother, who mostly ignores it; by Jackie, who instigates it; by John J. Allen, who ambushes with it. I brace myself, wobbling still. Once John J. Allen gets going, he does not stop. He will keep pounding and smashing with that mythical sledgehammer of his, long past the first direct hits that immediately leave me juiceless, any joy obliterated, reduced to fissures of dried mud at my feet. Why does he keep this up beyond all reason, constantly yanking more fresh insults from the yawning vault of his anger? But this is him, reaching, stretching, not satisfied until he is sure he has annihilated his target.

And now he yells, "You're going to be a secretary. You're going to learn how to type and take shorthand." He shouts this by way of punishment, imposing a lifelong sentence. He does this, I think, because he knows it is what I hate. How many times have I said that I never want to work in an office? Once, twice? Hundreds of times? Never? Maybe he simply possesses the eerie ability, like Jackie, to unearth my deepest loathings for use as lethal weapons. "A secretary, like the girls in my office." He gloats this command, and I believe he wants me to thank him for the privilege of this penalty.

Before I can stop myself, before I can in fact bite clear through the flesh of my cheek and taste salt leaching across my tongue, I am spurting tears and wailing because I feel the slingshot of chains whip around my neck, across my chest, shackling my arms and legs. "I don't want to be a secretary like the girls in your office."

Like the girls in his office. Girls who call him *Mister* Allen; girls with deep wrinkles and teased gray hair, old enough to be his mother, probably his grandmother. Stout girls in loose out-blouses worn to hide their fat, who laugh at his jokes, serve him coffee, and vote him Boss of the Year. Smiling girls whose ink-stained fingers fly across the keys of manual typewriters at ninety words per minute, pounding his words onto onionskin. Girls sitting cross-legged before him, perfumed and shellacked with face paint, steno pad at the ready, pencil poised, scribing every utterance he dictates. Girls bowing always to his power, submitting to his authority, serving his needs. The girls in his office.

He demands I be just like them, sodden and submissive, and he will see to it. He will make me be a secretary, one of the girls. Force my fingers, that are fluid when expressing sentiment and images, to clomp around an ancient Royal with keys that jam and ribbons that tangle. Impose on me the Gregg shorthand method that will reduce all the magic of words to indecipherable, soulless lines and squiggles, siphoning the pleasure from writing. He wants to bury me alive beneath fluorescent lights and ringing phones and file cabinets and dry annual reports. And the deathly nonstop kidding around and making nice to the men — no matter what, that define life tethered to a desk. That's my future. His say-so is final and unquestionable.

I have nothing left, no logic capable of seeping past the barricade of his made-up mind, no opinions worthy enough, no cries, no matter how pitiful or how earsplitting, able to drift beyond his deaf ears and discover somewhere a softness. My fight is gone and I fall into perfect silence, and before his very eyes, I shrink smaller and smaller into an invisible speck and I vanish, leaving only my bones on view. My mother rings her miniature dinner bell, signaling the beginning of supper and the end of my delusions, which were just bringing down wrath anyway.

The meat is tough, as usual. I swallow my peas one at a time, as usual, gagging between each one. There is the predictable silence at the dinner table despite the presence of seven people. The usual silence John J. Allen insists upon. And we all, including my mother, kowtow to John J. Allen's demands — to his face at least.

CHAPTER 5

Girl Unraveling

So my venture into the underworld of crime didn't last very long, caught as I was early on by two beefy goons in black suits and skinny ties — the dreaded store detectives who lifted me by the elbows and sailed me down, down into the bowels of Lit Brothers to a cement interrogation cell where they tried to browbeat me into confessing. The inquisition room was no more than a cinderblock basement office of some underpaid subordinate trying to work his way upstairs, though to me at the time, it might as well have been equipped with thumbscrews and a rack. Honestly, I did not steal anything from that department store where I was captured, but they accused me anyway, despite lack of evidence. I mean, there was evidence — the trinkets I stole did come from somewhere, just not there.

I admit I loved shoplifting. Not the act, which had the aura of shadiness and spoke of threadbare raincoats and scuffed-up shoes. What I adored was the sense of receiving delightful gifts, frivolous ·treasures — a pink faux-jeweled scatter pin, a golden scrolled compact — objects whose only use was to offer beauty and entry into a realm that seemed so unattainable. When a girlfriend introduced me to the five-finger discount, I felt as if I'd been asleep and had awakened as a princess in an enchanted land; all that brilliance was mine for the taking.

Being a Catholic, I was well versed in the Ten Commandments and knew "Thou shall not steal" held steady at number seven, but shoplifting did not feel wrong. Missing Mass was wrong. Eating meat on Fridays, really wrong. Being impolite could buy you a strong, swift punishment. But shoplifting defied definition. There was the "Finders keepers, losers weepers" rule — kid code for whatever trinket you found outside was yours. You didn't have to find out who owned it. I understood that one.

Stealing, though, was what robbers with masks and guns did in banks, and it didn't apply to regular life. The silverware and ashtrays and boldly embroidered green-striped towels my parents carried home from restaurants and motels were advertisement, there to be taken. And Aunt Bobby's cleaning Delmonico steaks out of the freezer at Howard Johnson's where she worked as a cook was a perk of the job. There were no hard-and-fast rules about encircling your wrist with a sparkly bracelet from the counter while the saleslady had her back turned. Well, there was one: Don't get caught.

But I did get caught. And the sight of it created a huge commotion just inside those revolving doors that deposited a constant flow of ladies with big hats and fat wallets right in front of Lit's cosmetics counter. Two more seconds and I would have been free. Well, not exactly. Those boys probably would have chased me all through the twisting alleyways of Trenton. And so, right before more startled eyes than I like to imagine, a great sweep of drama commenced to my strains of "I didn't do anything! I didn't do anything!" while I tried to break free as the big boys carted me away like a sack of bones.

Divine intervention had to have something to do with my short-lived life as a crook. Could've been God, could've been the devil. Half the time I couldn't tell which was which; between the two of them, it's not like anybody ever stands a chance — punishment will come from one or the other. Clearly, though, a stiff cuff to the side of my head was required. I was liking my new pastime too much, making every visit to a store an opportunity for a private birthday party, where I selected all my own presents from those vast, colorful displays. I guess I was getting closer and closer to actually believing I was a deposed princess, entitled to stuffing a brand new RCA television into my underpants.

Torture is torture, no matter how it's dished out. And the day after my detention, waiting by the phone for Lit Brothers to call as they pledged they would, was unadulterated agony. When it finally rang, the official woman on the other end of the line didn't buy it when I lowered my voice and claimed to be Mrs. Allen. In a dust-up of confusion and sobbing, I thrust the phone at my mother and raced upstairs to my bedroom and buried myself beneath my blankets.

Swabbed in terror and sweat, I waited for the guillotine to fall. It was coming; I knew it. And it was going to be horrible, the worst punishment I had ever experienced, because I was in line for a beating. One of my parents, my father or my mother, would storm up the stairs and burst into my bedroom and rip my flesh with a leather belt and forevermore I'd live without skin attached to my body. I was going to be tortured so unmercifully that I would be wishing the Communists had found me first.

So I waited. Hyperventilating hot breath into the blankets and sheets, I waited. I had to pee. But I didn't dare move. I had to wait. Just wait. And wait. And wait. At any second, foot thumps would thunder up the stairs. I'd hear the swish-tunk-tunk-tunk of my father's belt being yanked from its loops. The crash through my door. I waited. And waited. Listening. Holding my breath between pants. I waited. No one came. Hunger pangs and bursting kidneys led me to peek out my door and listen. Nothing. When finally I bolstered my courage and crept downstairs and meekly inserted myself into family life again, it was as if nothing had ever happened. My sin faded into the past.

I should have been thrilled by the skin-of-my-teeth escape. The lack of a bloodthirsty reprimand would have spurred any respectable criminal on to bigger and better heists. Instead, I mourned the loss of my access to all the exquisite gifts I longed for. I would never shoplift again. But I ached for the sophisticated abundance presented in those stores with their soft music and magical, orderly displays, now beyond my reach. The few stolen items I did have held no more charm. They had lost their allure, been tarnished by the ugliness of reality. Now they were just meaningless pieces of junk.

It was always the refinement, the beauty, that tugged at my heart, and I longed to be embraced by such grace. I wanted a ceasefire on scabs picked raw and boogers and boy farts. Wanted elegance in a house where my father stuck out his finger to be pulled, triggering his own fart. I didn't want to smell sweaty sneakers and see, even occasionally, a severed bird's head falling out of a little boy's pocket. I wanted the sweetness of swinging on the swing, melting my voice with the sky without someone staring, waiting to attack. I wanted to wear clothes without cigarette holes burned into them. I wanted my brothers to be obedient, polite, not so god-awful exasperating all the time.

I wanted my father to stop beating them, stop making us the spectacle of the neighborhood with all the screams that broke from the upstairs windows at nightfall. I wanted John J. Allen to stop destroying whatever nice thing crossed my path.

Where I got such a stuck-up attitude from, I don't know; maybe I was born with it. Maybe I was actually dethroned royalty from a prior life with vivid body memories. All I know is that I felt swallowed in ugliness.

Why the hell was I so damn unhappy when I had so much to be thankful for, John J. Allen demanded to know over and over. "You burn me up with that tear bag of yours," he'd say, lecturing me how I wasn't the only kid who wore hand-me-downs and shopped at Cheap John's and Atlantic Mills. Atlantic Mills — if you had two dollars and could stand the stink, you could spend the day loading your shopping cart with clothes yanked from mammoth piles dumped into wooden bins like they'd been belched out by garbage trucks. There was no order in that dive. Nothing pretty. Just ugly on top of ugly. Unwashed women and grimy kids clawing through the smelly mountains, pulling out irregulars and hooting and hollering like they'd unearthed precious gems. It was disgusting and degrading, and I wanted nothing to do with anything from that discount mart or any other dump where people with stained shirts and gray, scaly feet falling out of their dingy bedroom slippers shuffled though aisles crammed with rejected merchandise, licking chicken grease off their fingers as they shopped.

Too bad my hoity-toity attitude did nothing to change facts: I wore clothes found deep in those Atlantic Mills bins, and from the "final sale" racks in Two Guys and Cheap John's, though not even Chinese water torture could wring a confession out of me. But every time I left the house wearing wilted hand-me-downs or outfits from those bargain basement stores, I felt shoddy and blemished, trailed by the ghost of a carnival barker, his hair slicked down with tallow, constantly squaring his shoulders under a too-big suit, surrounded by blinking fairway lights. Did others hear the echoes of him hawking my cheap clothes as I walked down the hallway at school? *Hey Mudder, come closer. See this little item? This here's a real bargain. A little smoke damage never hurt nobody. C'mon, doll face, gimme a fin. Don't you want your little girlie to look just like a princess? What d' ya say?*

When it came time for prom dresses, they had to be either borrowed from a cousin who wore them in the 1950s, a decade earlier, or bought on credit, scavenged from a markdown rack stashed in an unlit section of a discount mart, next to crushed boxes of Kotex and the scratch-and-dent appliances. To ease my delicate sensibilities, my mother helped me invent a story about how we purchased my gowns in a fancy cubbyhole — and imaginary — shop on a side street in New York City she aptly named *Patricia's* — an ode to my mother's visions of splendor, I guess. The world of my personal humiliations knew no boundaries.

According to John J. Allen, my problem was that I was conceited, stuck-up, and associated with too many snobs like Margaretta. I didn't know how to be grateful, he bellowed. In the fertile ground of my idle fancies, I told him off constantly. I'd conjure him up in his T-shirt and boxers, holding that pipe. I invented the urban head bob, you know, and in my imagination, I used it often to enhance my fine retorts to all of his peeves.

Don't we take all you kids on day trips to the shore, to Washington, D.C., and to the mountains, where we swim in crystal-clear lakes? he would demand from his perch in my dream world. I'd lick my lips, preparing for all my delicious fictional comebacks. *Yes,* I would concede, *you do.* Then I'd add: *And five minutes into the car ride, don't fights break out? Then don't your threats start? Don't you start swinging that monkey arm of yours into the backseat until the kids really start screaming? Then don't you yell at everybody to shut up or you'll really give them something to cry for? But the fun day is only beginning. By the time we finally get where we're going, everybody's so sweaty and cranky that we all bolt from the car the second it stops. But don't you call us back to lug enough stuff to furnish a vacation house a mile over the blazing sand to your perfect fishing spot?*

Oh, the fun doesn't end there, does it? I'd say, inserting the head bob. *No, of course not, because the beach umbrella has to be set up, but it keeps falling over and the blanket flaps in the wind, whipping up sand that keeps stinging everybody's eyes. By this time we're all starving, but you will only dole out food after everybody's settled, which means we have to practically kill each other staking out one-square-inch claims of gritty blanket. Do you really think anybody besides you can actually eat with the stink of mushy Spam salad sandwiches and syrupy grape juice mixed with the stench of live bloodworms packed in seaweed?*

The fun day at the beach is the one time I wish you'd follow through with your threat of banishment. I would love to be sent to the station wagon for the rest of the day. Watching the steering wheel melt in the sun is a whole lot more fun than being eaten alive by greenheads and stung by jellyfish joyriding the waves while we wait for you to catch a fish so we can go home. Besides all that, I despise the sand that sticks to my feet and crawls inside my bathing suit. Mostly, Daddy, and I say this in my head over and over again with great flourish, *not that you give a hoot, but I hate being wet.*

When I got on a roll, I didn't stop. And on that mini television in my mind, I would incite John J. Allen to keep it up, keep trying to outdo my smart-aleck attitude, to work harder at bullying me into being grateful — which, by the way, I was never going to be anyway because the only thing that would please me besides his disappearance would be a steady stream of cash. No, in my imagination, I wanted him to perform for me. *Didn't we take you kids to the Gingerbread Castle, to the Land of Make Believe, to Luray Caverns?* he asked. *Yes, yes,* I would sigh, calling forth the forbidden eye roll, letting him know I was growing bored and impatient with his cabbage head of a brain. *Yessssssssss,* I'd groan. *And do you know whyyyyyyyy I'm always so miserable?*

In real life I longed for the courage to be rude to him, so since it was my fantasy and I had all the control, I granted myself permission, and just to be irritating, I crooned in sort of a sing-song manner: *I detest being part of a parade, Daaaaaaad.* Then I zeroed in on his eyes so he understood the gravity of my seriousness and said, *I hate marching in line with the boys. All those gawkers eying us? Besides, I don't give a shit about what grows up from a rock or leaks from some stone ceiling. Why should I smile at some damn phony Santa Claus sitting on a dusty throne in a clammy room on a sweltering July day pretending to be jolly?*

Kid profanity was unheard of in our house, but it had its place and I never hesitated to use it when I talked to myself, especially when I was frustrated. In real life, my father never gave up; in my imagination, I didn't either. Those were glorious moments. So he'd say, *What about your thirteenth birthday? Didn't we take you to the Steel Pier to see Duane Eddy? You're so high and mighty you didn't even appreciate that. And it cost me a week's pay.* In my blatant romp of impertinence, I'd cock my head and arch one eyebrow, looking so much the image of him, and fire back, *I doubt that. It's not like it was Elllllllvissss.*

Then, I'd look at him like he'd lost all his marbles — kind of like he looked at me all the time — and ask, *Didn't you have the nerve to drag Jackie along "on my birthday" and spoil my one and only chance to pretend I was a rich only child?* Hey maaaan, I'd say, using beatnik lingo. Need I tell you that cool slang was not appreciated in the John J. Allen household? Uttering it even in fantasy was risky — so completely disrespectful that I'm sure both God and John J. Allen were surveying my mind and that one of them was going to pounce. But I did it anyway. *Hey maaaan, I'm sick of being part of a circus troupe, maaaaan.* Then I'd act like a real beatnik, though I didn't snap my fingers and call him daddy-o; that was too hokey, even for fantasy. But a little head bob wouldn't hurt. So, rocking my head back and forth, I'd say, *Like, don't you get it maaaan? I don't want to be saddled with any damn kids. None.*

I could have stopped there, because I had him. In my little absurd frolic, he'd be shocked off guard by the mouth on me, quiet little me, and despite myself, I'd begin to feel embarrassed for him. But I'd keep going, because I always had more to say to Pops and I wasn't going to allow any softhearted guilt to shut me up. In truth, I wasn't tough and heartless, but in the privacy of my own thoughts, I certainly made myself so. Generously, I'd let him keep sputtering — not because I was being nice, but because I wanted him to do the setup. He was so pathetically easy to play off of. So predictable. *You always want more and more.* I'd make him whine like a little kid. Even though it made me a little uncomfortable to see him shaky, it showcased his weakness and granted me power. *You're never satisfied. Never.*

I made steam shoot from his ears like in the Saturday-morning cartoons. Made his face beet red as he grasped for a good insult he could hurl at me. Being John J. Allen, he always found something, so he'd snap, *Don't we always stop for ice cream on the way back from the shore? Every time, without fail?* That was good. What kid didn't love ice cream? At last he found something even I, in my pitiless, thankless attitude, could not grumble about. But of course it was my script, and I had him trumped — rock, paper, scissors. I win.

I exaggerated my politeness, strummed out my response in a long, slow drawl. So I said, *Yes sir; yes sirree. Yes, you do take us out for ice cream.* I let him relax a bit, let him think he's won as I revel in my relaxed confidence, glaring down at him — in my imagination, I always towered over Jack. Then I'd speak as if I were the Queen of England herself. *First, let me say, I deplore your laziness and impatience.* I really wanted to swear at him here, but I figure that would've spoiled the cadence of my pompous melodrama, so I just lifted my chin higher and said, *Bulk ordering seven vanilla milkshakes makes you an inconsiderate skinflint — I hate milkshakes, Jaaaack. And anyway, even if I didn't, I only like chocolate. Secondly, they always smell like your fishy hands, and who wants to suck that up through a straw, huh?* In the soft focus of my inner landscape, after begging my forgiveness and making promises, all of which I grudgingly accept for the good of the family, John J. Allen would finally, finally shut his mouth — permanently. Ahhhh, the heartwarming sound of success.

Imagination only took me so far, and somewhere between desperate measures and absolute insanity, I began sneaking kids in the house while I was babysitting my brothers. Those kids included boys. These acts of daring were not only beyond reckless, but completely forbidden and punishable by death, a fact I conveniently ignored. Something must have worked loose in my brain; maybe the screw that held in my common sense backed its way out and left a flap open enough to let in too much stupid dust. It wasn't defiance or a hip act of teenage rebellion. It was a simple, desperate struggle to breathe, to suck in whatever oxygen I could from the vacuum inside 14 Beaumont Road — somehow wedge space between the commands and rules in John J. Allen's house, a house where I felt bound so tight with tape that my heart pinched when it beat. I knew well the consequences of such risk, and I gambled anyway.

First it was girlfriends I sneaked in through the backdoor while my brothers ran around crazy wild in the dipping evening sun. Having friends over did not make me less attentive to the boys; I was never attentive in the first place. I didn't care if they fell and shattered a limb or gashed a huge gaping wound into their skulls. When I had to mind them at the local lake, I kept myself amused by flirting with cute boys, far out of sight of my unsupervised brothers. There was a lifeguard, so I wasn't completely irresponsible. And there were lots of other parents available if a hurt and crying boy needed some help.

Which, it turned out, one of them did. But those boys got hurt all the time, so I was unmoved when a neighbor man came running up the hill in a condemning, quasi panic, yelling that I'd better get down to the lake because one of my brothers was hurt. I just rolled my eyes and sauntered down the hill, taking my sweet time. I hated being interrupted. I might have been tethered to those boys, but the leash was long, and I didn't want them to bother me, even if they were bleeding. Who but negligent parents would leave their young children with a sitter whose heart seethed with hate and anger? Maybe desperation made them completely oblivious. I guess the call of the bowling alley was pretty strong.

My girlfriends and I would tell dirty jokes and laugh ourselves into stitches. If we could scrape up enough money, we'd order pizzas and sodas, and sometimes snatch old dinner plates my mother would never miss and smash them on the concrete walk outside the back door. Though I don't know why, my parents never spotted the shards gleaming in the grass the mornings after. And, oh yeah, we'd cuss, too. It made us feel strong and potent, and older than we were. Then there were the prank phone calls, and when we had a mind to, we could get really raunchy. My brothers could have burned down the house and I wouldn't have noticed. As long as they were quiet, I didn't give a damn what they did.

Sneaking in boys was a different challenge altogether, a stealth operation that required lots of preplanning. Where girlfriends might have earned me a reprimand I probably could live with, boys would have meant my sudden death. Darkness and sleeping brothers were absolute rules. So, over the brief course of a crush or two, a boy would hide his bike alongside the garage, climb over the Cyclone fence, and tap on the utility-room door. It was all so clandestine and terrifying and incredibly sentimental in a forbidden-romance kind of way.

Those sweet kisses and awkward embraces connected me to kindness and hope, ferried me into a dreamland of smiling faces and warm hearts. Until an unexpected flash of headlights lit up the family room one night and sent me into a panic of pulling and pushing the boy out the back door. *Oh my God*, I had no more than thirty seconds, forty-five at the most, to shove him out, smooth the wrinkles on the old couch where we had been cuddling, and ditch every single telltale sign, including cigarette smoke. Waving my hands in the air, I grabbed the ashtray, but didn't know what to do with the butts. My mother smoked only Raleighs, and these were Winstons. *Oh my God.*

I raced to the powder room next to the washing machine and dumped and flushed, praying that those butts didn't float like corks and hang around the bowl dipping and bobbing. Car doors slammed. Muffled voices drifted in through the curtained windows. Twenty seconds. I heard the tumbler release, and a cool draft smacked my scorching cheeks, fiery not from passion but from terror. *Oh my God.* What else? What else? Two glasses on the coffee table. Too late. Too late. *Oh my God.* I fell into the corner of the couch and stared straight ahead at the television, heart pounding so violently that it threw me into spasms of coughing. My father hit the stairs hard and clamored down fast enough that I thought he was going to take a header, which would have been a big save for me. "Whose bike is that outside?' he demanded.

Oh my God, I was dead. And so was David, who obviously didn't escape in time and was at that very moment probably cowering behind the juniper bushes by the fence, shaking so badly that his skin was coming loose, making his own private deal with Jesus and anybody else up there who would listen. *Oh my God. Oh my God.* I was caught. I was caught.

Disaster was so close that I could smell my blood spent on the scuffed eight-by-eight tiles under my swinging feet that were supposed to be making me look relaxed. If John J. Allen determined I was lying, he could lunge into an uncontrollable rage and finally, after all the years of restraint, justify the backhand he would at long last get to crack across that smart mouth of mine. Plus there was the remote possibility that my mother could leap from the shadows slapping and clawing at me, making me swear that I had not just been in the arms of an unknown boy, when she knew deep in her gut otherwise.

How much clearer could the evidence have been? It was practically scrawled in red letters across the knotty pine paneling. A couple of half-empty jelly glasses on the table. Since when did I drink from two glasses at once? Would I actually lounge on the couch sipping grape juice with one of my brothers, discussing world events? And the pungent sulfur from a just-lit match burning into tobacco? Given that no one else in the house smoked cigarettes, how could the stink from one of my mother's have stalled in the recreation room for hours? Especially when she didn't even spend much time down there? No need to look in the mirror to know that my lipstick was smeared. *Oh my God.* I may as well have been an ant on a busy sidewalk. I was about to be annihilated, and with my heart thrashing against my ribs and a swarm of bees in my ears, I could barely process that notion fast enough.

"Answer me! Whose bike is that outside?" Dread twisted and yanked, stretching itself into a play-act resembling composure as I battled to keep from shuddering. Shrugging my shoulders, I looked my father straight in the eyes and without so much as a quiver in my voice said, "I don't know. Maybe one of the boys' friends left it." Raising his chin, he arched one eyebrow, and I knew I was in for the hate stare. A laser-beamed, eyelids-lowered, unblinking glare that always landed on my cheeks with the hiss of a branding iron and pooled sweat onto my upper lip and into my armpits and left me wilted, in danger of disappearing like a snowflake facing boiling water. How could I ever expect myself to stand up to wrath with a personal grudge, even if it did wear a bow tie and comb its thinning hair into a three-strand wave?

I had no choice. It was either force myself mightier than I was to buy a few more injury-free seconds or face immediately the potency of John J. Allen's venom. Two things we had in common, John J. Allen and I. Love for my mother. And hate for each other. I knew the twitch, that urge to charge into territory from which there is no return, that longing for the physical payout of rage that would guarantee a good's night sleep. I would have loved to batter John J. Allen into oblivion with the power of my own fists and fall into a dreamless sleep like a satiated newborn. Just like he wanted to do to me. Violence. It's such a convenient, low-cost portal to emotional ejaculation.

Forcing myself calm, I glanced at the TV droning on and on in the background, and again at John J. Allen, trying to ignore his huffing, the anger burgeoning on his face, making believe I wasn't holding my breath and bracing myself for an onslaught of such gargantuan proportions that surely I would be using crutches for the next six months. Maybe in those few agonizingly long seconds while he had me gripped in his death stare, my father was trying to concoct a worthy punishment equal to a good beating. Take away the one three-minute-per-day phone call I was permitted? Exile me to my room, which I never wanted to leave anyhow unless I had someplace to go? Warn me that if I didn't shape up, I would be forbidden to babysit his kids? What else besides a walloping was left? He could do some nice dream smashing, but I didn't have any good ones left. And how many times could he belittle me with the same old insults and expect them to bite as hard?

What John J. Allen did not know existed, and therefore made him nearly impotent, was that my mother and I had a little collusion going on — I carried on an entire social life behind his back. Not even John J. Allen with all his blustering antagonism could destroy an invisible foe. So with no crushing punishment rising to his mind, a licking was the only thing left. The fact that I was a girl did not guarantee me a pass, and I knew it as his stare bore into me while he wrestled with what action to take. Then, in what could only be termed an epic miracle that deserved prime-time news coverage, John J. Allen turned and walked back up the stairs, and I was free. As free as the puny blowfish he unhooked from lures and threw back into the Atlantic. Suddenly I had to pee so badly that I thought I was going to wet my pants. Another miracle: there was one free-floating butt. A fast flush and the last telltale piece of evidence swirled its way to a safer roost.

My brother Jackie's escape from his pain was heroin. Mine was freedom — a world minus John J. Allen and his eyes and his endless threats of punishment. I don't know what Jackie got from his drug, but mine, the tonic of freedom, intoxicated me with such ebullience that if I could have purchased it from a shady character trolling a dark alley and injected it into my veins, I would have. I was a junkie; I just had not discovered illicit drugs. And like any addict, I took risks to get jacked up. Because when I was high with exhilaration, I was superhuman with a power I had never before known. So powerful, in fact, that I believed I was invincible. That I could heal the world with my humor, with my laughter.

In that chaos of emotion, I believed that within my circle of friends, I was loved. Not only loved, but cherished. And as if at any moment freedom was going to be stolen from me, I attacked it with brazen spunk and ferocious energy. I danced until there was nothing left to do but collapse. Laughed until I was hoarse. Made wild, reckless jokes that left my friends shocked and me the center of attention. Without a doubt, if John J. Allen had known of this abandon, he would have boot-stomped it into dust, and me along with it.

In my mania, I did not recognize the warning signals; nearly getting caught the night I shoved David out the door was one. There were others. I'd make outrageous remarks to boys that had one friend cautioning me, "You shouldn't talk to him like that, and you shouldn't let him talk to you like that, either." I didn't understand what she meant. I was just joking. Then, when I rebuffed a boy's sexual advances, he bitterly complained, "You're all talk and no action." I was always, always just kidding. Didn't they get it? I was all mouth. "You're a tease," boys would say. Of course I was; in my house, teasing was a blood sport with one rule: you took with a smile whatever John J. Allen dished out.

And that's what I expected of others — that they'd just laugh and never, ever take my loopy, hard-edged teasing and bantering for more than it was: extravagant displays of sarcastic wisecracks I used to get my fix — that heady, brain-swirling joy-high I was addicted to. I lived in a frenzy of feeding my obsession. In my manic state of freedom, I was the all-powerful Oz jostling smoke and mirrors. Strip away all the gusto, though, and I was just a desperately sad, vulnerable girl. And it would take a predator but a scant few minutes to figure that one out.

CHAPTER 6

Plunge into Darkness

I thought I could help him.

In the mysterious ways of a young spirit with an anxiousness to comfort, I lent him a shoulder to weep on. At eighteen, he was three years my senior and the subject of vicious schoolhouse gossip that grew worse with each telling. He'd gotten a girl pregnant, they said. That sweet Mary Jo. What did you expect? Look at him. Lives in the slums. Nothing but a punk.

Flush with indignation at the unfairness aimed at him, I took up his cause and missed all the cues. I didn't sense then his cruelty. Didn't identify the callousness behind the narrowing of his eyes or the mental illness that set them deep into fine webs of purple and umber that would soon land him in a locked-down psychiatric ward. I saw nothing of the meanness coiled inside him, the tongue of it quietly licking and snapping. I saw only an opportunity to help, maybe bloom beyond my destiny of being chained to a desk beneath fluorescent lights.

As I took those first steps toward something I thought I understood, how could I have recognized that I was walking into a darkness from which I would never escape? Not. Ever. Escape. If only I had turned my head, looked back, maybe I would have spotted the barred door about to clank shut, heard the iron lock being readied to slide into place, while there was still time to flee. In TV land there was always a blind girl, hands outstretched, wandering in the woods, about to fall into the pit of quicksand where she'd meet her certain death. If you weren't busy shouting, "Look out! Turn back!", you would have heard the collective cries of your neighbors up and down the block yelling the same alarm.

There was no Greek chorus caroling its warning to me as I laid my hand on his arm and said, "It's not fair." Maybe I thought I was answering the call of some unchanneled ability pushing up through the bedrock of my father's restriction. A dandelion determined to grow despite the layers of cement smothering it. Or possibly, looking to create happiness in the midst of this unpolished boy's sadness. In spite of everything, I was gifted in the art of the smile and the ability to turn a laugh, especially at myself.

Or just maybe it was the urgency, my frustrated intensity to transform ugly into beauty. If I couldn't do it for myself, maybe I could do it for someone else. Because he was ugly with dirt-encrusted fingernails and body odor that spoke of things unwashed, teeth unbrushed. Hair oiled with sweat. Where I should have seen danger, I saw pain, and the nakedness of it drew me down, unafraid, into its cavity. Its cry was so recognizable, kin to what lived in my own heart.

Maybe that dwelling place of hurting seemed so familiar that it could have been my own, and in my need to offer support, I leaped before I understood that I was mistaken. That what I took as pain was something far darker than I could have ever conceived. So it was that I jumped freely into his rescue, not knowing that there would be no getting away. Maybe it was preordained—fate toying with human destruction, an experiment to see how long it would take for a teenage girl to break beyond repair. But I heard no alarms blaring as I hurled forward in my role of counselor extraordinaire. It would not take long before I heard the sounds of my own death.

One day he was not in my life. The next day he was. And refused to leave. One by one, he turned out the rest of the lights accidentally left on by John J. Allen. Maybe you would like to believe that this is a love story gone sour. A little Romeo and Juliet tale that started out with the coy dance of flirting, a little game of hide–and–go–seek until the prince won over the damsel. Maybe you think all circumstances are variations of perception. That evil doesn't exist. All can be reasoned away or loved into better. Maybe you don't believe in the bogeyman. Maybe you should.

He crashed into my life with mission and purpose, John J. Allen minus all restraints, only not smelling of Old Spice. While I was still rattling around in the confusion and disruption of his intrusion, he strutted through my bubble of fog and anointed himself authority, early on claiming me for marriage—a marauder marching in and seizing the goods he had coming to him anyway. And because he declared me his, I was obligated to him, he said.

The racket and bluster of his demands left me dazed, a shell-shocked wanderer lost on my own street. Being locked inside a metal barrel with exploding gunshots could not have raised more pandemonium inside my head — booming echoes ricocheting, over here, over there, back again and again and again. Flinging me side to side, tossing me up, then hurling me down, until I could not collect a rational thought and craziness began to make sense.

He overpowered my present and future, commandeering what he considered his property, badgering me about his entitlement to my body with nonstop bullying about how he would get me to give in. Kissing became an epic battle, and I did not have enough arms to thwart his hands. The word no was not part of his plan as he turned me into his appendage. One afternoon, he demanded my diary. After he read its pages full of musings over boys and girlfriends and rock-star idols, he tore it up in a rage, despite my pleading and promises that those boys meant nothing to me. It was John J. Allen gone mad.

There was no air to breathe as he glued himself to my days, impounding me inside his orbit. The boundary between what was my own and what belonged to him became forever extinguished. This stranger, with his crude behavior and his keenness to bulldoze whatever stood in the way of what he wanted, carted me into his culture on the opposite side of the township with its backdrop of dilapidated houses and its coarse, vulgar tenants. He raised homing pigeons in a filthy coop that you couldn't get near for the smell, and he boasted about snapping their necks. I was never sure what heading this belonged under — Torturing Animals or Rules for Raising Pigeons — but it felt unsettlingly cruel to me. His friends were outcasts, hoods who jumped from their cars and bloodied their fists in pickup brawls and knew how to pocket money from unwatched cash registers.

He arranged double dates with these roughnecks from the streets, black couples who had musky-smelling sex in the back seat of his car while I fought him off in the front. *Come on, come on. They're doing it. You owe me. You're mine. You're gonna marry me anyway. You're gonna marry me,* he'd say over and over. He crowed about Spanish fly and its effect on girls who would throw themselves onto floor-mounted gearshifts in orgasmic frenzies, or abuse themselves with coke bottles in a craze of sex heat when they had nothing else. How once a girl got *it* she had to have it all the time. With bitterness as caustic as acid, he blamed me for the agony between his legs that he termed blue balls, and how it would be my fault if he got a horrible disease because I didn't love him enough to relieve his pain.

And there was no breaking up with him. He wouldn't leave. I was his. That was the end of it. No more questions. He wasn't going anywhere. I had to learn that. He was staying.

Twice I nearly escaped—so close I could taste the sweetness of freedom hovering just above the skyline. Gentle dreams began to play shyly at the edge of my consciousness as I began to believe I just might be able to get away. I could nearly smell the rising of grass pushing its shoots through meadow dust, envision roses blooming within songs. And I began to imagine that if he would just let us break up, I could get back to *before*. I steadied myself and pleaded my case. And off I went to a sorority meeting with my girlfriends, where I sucked in the air of laughter and the liberation of twirling in dance and the bright joy of leeway. It lasted less than an hour.

"Someone's here to see you, Kathy," my friend's mother said.

We all knew who it was. "Don't go down there," my girlfriends begged. "Don't!"

I felt bound, responsible, and slowly descended the steps and dragged myself out into the night. He was waiting in the dark, standing on the sidewalk. "I just tried to kill myself because of you," he claimed. I looked at him, trying to steel myself against his persistence, and began crying. Crying not because I cared, but because he was laying down another trap. I could feel its spikes cracking my bones, hear the crippling, brittle dry snaps as it crushed me in its grip. "I almost swerved my car in front of a station wagon full of kids. I would've killed them all, too. It would've been your fault. Your fault. If you don't go back with me, I'll leave right now and make sure I do it this time. I'll kill myself and a car full of little kids. I'll do it, and it'll be your fault."

The night pressed against me, swamping me in its weighted closeness. I could hear his breath—short, hard pants. Smell the stink of his sweat wafting toward me like menacing fingers. I visualized the family, maybe on their way back from a movie and a pizza. Everyone singing silly nursery rhymes. Then the daddy suddenly wrestling for control of the steering wheel, fighting, fighting to right the car. The kids silent at first, then screaming as the mommy reached back just before the car flipped and slid across gravel and dirt, skidding to a stop against a tree. Low moans. Then silence except for the slow tick-ticking as the wheels spun slowly to a stop.

I climbed the steps back into the house. "I have to go," I told my friends.

"Don't! Don't go with him," they begged.

"He's going to kill himself," I whispered, gathering my things, staring at the floor.

"Kathy, he's not going to kill himself. He's just trying to get you to go back with him."

They didn't know him. "He said he'll swerve his car in front of a car with kids. He'll kill everyone. He will. I know he will."

"He won't do that. He's nuts! He's nuts!" they cried.

I stepped away from the protective circle of my friends that night and into his car and sat very still while he drove me closer and closer toward the life he was preparing for me.

If I had noticed, I would have seen the day gorging on sunshine, skipping it like flat stones across the ripples on Gropp's Lake, drawing the trees — crimson and goldenrod, apricot orange — into its beams. The air, crisped and dry and nipping my cheeks, should have brought me stirrings of joy as the year settled into its majesty and exploded all the horizons into splendor. The scent of apples and damp earth and pungent smoke curling from raked mounds of fallen leaves should have intoxicated me with pleasure as I pulled on the first woolen sweater of the season and anticipated upcoming high school football games. The cheering. The uniformed band marching in formation.

But I had just smashed my fist through a window. In fact, it was a windowpane on the side door to Yardville Heights School, and the index finger on my right hand was bleeding.

I watch blood ooze from the opened flap and wonder why it doesn't hurt. He is waiting for me down past the parking lot. I wrap my finger in a tissue and shuffle toward him. Down the street a ways, I lean against the pebbled concrete bridge and stare at the lake that, despite the brilliant sunshine, lies shrouded in misted grays, its shoreline dusted in ash.

He grabs me by the arm, the one with the bleeding hand, and sidles in close, fixing his lips to my ear. I feel wetness from his saliva and can smell his breath stale with cigarette smoke. He is leaning in tight, pressing against me, digging his fingers into my arm. He's too close. Too close. Too close. I feel the rise of panic blistering me in places unseen and I don't know how I am going to stay motionless, silent, because I have to run. I have to run. But I can't. I can't. I have to stay still. Not move. Stare straight ahead. Into the water. Into the water.

"*Do you know what I'd do to a girl who cheated on me?*"

I don't see his face, but I know one eyebrow is arched, his lips pulled back in a snarl. I can read all this in the tone of his voice, feel it in the squeeze of his hand around my elbow that would leave a bruise if I weren't wearing a sweater. I don't react. His question reminds me of John J. Allen's, ominous and unanswerable. I want to rock back and forth. Soothe myself with motion. Make believe I'm home, in my bed daydreaming.

"*Huh? Do you know?*" *he asks again.*

Where am I going to pull words from? I chase them, but they scurry away, refusing capture. Then they are gone and I am abandoned, swallowed up in my silence, cringing in the space left empty. I hate this. I hate this. This is what John J. Allen does.

"*Come on,*" *he urges.* "*Answer me. Do you know what I'd do to her?*"

I just shake my head and try to picture her. The girl. The one that made him mad.

"*I'd kiss her real gently, at first.*" *He whispers this, but his tone is flat.* "*I'd tell her how much I love her. I'd keep kissing her. Touching her. I'd have my fingers down there, softening her up. Making her hot. Getting her nice and wet. Then you know what I'd do?*"

I dare not twitch. Not an eyelash. Not a muscle. The world does not exist beyond his words.

"*I'd surprise her. She'd be all hot and bothered, thinking I was going to fuck her. I'd fuck her, all right.*"

Nothing works inside my brain. My bones refuse to move. My heart is stalled.

Nothing lives inside me. Not oxygen. Not blood. Nothing. Nothing.

"Oh yeah, I'd fuck her," he says. There is glee in his voice. "I'd fuck her with a knife. What d' ya think about that? A real sharp knife. Good and sharp. I'd shove that thing up her so hard and I'd keep shoving. I'd rip her apart. No bitch is ever gonna cheat on me."

Where dreams go when they stop their visits, I don't know. I guess I wasn't fun to play with anymore, and mine dashed away to find a girl who could make them come true. Between him and John J. Allen, there was no room for gentle musings. What chased me into sleep that night of the threat and countless ones thereafter was the image of that girl and the shocking agony she would have to endure if she somehow slipped up. Or if he thought she slipped up. I knew that girl was me. It was me he would butcher if he got mad. Not some faceless waif. It was me.

He had a plan. I knew what a bully could do. I'd heard the screams of my brothers facing the attack of John J. Allen's belt. I lived every day with my father's emotional cruelty and folded constantly under the weight of his temper. Yes, I believed fervently in the threat of bodily mutilation at the hands of a street tough, heard the foreboding warping his voice, the cold relish of his calculation. He frightened me, and I collapsed like a dog beneath one too many kicks. Because I believed it would not take any blunder for him to take up a knife against me. I knew he would do it whenever he felt a strong wind of suspicion brush up against the jealousy he lugged about. He would harm me anytime he had a mind to.

There is a place beyond fear. Beyond despair. Past panic with its racing heart and unbridled urgency to bolt. Farther down even than disgust and revulsion. It is a vacuum of utter silence. A quiet so silent that the sounds of breathing cannot be heard. It is a state of paralysis where the elastic motions of living become deliberate acts of might — staring straight ahead; staying upright; speaking coherently; smiling. And in those nights of fitful sleep, I drifted there — tumbled, actually — into it.

Into acceptance. The simple fact that this was my life. There would be no God swooping down on a thunderbolt, or gallant knight riding rescue on a white steed. Not even a mother reading the unspoken words I could not cry out loud. I did not need to feel the poise of a blade against my privates to understand what I had to do. I fell into what I knew — obedience with its practiced flattery and feigned interest, and moves that guarantee no wake.

During those dark years, I believed that obedience was my protection, that my compliance bought me safety from harm. After all, politeness, a smile, and acquiescence mostly kept John J. Allen's unwanted attention at a distance. Though with John J. Allen, I found ways to live behind his back. In this situation, I wouldn't dare. I existed tiptoeing lightly about the fringes of his harshness, just like I learned to do with John J. Allen, trying not to raise his ire. Never could I have understood that hiding in the depths beyond obedience was something far more sinister. How could I have known that when my will to fight crumbled and melted away and I took up the dance of disappearing in plain sight, I forfeited myself to a greedy beast who would usher me straight to the bottom — a point so low, so degrading, that its only equal is a gutter slicked with refuse? A place where even the Catholic God with all His ceremonial vestments and trumpeted hymns would not show His pretty face?

Some time ago I met a woman whose boyfriend literally kicked her out of the car onto the street and forced her to crawl in the gutter along the highway. The gutter with its sewage — the stench of liquefied human waste and animal droppings and slimy gobs of phlegm and decaying food. GeorgeAnne cried but never complained. So there it is. You do not have to die to go to hell, because if you are crawling in the gutter without protest, you're already there.

And once you are there, that is where you stay, always. That's the untold truth. It is where you secretly live forever. Despite your fancy clothes, your expensive purses, or your New York-style shoes. Far-away removed from the sight of the rest of the world, cowering in the shameful darkness, you are the sad, weeping sister of rage.

I was my own dearest enemy, and my most sordid agony was participating in my own abuse. And the shame of that collusion, my complete failure to defend myself, plunged me into lifelong despair that could not even be healed by the power of unconditional love. If I believed in the devil, surely the gutter was his home. And I became his whore.

CHAPTER 7

Evil Deeds

"Shut Up! Shut Up!" he shouted. I was screaming. Screaming. In the front seat of his car, screaming. Flailing. My screams spewing agony. A bellowing storm of pain. "Shut up, I said," and he jerked his arm back and let loose, smashing his hand into my mouth. That should have made me shut me up. The instant shock. The immediate throbbing ache as my lips ballooned. The salty blood leaking onto my tongue. The sting racing across my cheeks, blossoming them red. But it didn't. In that car that smelled of swamp water and body odor and his foul breath, I couldn't shut up. I couldn't.

~ ~ ~

The voice watching and listening from inside my head says, "One foot in front of the other. Just put one foot in front of the other. Don't think. Just do. No looking down."

He is ahead, leading me up an unlit stairway, the heat of the muggy afternoon trapped between the walls that have long ago peeled their paint and are now just smears of grease and grime from countless dirty hands. Collected in the corners on each step are tufts of dust and debris, sloughed-off flakes of skin, human hair, dog hair, bits of fallen food, all baked into moldy clumps by the day's hotness.

"Don't think about it. Just breathe through your mouth," the voice says, soothing me.

The room is stifling. It is his bedroom. And the worn sheets on the mattress are limp and crumpled, soiled with stains, smelling of stale body fluids that he has not bothered to wipe up.

"Just stare straight ahead. It will be over soon. Don't think about it," the voice cautions. But the dirt. The filth. The stench. I don't want it to touch me. I don't want it to touch me.

"Just stay quiet."

So I stare straight ahead, not seeing, not feeling. I am obedient — to him, to the voice. I am half stripped. My shorts and underpants pulled down. I am lying on top of filthy sheets, not wanting them to touch me, not wanting him to touch me. It's so ugly. So ugly. I have to get away. Have to run. Panic pounds my chest with hammering blows.

"Stay quiet. Be still," the voice says.

But I am being ripped in two. My body is tearing, splitting apart.

"Listen to me," the voice commands. "Calm down. You have to calm down. Don't think about it. Soon it will be over. Calm down. Just breathe. Swallow. Swallow. Don't make noise. Just be quiet. Disappear. You can stay still and run to safety," the voice says. "You know where to go, where none of this can touch you. Just go there, go to safety."

I want to shriek bloodcurdling screams and never stop. I want to live a life of screaming. A lunatic girl wailing and banging her head against the wall, right at home in an insane asylum. But I obey and am silent. So silent. So polite.

"Yes, that's it, breathe through your nose. Stay calm. Stare out the window," the voice says.

But bugs are decaying on the rotted sill. And there are eyesores outside — drooping wires strung house-to-house; sagging rooftops; chimneys leaning, ready to tumble.

"Then close your eyes. Just stay calm. Don't think about it. Soon it will be over and you can go."

"Go where?" I ask. "Home to John J. Allen's fanatical bullying?"

"Sssh, sssshhh. Soon. Soon it will be over."

I am flawless: a perfect victim, primed under John J. Allen's tutelage of no complaining, ever. What rapist wouldn't love me? I make no sounds. I lie still, my limbs pliant. I am patient. Polite to a fault, taught so well. I display outward grace. Poise in rape. Dignity while being degraded. Its oddness is lost to me. It is all I have, so it's what I use to distract myself from the truth: that I am filthy, like a debased princess pretending her gown is not ripped to shreds, pretending she doesn't stink. Pretending I am not a slut. But the stench is devouring me; sweat and the gummy insides of him cling to my skin. Stink that will never wash off.

"Get up! Get up!" he shouts, and yanks me hard by the arm. "My damn mother is home!"

He jerks me awake from my stupor and I scramble to my feet on rubbery legs. I pull at my clothes, trying to cover myself. He shoves me into a tiny closet where the heat and the smell and the fear slam my heart against my ribs, and I quake so loud that I am sure his mother will hear my bones rattling alongside my panting. Last night's dinner rolls in my stomach with a powerful threat. Fuzz and cotton cram my head, and I am so woozy that my knees begin to buckle.

In the dark, I stumble over the tattered sneakers and heaps of soiled clothes piled on the floor and thump against the back wall. Weak with terror, I slide to the floor, cowering like a wounded animal. The stench of him is glued to me like paste and now wafts up from the rank pile I have fallen into, taunts me from his clothes dangling in front of my face. The nausea thrashes wild in my stomach and hurls upward toward my mouth, and I battle not to retch. My heart and bones are a helpless mutiny of ever-increasing deafening booms and clatters inside my skin, drowning out the voice. Where's the voice? I can't get a hold of myself, my body. I don't know if I can stop from exploding and firing my innards all over the walls, the floor, splattering them on the ceiling.

She's going to find me. Never mind that she's a social worker in charge of repairing lives. That bulky woman with her thick arms and tree-trunk legs, shouting, cursing — goddamn this, goddamn that — is going to bound up the stairs straight to this closet. When she wrenches ʻopen the door and discovers me trembling behind the pile of dirty clothes, she will jerk me out so fast that I will be no more than a shivering blur stinking of hymen blood and filth and of the shit that will surely course down my legs at the sight of her.

I hear her bellowing threats, pounding up the stairs, barreling closer. And closer. Just outside the room now with its bed of rumpled, clammy sheets and dank scars of his ejaculate and my hemorrhage. She is yelling. Screeching within feet of me, just beyond the closet door that rattles from the force of her rage. Drenched in the sweat of panic, I cringe tighter into the wall with a dread so ripe, one tiny prick and it will erupt. He is yelling back, cursing at her. Unafraid of his bluster, she does not retreat, just keeps shrieking her threats, her profanities, on the way back down the stairs and out the front door that she slams to this dirty house of dirty people where I only narrowly escape discovery.

~ ~ ~

And so I did explode after all, less than an hour later in the front seat of his car. I exploded into earsplitting screams. Into hysterical flailing. All the seams of my body popping and bursting in a messy gush of agony, spouting the bottled fear and terror of the bed, the closet. Of his mother. Of him. Howling at my shredded, bruised vagina stinging of brush burns, sobbing at the spasms in my gut from him. From him. The heat and racket of my screams besieged that car. Then suddenly with a muffled *woomf* and a sizzling crack, his hand smashed into my mouth, unleashing salty blood and triggering the swell of tissue.

But that blow did not stop my madness, not when my heart was splintering under a truth. The truth of my compliance; my contemptible obedience; my despicable collusion with him against myself. All of me ruptured with grief at my unvoiced protests swallowed and buried under politeness and watery smiles. I despised the body that lay docile and pliant in filth while inside I screeched like a maniac. I screamed in the front seat of that car with unspeakable anguish, anguish born from my silence. The silence that granted him permission to destroy me. And that truth was so haunting, so depraved, that it would remain forever unforgivable.

When my mother asked about my blowfish lips, I told her I was hit by a hockey stick. That's what I wanted to have happened, to have taken one for the team, been fearless in a tough game. Courageous enough to jump in the huddle swinging, unafraid to risk it all. In school, that's what I told everybody. I'd been hit by a hockey stick. It didn't matter that I didn't play on a hockey team or that the only time I played at playing was in once-a-week gym class where mostly I dodged whatever came toward me. Nobody questioned that.

Everyone bought what I told them — even John J. Allen, who teased me about my fat lip. And there I was, issuing him the obligatory chuckle, because that swollen lip was kind of funny, wasn't it? I liked the bit of lighthearted drama that made me seem like a klutz instead of a whore. Besides, who would ever want to hear the unfunny reality? Who would ever want to know that I was belted in the mouth by a boyfriend and abused in a way I could not even face, much less confess? Who wanted to hear that the shame I carried was worse than the sludge clinging to the sides of an unflushed toilet?

So I used my injury to make myself a star in my own eyes. I cleaned it up, made it pretty, and to give it real brilliance, added a touch of bravery. It would have been a great story if it had been true. But for a few days, I basked in the sun of hero status. It was known that Kathy Allen was willing to take a hockey stick to the mouth for the win. From that day of terror and abuse, I managed to score a few *attagirls*. It wasn't much. But it was something.

It takes flight like a preening vulture, abuse does, and grows fat by gorging on silence. Unchecked, it rides the winds, landing wherever it wishes, enjoying a glorious berth of freedom inside the boundless territory of someone else's fear and misery. What did it matter where he decided to affix his talons? If the police came upon his car in the woods where I cringed, rumpled and exposed, sobbing, he managed to sweet-talk his way out of a statutory rape charge—*Ah, you understand, officers; it's young love.* What difference to him who was within earshot or sight distance when he asserted his claim? Cocksure, he took what he wanted whenever he felt like it, and he reduced me to a piece of cheap meat. I made peace with the duty rapes. I knew what to expect. Stillness and silence were my only allies, so I clamped my eyes shut, clenched my fists, lay still, and kept quiet. And blocked everything out.

All except the terror. The merciless terror of discovery sank its teeth deep and rode roughshod with me everywhere—a maniacal, screeching phantom, clawing at me relentlessly, petrifying me with detailed visions of my capture. Its favorite: me being caught naked and spread-eagle while he used me. I melted into the background of my life, a shadow of my shadow. Long gone were my spirited antics, my friends. No more joyful exuberance at being out of John J. Allen's line of vision. If I wasn't under John J. Allen's scrutiny, I had this street tough stuck to my side—and always, always clinging to me was the terrifying dread of being caught.

Then, unexpectedly, hope dawned. He was going into the service. He gave me a framed picture of himself decked in a Navy uniform—so that I wouldn't forget him, I suppose. But secretly I sagged with relief, and in the privacy of my bedroom, I fell to my knees in prayerful thanksgiving to God that he was going away and I would be free. Well, not exactly free, but free from his physical presence at least. He expected me to write him every day. And then there was that whole knife-shoved-up-the-vagina thing I had to be concerned about. And the threats to slaughter families on the highways. And I dared not ignore his rage and proven willingness to hit me.

So I entertained no crazy notions of cheating on him. But like a sweet, patient friend, hope began to nuzzle me, purring softly in my ear, and bit by bit I began to unfold and look forward to uncomplicated pleasures — the phone ringing and it not being him. The joy of reading a book without being preoccupied with worry or dread. All tiny steps toward reclaiming some of myself. Maybe, I thought, my daydreams would return.

The day he left for his stint, I picked up a magazine, sank into a living-room chair, opened it, and just breathed. And breathed. Clean air washed over me, and while I could never really be clean again, I could inhale its fragrance, loosen myself in its promise. For a long, long time I sat like a bag of wilted bones in that chair, silent, grateful, and spent, luxuriating in the downy, tender shoots of hope. Those were good moments.

Not that they lasted. Within days he was back on my doorstep, and my second attempt at escape deflated like a worn-out balloon. Discharged from the service. Dishonorable? Medical? Psychological? Did it have something to do with the episode of mental illness that had put him in a locked-down psychiatric ward not long before he embarked on his big-talking, he-man, patriotic stage show? I don't know, but like a chronic disease, he charged back into my life, and that hope that had begun its bloom turned as black as decay.

It was the mattresses that frightened me. Pockmarked with broad yellow stains. Smelling of pus and sweat — of substances excreted, oozed, and shed from unclean bodies. Wiry scatterings of pubic hair. Streaks of stool. Dribbled urine. Fingernail grease. Scabs. Strands of oily hair. Mattresses were a repository of filth in which I lay skin-down. I thought the gutter was as low as you could get. But I was wrong. It is the mattresses, a hell unto themselves harboring their own brand of double-sided torture. Rape and squalor. That was the paralyzing, terrifying height of torment. And I had to touch them; my body had to touch them.

Inside my head, I shrieked and screamed; begged, prayed, *please no.* But they touched me anyway. *He* touched me on those mattresses with his filthy hands and his sweat and the crud that spilled from his penis, and I was contaminated as surely as if I'd been thrown into a cesspool. If those mattresses could have mustered up laughter, it would have been shrill and mocking, as they petted my skin with all their refuse and ogled the goings-on.

His father was as dirty as he was. Pot-bellied and dressed always in janitor greens, teeth rotted from tobacco, he lived in a welfare motel. He reminded me of my Uncle John, except he didn't have a humpback and Uncle John's teeth weren't rotted—they were gone. At midnight on the New Year's Eve I was thirteen, Uncle John pulled me into a tight squeeze, grinding his body into mine, and French-kissed me, sticking his tongue far into my mouth until I gagged. My mother and father and his wife, Aunt Irene, thought it was hilarious. It made me sick.

His father never touched me; he just leered a "you go get her, boy" smile and lent his son the use of his bed in the one-room pigsty he called home. Home of the mattress where the old man flopped his oily body and belched and farted his way into sleep. A cell with one lone window hung with dingy makeshift curtains and a rug plaited with the slag and muck he dragged in on his boots and left there to putrefy. Piled in a sink in the corner by the hot plate were dishes and pans encrusted with the leavings of a week's worth of feedings. I don't need to tell you about the stench in that room.

He was driving me to school and decided to take a detour. Though I didn't realize it at the time, it must have been planned. Because his father stood outside the row of forlorn rooms that seemed to bear the end of all hope, where dreams of the fine job and the cute little house in the suburbs came to die beneath the trash swirling in the gutter outside the doors. Leaning against a pole by the curb smoking a cigarette, the geezer tossed a smirk and a half wave when he saw his son's car. Proud of his boy, he was. Willing to do anything for the kid.

The son led me into that room where nothing lived except ugly and steered me, dressed for school in my red-and-black plaid skirt and white blouse pressed crisp with pleats, to the mattress crawling with vile. I disappeared then — into the arms of a protective angel, I would like to say, but that would be fiction, a feel-good fantasy. No, I sank deep into the forces that patrol the darkness, swallowed up by what lurked inside that mattress, where I died as I breathed, as rancid as all the garbage around me. Hell would have been a blessing.

CHAPTER 8

Not Kathleen, Not My Daughter

My periods stopped. The abuse did not.

I didn't want to go with him. The World's Fair had descended upon New York with trumpets and newsreels and fancy promises. Fanfare has a way of stirring up frenzy. Everyone wanted to go. I wanted to go too, but not with him. I didn't want to go with him. I didn't want to. But I went. Without complaint, I went. Despite the brilliant colors of the flags and plantings of lush blooms carpeting the grounds, the smells of popcorn and cotton candy meandering down the fairways, the sights of so many different countries parading their cultures, I could not rise above the misery that left my head too heavy to hold up. That felt like sodden bricks wedged inside my chest, hampering my breathing, weighing my limbs so I could barely lift them. All I could manage was silence. Leaden, submissive silence.

Of all the fair's marvels, I remember only the escalator. How high it soared, dizzyingly high, straight into the sunlight, crafting a moving quilt out of the shapes and colors below. It crawled upward in a long, endless climb, rewarding riders with a spectacular panorama — a sumptuous vision of manufactured design. I heard the *oohs* and *ahhs* of the spectators around me, heard their *look at thats*, sensed the crush of bodies as they pointed fingers and strained for even better views.

Gliding up that escalator, I was not a tourist fawning over the festivities. I stood immobile, folded into myself, staring straight ahead, begging time to *hurry, please, please hurry*. I needed the ride to be over, because his hands, as dirty as if they'd been raked through manure, were on me. Every now and again in a feeble grasp at dignity, I'd run my hands down my shirtwaist dress with a surreal calmness I did not feel and smooth the wrinkles, making sure it was tidy. Tidy despite the filth mauling it. Trying to keep immaculate the crisp violet cotton that my mother had starched and steam ironed so it would be pretty for the World's Fair.

But the dress was hopelessly tainted from his hands, as was my body, and what my mother did not know was that I was hiding something beneath the full skirt of that freshly pressed dress, and that the dread that consumed me, the terror of her finding out my secret, was so raw that it was a fire blistering my skin. The horror of my mother or anyone knowing of my shame was so vast that nothing existed beyond its horizon. But he knew, and he was devising plans. And on that day with its otherworldly backdrop of bright blue sky and the call of families with their intimate conversations close by, the slap, slap of rubber soles against cement so achingly innocent as folks rushed from exhibit to exhibit, I was encased in such gloom that I could barely stand upright as he rode the escalator behind me.

In an orderly world, nightmares would only visit under the cloak of darkness, not pounce in the shimmering light of day surrounded by the blind exuberance of sightseers. But I knew that sinister things could happen just at the edge of the ordinary, even when you were wearing a cute dress and the people around you were laughing and licking ice cream cones. Still, I had not been prepared for the slide of cotton against nylon and the shock of open air hitting my backside. I twisted to the side, but he gripped my waist with one hand, while with the other he held up the back of my dress exposing my flimsy underpants, my bare buttocks beneath.

A dog will bare its teeth and snarl in protest against aggression. Even a rat, a creature of the sewer, will scurry away when threatened or attack when cornered. All I could offer was a weak nudge at his hand — an old woman shooing away a fly. At my measly protest, he pressed his mouth into my ear. *I own this*, he said, and yanked my skirt up higher, displaying all I owned below my waist while he hooked his fingers under the elastic of my underpants, pushed it aside, and began poking and digging, crawling his hand across my bare bottom, trying to get his fingers into me.

I wanted to slide to my knees and weep in despair at the degradation I could no longer endure, to cross my arms over my head and just sob. Sob away the solid mass of pain lodged inside me. Sob until I dissolved into nothing. I wanted to cry over the breathtaking beauty about me now turned ugly. Over the suffocating humiliation of him hiking up my dress and shoving his hand beneath my underwear — not in the seclusion of a dank room on a stinking mattress, but in public. In front of decent people. Moms and dads toting cameras and maps. Children. Small girls in frilly dresses. Little boys in coonskin caps. Grandparents reaching hands out to keep toddlers safe. Families like my own that bathed every day and wore clean clothes and would never expect to see a girl on exhibition as a gutter tramp within feet of the United States of America Pavilion at the New York World's Fair.

The weight of that disgrace was more than I could bear. The torment of being trapped between him with his unending cruelty and John J. Allen with his incessant, merciless bullying and crushing authority knocked me to my knees. But I stood erect and did not move, not an eyelash. Did not allow a tear to roll down my cheek. I just quietly sucked air into a throat constricted with such pain that I could barely wheeze and stared straight ahead. Stone still while his fingers roamed my flesh. I could have been a statue staring into space, fronting an exhibit. I was nothing as his fingers dug and probed. Nothing except a corpse inside a cotton dress. When at last the escalator reached the top, I stepped off, smoothed my hands down my dress, and like a zombie unearthed long after death, kept walking.

~ ~ ~

I claw at my stomach, punching, hitting, beating it. I have to dislodge it. Have to make it go away. That thing that is growing inside me. It has to go away. It has to. I have to get rid of it. I rock and sway and punch and beg God. "Please! Please!" I beg. I plead. And I punch. And punch. But it won't go. I want to bang my head against the wall, my bedroom wallpapered with tiny flowers and thumb-tacked with pictures of Elvis and Ricky Nelson. I plead for help from the souls in purgatory. Such a desperate Catholic thing to do. I want to have the guts to plunge a butcher knife up my vagina, but I can't even muster the nerve to use a coat hanger. I want to swallow pills, bottles of them. Slice a razor across my wrists. Throw myself down the stairs. But I'm scared. So scared.

Downstairs my mother is preparing lunch, spreading peanut butter and jelly across Wonder bread. A dozen sandwiches will be wolfed down by the boys. I hear them running across the wood floors, slamming doors. The phone rings. "Hello?" my mother answers. Please, please don't let it be for me. A few feet away is my vanity, skirted in starched pink cotton and topped by a triple mirror where I used to make faces at myself. I catch a quick glance at my reflection. It is contorted with agony. Throwing my head back, I pinch my eyes shut and wail a scream so loud that the veins in my neck bulge, my face blazes hot. The scream is piercing. Piercingly mute. Only the thump, thump of my fists beating into the downiness of my stomach make a sound. Thump. Thump. The sound of beating a stuffed animal. Thump. Thump. Thump. The screams, deafening, erupt in silence.

I grab my coat, a black trench that I keep wrapped around my ballooning self every time I leave the house. It is my hiding place and I wear it everywhere, a reincarnation of batty Aunt Nellie, who always kept herself locked inside a black coat until the day she died. I want to die today. Today.

"I'm going out for a walk," I call to my mother.

"What about lunch?" she asks from the kitchen.

"I'll eat when I come back." She has no idea. It's been months since I've asked for sanitary napkins, and she's never even noticed.

Outside it's spring, but I ignore the crocuses popping their heads up and the daffodils dancing to the rhythm of the wind. Spring, the season of new beginnings. I thrust my hands into my pockets and beat my fists against my thighs, my waist. I am freezing, shivering, clanking, and rattling inside my coat, despite the sunshine trying to envelop me in its warmth. He is taking me to Maryland tomorrow, dragging me further into the nightmare. He is going to marry me. He has a ring. Elkton, Maryland. It is where everybody goes to get married, he has told me. It's fast, no questions ever asked.

I force back the cry welling now in my throat, urging itself upward, trying to pry my mouth open. Tomorrow is roaring toward me, gathering pace and speed, the sound of hoofbeats rushing toward stampede. My body weakens at the tremors rumbling under my feet as it races in my direction. And I know with utter clarity that tomorrow will bring one moment so savage, so brutal, that it will be like a garrote twisted tight around my neck, a sledgehammer slammed into my solar plexus. It will be the second my parents learn of my…of my…that I am….

I can't even think the word, or pull it together with letters; for them as well, the shock of just the word will blanch all color from their faces. Then ashen will give way to pink as the horror sets in and their disbelieving glares bore into me. I will writhe in anguish as my secret shame prances and howls its silent shriek of victory — the maniacal phantom triumphs at last. And in a voiceless scream I will beg for death. But I won't die; I will be locked into their stares, shamed further by their words. Then I will be inked by more humiliation as the truth gathers steam and bursts like nighttime screams from 14 Beaumont Road, races up and down the street, crashes through the school doors, works its way into the homes of friends. Relatives. I will be naked in my shame before all of them. And not one will reach out with kindness. Not one. I know this. I see the future as if it is spooling across a television screen. I am not wrong. The thunder is rolling toward me. It is coming and I cannot stop it.

With brilliant sun glinting off the hood of his two-toned Chevy, a neighbor drives by, honks, and waves. Briefly I rise from my trance and return the wave, tossing a full-size smile along with it. Then it hits me: traffic constantly zips up and down South Broad Street. I could hurl myself in front of a car, a speeding car. Or into the path of a delivery truck maybe on its way to Gropp's Lake Store with this week's supply of ice cream. Let the driver do all the dirty work. One giant leap, and poof! I'm gone. What is inside of me will be nothing more than a heap of steaming entrails lying pulsating in the gutter not far from where it was begat.

One blast of pain and I will vanish. A quick, easy shortcut to freedom. I will be free. Free from myself and the humiliation — that thick sewage of paralyzing shame that clings to my skin, my organs, that tastes like rancid perfume in my mouth and has disassembled my spirit and destroyed all the beauty that lived within my heart. I will be free from the unending swell in my belly pushing me further and further into despair. Free from him, his mauling hands, and his stinking body that keeps at me and at me, smearing me with more and more filth, until I can't tell the difference between what rots in the garbage can and the girl that lies beneath him.

The whispers and stares at school drench me in shame so unbearable that I can hardly lift my feet. I skulk around the halls, clutching books tight against my midsection, disappearing as far into my black coat as I can get, willing myself smaller and smaller. But I can't get small enough, not with this thing pushing and pushing at my skin. I see them, the kids, especially the girls, pointing, smirking, raising their eyebrows as I shuffle by, trying to be unnoticed. I have become a target of such vicious gossip that I believe no one will be satisfied until they witness the spectacle of me collapsing to floor, as the object that has siphoned the marrow from my life slithers out of my body like a bloody, cancerous tumor.

Wonder-struck, students and teachers alike will gawk with great satisfaction — the same premium contentment John J. Allen treasures when he zeroes in for the kill — as I bolt, screaming like a banshee, out the double doors, leaking clots and membrane, fleeing the mess for some hapless janitor to swab away with his string mop. "See? Told you so. She is a slut," they'll say, stepping over the gore, shaking their heads, so delighted with the prize of a good story to tell and retell.

The traffic flirts with me, luring me with its bold colors and shiny flashes of chrome. "Come on. Come on," it seems to be saying. "Just do it."

"God," I beg, "please, please give me courage. Blessed Mother, please."

I keep walking — shuffling, really — alongside the traffic, waiting for the nerve to jump in front of it. The school where I pushed my fist through the window is right here. Maybe this time the glass will sink deep into my wrist, make a good clean incision, sever a vein or an artery. Painless. I could hang my arm and let the life force leak silently onto the blacktop and I could disappear. But I can't marshal the energy to walk up the drive and through the parking lot to the building, much less garner the strength to ram my fist through thick glass.

"Souls in purgatory, please, please."

Maybe I could just run away. Run until my body drops to the ground, where I could melt into the dirt. Quietly. No eyes peering, laughing. No sneers. Unlike my brother Jackie, I don't have the guts to cross over into the netherworld, where kids wander the streets and beg money for dope and food, stealing if they have to. Where girls trade sex for the services of a backstreet butcher. And there is no one I can think of to turn to.

I try and try to think of someone, anyone, who would not recoil in disgust at the sight of me, passing through an alphabet list of aunts, briefly considering the aunt who made a big story out of my first period. If the sloppy onset of my menses was a news flash, what would she do with this? Phone up every relative she could think of and report the scandal? Did you hear about Kathleen? Yes, that Kathleen, Pat and Jack's daughter. I keep moving, slowly pushing my feet forward, racking my brain for a plan, but it is dull and lethargic, making me want to curl up in the gutter and sleep.

~ ~ ~

I didn't kill myself that afternoon, blowing a good opportunity to rise up and lay claim to my body, to myself. That night, I sat before my vanity as the failure of the day settled in and just stared at the unfamiliar girl in the mirror. The one with the once-bright blue eyes, now sunken and filmed over with gray; the girl with the thickening body. I stared eye to eye with that girl and cursed her cowardice.

Angry rain, its pings tapping hypnotic beats, pelted the car as it sped toward its destination. I huddled against the door, staring out through the rain at the drab fields and cement buildings passing in the dusky daylight. Colorless quiltings of grays and blacks. Every now and again, the rivulets racing down the passenger-side window caught my eye and I squinted, fascinated, as the water rushed down in torrents, gulping up all the lonely little droplets in its path. The glass was cool against my forehead, and I rested my head against it, keeping my eyes closed for miles.

Occasionally I drifted off and startled, waking myself. Confused, I thought I was in the car trapped next to John J. Allen, enduring one of his tirades. Or sitting safely next to my mother as John J. Allen swung his arm into the backseat of arguing boys. But no, I was in a car barreling down the road to Elkton, Maryland. I felt like dense, heavy cargo being hauled down the interstate. But really, I was no more than a carcass giving shape to a black raincoat. Stripped remains — what was left over after he had feasted, and what he had implanted had gorged on the rest. There was no me left.

But there was one last chance. Maybe he would steer the car into oncoming traffic or into a ditch or a telephone pole. The rode was wet and slippery. It would have been perfect. I wanted to pray for such a horrific accident, but I couldn't formulate the words in my head. All I could do was slump against the door and wait for the day to end.

He stopped the car and got out somewhere in Maryland, the place where kids could get married, no questions asked. But he wasn't a kid. He was draft age. He could drink in New York City. I was the kid — a stupid, gutless kid. I waited, gazing at the sad little raindrops sliding past as they disappeared into oblivion. By now it was dark outside, the street lamps sending small shafts of light across the slick, shadowed sidewalks. He got back in the car. No. Not here. Not today. I didn't ask questions. I should have been relieved, but I wasn't. What difference did it make if it didn't happen today? It would happen tomorrow, or the next day. I was not getting away.

It was time to tell my parents, he said, shifting the car into gear and swerving it into traffic. If I wouldn't, then he would. I jerked my head toward him as panic and dread welled up, squeezing sweat from my pores that washed down my chest in an oily waterfall.

"No!" I screeched, fighting the urge to jam my hands beneath my clothes and claw at the itching wetness. But his Elkton plan had failed, and all my pleading and begging were a hopeless waste of time. He was going to tell. Unless I could summon the courage to fling myself out the car door, I was on my way to drowning inside this nightmare.

Those hoofbeats slammed into my chest as he turned the car into the driveway of 14 Beaumont Road. The rain had stopped and the night was dark and hushed, the porch light on, welcoming me home. I slid from the car onto legs burdened with lead, unable to move, glued fast to the blacktop. "Come on," he said. Each step was a drag-and-heave struggle.

They were there in the living room, ready with greetings, when they must have spotted the boot print of unconcealed agony stamped on my face. Before they could utter them, their *Hellos* and *Did you have a good day?* fell mute on their lips, and as I had seen in my vision, their faces grew ashen.

There is an eerie standstill at the cusp of calamity, it seems, when all energy stalls for a millisecond to align its charges before erupting into catastrophe. It's the hair that stands up on end just before the lightning bolt strikes you dead. That instant of suspended movement through colorless mud, where sounds are thick and garbled and limbs sluggish. It's the hands that can't reach the child before he falls headfirst onto the rock; that slow-motion flash of blond ringlets and gray stone just before screams ignite your universe — the split second before life as you know it is forever changed. Then suddenly the tattletale omen vanishes into an explosion that unleashes a sonic boom and bombards the air with flames and scorching embers.

Pregnant. That's the only word I heard him utter, and the echo of it roared into the living room, bouncing and crashing against drywall and unsuspecting faces, and chased me up the stairs in a gasping frenzy of thrashing and stumbling. *Pregnant.* A word I had never been able to whisper or even allow into my thoughts — not through missed periods or wretched nausea, not even as my clothes pulled tight across my belly. *That* word was the neon sign pointing to my shame, the public proclamation of my sin. The word that made me as foul as the stained, sour mattresses he used me on. *Pregnant.*

I was up the stairs and curled on top of my bed before he had finished his sentence.

I heard my mother cry out, *"Not Kathleen. Not my daughter."*

My father shout, "What are we going to tell the neighbors?"

Then my mother screech, "I'm not worried about the neighbors!"

I buried my head in my pillow, slapped my hands over my ears.

"Where do you think you're going to take her? To live with you in the slums?" my father yelled.

There were muffled shouts. Thumping around. The front door slamming. And then my mother was standing in my doorway.

"How could you do this? How could you do this to us?"

Was my mother screaming, or was she slumped against the door jamb, mumbling, all the air hissed from her? I couldn't tell. Her image was fuzzy, out of focus, her words a slipstream of rising and falling notes. Screaming would be better. I deserved her wrath. I wished she would beat me. Beat me until my bones broke, until I spit up blood, until I was no more than pulp lying on my bed. I wished she would use her fists to destroy me instead of using her anguish.

Not Kathleen. Not my daughter. The sting of that cry, worse than a scalding hand smashing my face, burned an evermore flashback right into the lenses of my eyes. *Not Kathleen. Not my daughter.* I'd heard the sob in her voice, her cry of disbelief, her low moan — all now gaping, bloodless slices into my flesh.

Maybe she was on her way to death as she glared at me in pallid shock, and I would be responsible. Me, who loved my mother more than I loved anything in my whole life. My mother, who rose far above Jesus. I wanted her to kill me, do what I hadn't had the nerve to do. I couldn't bear looking at her, at her pain, at the revulsion in her eyes. At the disgust she felt for me. The sound gushing from my throat was not human. How could I be capable of such noise? It was not the hulking, choking cries that steal breath. No, the sound was savage, feral. Animal. It was a keening. A cry beyond sadness, far beyond heartbreak. It was a primitive wail of grief.

She did not come into the room. Did not move any closer to me. I was glad. I wanted wrath. I wanted hate. It is what I deserved.

"How many times?" she asked. Then yelled, "How many times?" Her eyes bored into me from that long, long distance across the room.

I heard the answer in her question. The correct response was my only salvation. If I dared answer wrong, I would be thrown away with tomorrow's trash. My parents would have no more use for a girl who whored around, a girl who could be easily taken in the backseat of a car. Such a girl could never get taken home to meet the mother of a good boy, or wear white at her wedding — if any young man would have her, that is.

My mother would allow me one mistake. I heard it in the undertone of her question. I had one chance to hold on to her love. Only one. I would have to claim that a one-time foolish dalliance in the backseat of a souped-up rattletrap got me in this mess. A single, solitary fuck was all that my mother would tolerate. Paralyzing obedience on squalid mattresses would offer no excuse. One fuck. That is what I heard. That is what she meant. Beyond that, forgiveness would be withheld. Forever. I could count on it.

"How many times?" she yelled again, her voice cracking into a squeak.

"Once," I uttered. All those filthy, stained mattresses, grayed with sweat and grease, swam before my eyes.

"Once?" she yelled. "Once?"

Her rising panic betrayed her; confirmed my understanding that I could not answer any other way. No other reply was possible. One fuck. That was all. One.

"Once," I sobbed. But I felt his grease-packed fingernails crawling like cockroaches over me again and again. Smelled his sour odor imprinted on my skin, flinched again at his unwashed, oily hair.

She stared at me.

"Once, Mommy. I swear." But hooting and hollering in my ear was a mocking, sneering voice. *Once? Once? You liar. You filthy, dirty liar.* The ruthless phantom that followed me everywhere, cataloging my every move, every fault, each mistake, cursing me even when I tried to do something good. The booming voice of absolute authority, sounding so much like the voice of John J. Allen.

"One time. That's all," I sobbed.

I grasped onto that lie, squeezed it so tight that surely my mother could see it was no more than a hopeless wish. But I lunged at it, made it true. Grabbed onto its offer of one last shred of dignity — no bigger, I knew, than a tattered scrap of rag — and shoved that flake of protective armor over my ruined privates. And heard the hysterical cackle of my desperate secret growing fat on my lies.

"How many periods have you missed?" she demanded.

"I don't know," I cried, burying my head deeper into my pillow, not wanting to say, not wanting to know.

"You *have* to know. How many?"

"I don't know," I wailed. "Four. Five. I don't know."

"Oh my God," she said, and fell into a silence that seemed endless. Finally, in a voice twisted with anger, she said, "If you'd told me sooner, I could've had this taken care of. It's too late now." She turned and, slamming my door behind her, marched away.

The world's darkness closed in around me as exhaustion tugged at my eyes, forcing them closed, and pushed me further and further into the blackness. Just before I sank into a deadweight sleep, I thanked God for finally showing up, not bothering to ask why He'd taken almost two years to throw off His robes and get down to business — He was no Superman, that was for sure.

There wasn't much to be said for the day except that I knew with all certainty, beyond all doubt, that God had reached His hand far into the pit and rescued me. The rapist was gone from my life; I would never have to see him again. I knew this with complete clarity, and with this perfect knowing, wisps of relief began to settle about me like puffs of fragmented mist. It didn't matter how my parents reprimanded me, what kind of hideous consequences they would devise. Because whatever punishment they dispensed, I deserved that and more, much more. I deserved to die. My anguish at the pain I had caused them throbbed like a festering ulcer, and I would never, ever forgive myself. It was not possible for them to hate me more than I hated myself.

John J. Allen visited with me the next day to lay down the rules. Subdued, he lacked his usual bluster; somewhere he'd abandoned his honed ridicule, because when he spoke to me, he was eerily calm. I wouldn't be permitted to go back to finish the final weeks of school. I was not to contact any of my friends. Lastly and most importantly, he said, "You are forbidden to see him ever again." I raised my eyes and stared at him from the long dark hollow I was lost in. He was serious. I cast my eyes to the floor, not knowing whether to laugh hysterically or cry uncontrollably. Or do both at the same time. Or just crumble into a ball of dust and blow away.

"You're not to see him; is that clear?" I was too exhausted to pull more than a mumble from my lips. He *was* serious. He actually thought that unless I was chained to the doorknob, I would flee out my window under cover of night and have a little romantic rendezvous with the rapist. I was alone in a foreign land. I didn't know the people. I didn't understand the language. I didn't even recognize who I was any longer. But I didn't care. Because *he* was gone. Finally. And there would come a day when I would be free.

CHAPTER 9

Catholic Charities

It was the sixties, and homes for unwed mothers dotted the cities and towns across the country. Girls in trouble needed a hideout, something worthy of the likes of Bonnie and Clyde. It was the days before women marched for their right to own their vaginas. And if you were Catholic, it wasn't just the government that wanted control of your vagina; the Pope had a vested interest as well. Murder was pardoned more easily than the mortal sin of getting pregnant out of wedlock. Forgiveness and happy endings were for Saturday-afternoon matinees, not for a girl who had made a mistake. And since rape and sexual assault had not yet been invented, when a girl found herself pregnant, well, she had only herself to blame.

No mercy. No parole. The penalty for a girl's fall from virtue was public scorn, the banning of ever wearing white at her wedding, and a life sentence of shame. The girl, no matter how her condition came about, was considered a slut and had a lot in common with a convicted criminal. She, too, would be banished from society.

St. Elizabeth's Home for unwed mothers was rumored to be run by German nuns. An elongated yellow brick building, three stories high, it sat smack in the middle of Yardville, a little outpost a few miles from my house. Yardville wasn't exactly a bustling town, but neither was it remote or unpopulated. So the fallen girls sent there from somewhere else were hidden in plain sight, in view of plenty of eyes, but at least those eyes belonged to strangers.

On their way to Lou's Grocery, where I used to walk to get my supply of Nestlé Crunch bars, or to the Beacon Restaurant with its fake lighthouse and cheap eats, everybody gawked at St. Elizabeth's. On a lucky day, the girls in trouble would be strolling the grounds, their bellies stretched far out in front of them. They were the circumstances without the pomp, terrifying and fascinating. You could not pull your eyes away from them. They were the wreck on the side of the highway, the six-foot man wearing lipstick and falsies and his wife's earrings. Pregnant teenage girls, sad and scared. Pull a neck muscle straining to see them waddle about. Then grab some burgers and fries at the Beacon, and stop by Lou's for milk and bread. Great Saturday-afternoon entertainment, as long as it wasn't you caged like a sideshow freak on display.

Sister Social Worker was a real-live Catholic cliché, stern and menacing. Sheathed in black, she sat behind her desk, centered directly below Jesus nailed to the Cross, his head slumped in death. Having little patience with my silence, Sister Social Worker would have cracked a ruler across my knuckles if she'd had one handy. Her office at Catholic Charities was cheerless, the sunlight and fresh air stolen by solid cinderblock walls and sputtering fluorescents.

There's something about dented file cabinets and worn vinyl chairs assembled under dim lights that brings foreboding to a room and makes you want to flee before you even enter. I sat hunched over, shielded by my black raincoat, listening to Sister's ballpoint scratch the paper in front of her, staring down at my knees, my sneakers, at the fissures in the worn floor. How many girls had slouched in this very chair, their shoes, like mine, scuffing a swath into the vinyl? She wanted *his* name, but I sat mute, voiceless. Her glare bore down on me, into me, heating my face, prodding sweat into my armpits. The sensation was so familiar.

Maybe she thought I was being stubborn. But I couldn't think about him; I just couldn't. Saying his name out loud petrified me. *Please*, I wanted to beg her, *don't make me say it; don't force me to make him real again*. It was as if by uttering his name, some twisted force of magic would conjure him up and suddenly his filthy hands would be crawling all over my skin.

Sister Social Worker didn't understand that at any second *he* could waltz into her office, and within minutes she would be congratulating *him* as he whisked me off to Elkton, Maryland, where this time there would be no confusion about local ordinances. I didn't say his name, because I was panicked at being forever chained to him by the permanent ink flowing across those official forms, binding me to him in some evil spin of devilish torture. But it wasn't as if I actually stood a chance against Sister Social Worker; she knew exactly how to get what she wanted.

"You know, if you don't give me his name, I can't guarantee you confidentiality," she said, leaning forward over her desk toward me. Did the dead Jesus actually lift his head and smirk at me at that exact moment?

I was in the office alone with Sister, my mother somewhere beyond the closed door. Maybe flipping through a *Good Housekeeping*? Wringing her hands? I don't know, but she was absent, and Sister had me all to herself. And I was no match against a divine bully who wanted to crack me with a metal ruler. I reeled in silent panic, the dizziness hurling me into a bottomless vortex.

Sister had her black-heeled ankle boot planted on my neck and would not let me surface until I confessed. So I said it. I said the ugliest words that could ever cross my lips, besides the word *pregnant*. I said *his* full name. I said it because Sister Social Worker dangled my survival over my head, as easily as John J. Allen had suspended my diary out of my reach until I begged and cried with hysteria. I said it because without the promise of confidentiality, I was left on display like those girls at St. Elizabeth's, only naked and spread-eagle.

Sister had the power to erect billboards with that image and the details of my shameful offenses all over Hamilton Township where I lived and went to school, and in Trenton where my father worked. Where my relatives, my family, my friends, could gape and point. I said *his* name because I was too scared not to. And I despised myself for being so obedient, so desperate. I wished I could have found the nerve to kill myself. I wished I were a girl with tattoos, who smoked filterless cigarettes and said *fuck you* and could kick the ass of a six-foot woman dressed in black representing Christ.

"When was your last period?" she asked, driving that pen across the paper, checking boxes. "Any previous pregnancies?"

Her questions weren't questions at all. They were stab wounds. And I didn't know how to reply, how to keep mouthing words, when the only thing inside my head was a live animal ramming against my skull. In the space where there should have been vivid pictures and sentences properly structured, ready to be conveyed, nothing lived except a migraine and a void blacker than Sister Social Worker's habit. She saw me pull my raincoat tighter around my middle, trying for protection against her interrogation.

"Look, you're not going to be able to hide in that coat forever," she said.

Somehow I managed to mumble answers that satisfied her, neatly packaged answers — some that came by rote, others I made up for her pleasure — just to get her to put down that pen and shut up. But I was sickened that she was stealing parts of me and attaching them to her official papers where I would be permanently imprisoned. Yet I knew that only my obedience would buy me her guarantee. I needed anonymity more than I needed oxygen.

Sister finished writing on her forms and looked up at me, her hands clenched as if she were going to recite a fervent prayer. Instead, she forecast my future. Her words, quick and monotone, were like buildings zipping past a train window, a crazy rocket burn of commotion spinning off only tiny fragments of sense.

Maternity home. Adoption arranged. Completely confidential. Records permanently sealed. Nobody will ever find out about this. I needed her to slow down, let her speech unwind slowly inside the dry veins encircling the blankness and the drumbeats inside my head. Because I thought that, hidden in the blur of her lecture, I heard her *promise.* Her guarantee. A pinprick of light nibbling at the dark.

"Do you understand?" Sister asked, when I looked at her, confused. "We're going to send you away. You'll give birth," she said, "and when you return, it will be as if nothing ever happened."

I stared at her, into her eyes, searching for the lie behind them, waiting for her to make a ridiculing wisecrack so she could laugh at my reaction, as John J. Allen liked to do. There was nothing there except boredom and business and the untidiness of dealing with yet another girl in trouble. "You can put this behind you and no one will ever know."

I gulped her words as if they were life-sustaining water pouring down my parched throat. I wanted to hear her say them again and again — *You can put this behind you and no one will ever know* — but I dared not ask. I strained harder and harder, fixing my eyes to hers just to make sure I'd heard right, straining to understand, starved for a morsel of hope that only she could provide. She was throwing me a lifeline, tossing me a second chance, and I would do anything, anything, to get it. To keep it.

"You have one chance at a new beginning," Sister Social Worker vowed. "No more mistakes after this. There's nothing I can do for a repeat girl. After the first mistake, a girl's on her own." Sister Social Worker — the flashy ticket scalper offering a one-time and one-time-only deal of a lifetime never to be presented again. Take it now or leave it. I bobbed my head up and down.

"This will never happen again, Sister. I promise," I whispered. I was a beaten dog grateful to the dogcatcher, and I wanted to crawl across her desk on my belly and lick her hands in appreciation.

Unfortunately, I couldn't see into the future, where Sister Social Worker's promises and guarantees were as useless as the turds bobbing and weaving down the currents of Gropp's Lake. If I had known, maybe I would have sprouted a backbone and begged her for mercy, thrown myself on the floor at her feet and pleaded with her to put those promises in writing, begged her to swear on the Bible that she would keep me safe, keep my degradation from becoming fodder — keep it away from my future.

I was frantic for her protection. She had to be able to smell my desperation — the swampy tang of it curled up from my skin, wafting in the air like marsh gas. But I had no warning visions, and I walked out of Catholic Charities clutching Sister Social Worker's promises, determined to work off my penance and atone for my sins. What maternity home I would end up in remained a mystery. But if I had to go to St. Elizabeth's in Yardville, I would go without complaint and never show my face in the light of day if that's what it took. I would go anywhere she sent me, live in a locked cell if she required it.

I didn't care. I was crazed for that second chance to be a good girl, desperate to have my sins erased, buried where no eyes could see. I ached to be clean again, to walk in the sunshine and feel its heat sterilize my skin, bleach away the imprints left by hands that felt free to molest my body. I yearned to see my parents look at me without the shadow of disgust and disappointment in their eyes. I needed to be punished and I would accept it without complaint, no matter how harsh. Whatever they asked, I would do. Scour floors on my hands and knees, clean toilet bowls with a toothbrush. Whatever penalties they heaped on me, I wouldn't complain. I deserved worse.

And with my obedience, maybe I could scrub the sin from my heart, from my body. Sister Social Worker was offering me a chance to suffer my shame in private, away from staring eyes. Then a chance to be a regular girl again. Maybe someday I could make new friends and feel the bliss of laughter. Laughter that wasn't aimed at me. Maybe I could walk along the streets near my house without people pointing and gawking. Maybe there was an end to this torment of shame. Maybe *he* really wasn't coming back. Maybe when it was over, they would set me free. Maybe I could be a bad girl made good once more. Maybe at the end, I could once again be clean.

Heights throw my head into a spin, my body into drunken waves of wooziness. Maybe it is the terrifying thought that just one falter will hurl me into the crevasse below, my screams a fading echo into helpless oblivion. I never look down. Not on a ladder beyond two rungs. Not on a cliff overlooking a valley. I stare straight ahead, willing myself still. I ignore the ground below, always.

What had attached itself to my body terrified me with the same spiraling turmoil — its repulsiveness, its shame, its rise, cemented onto me like a living deformity struck with contagion. It was a disease I dared not look at. So I didn't. I stared straight ahead, just as I did when I was up far above the ground, ignoring what was below.

Nothing existed below my neck. Except for showering, I never even touched my belly. Never. It was the grisly abyss that would devour me, and I wanted to screech and slash at it until it was raw meat and would fall off me in bloody, cleansing shreds. But I quelled my panic, placed it in the hands of my mother and Sister Social Worker, who made their promises. Promises of secrecy and freedom that I clung to, the only lifelines I had. My only way back to a tattered version of *before*.

The home for unwed mothers where I was sent wasn't a home at all, but a hidden room on an upper floor in an urban hospital far away from the suburbs of Trenton. I had counted the weeks, the days, then the hours, until I could go, anxious to serve my time in purgatory and to suffer the punishment that would finally cleanse me of my sins and deliver me from my sordid degradation.

It should have lived up to certain reputations of Catholic institutions earned by terrorist nuns and their penchant for lockstep order, thunderous decrees, and fanatical enforcement of the "cleanliness is next to godliness" law — not to mention their pioneering application of humble weaponry, including the unauthorized use of state-issued rulers. Instead, that unadorned room with its medicinal scent and scrubbed floors and four institutional beds was quiet and sheltered. And finally, finally, I felt safe and protected. It was as if I'd been holding my breath since Sherwood Avenue and now, slowly, bit by bit, I was exhaling. No longer did I have to worry about gamy mattresses or grease-soiled hands or John J. Allen's bullying. It was hushed. Still. No one yelling. No kids getting beaten. It was a place where I didn't have to plaster on a smile or pretend to be nice. I had no one crawling all over me with demands and orders.

For the first time since I was very, very young, I felt what it was like to calm down. To be away from laughing, ridiculing eyes. And leering stares. And holes poked in the shower to watch while I was naked. And hands pawing at me. And John J. Allen bursting through my bedroom door with his decrees and lists of my wrongdoings. The room was so tranquil. Peaceful enough to read magazines and books uninterrupted. To gaze out the window. To nap unassaulted. It was a place where I didn't cry. It was a room where I began to have genuine hope.

When I arrived toting a suitcase of muumuus and a paper bag full of quiet distractions, there was someone lying on a bed by the window, her head buried in a book. At first I was confused. This was supposed to be a hideout for girls, and she was a woman. Twenty at least, maybe older. Overweight, not including her condition, with a large, pockmarked face and thick glasses, she looked like the type that boys would mock and men would use for their convenience, as long as they didn't have to look at her.

It turned out I was pretty close to right. She'd fallen in love with her boss, who promised her marriage as soon as he could manage a divorce.

Her pregnancy inconvenienced his little arrangement, and she was cast out as if she'd never existed. There was such sadness in her eyes as she professed her secret. She'd made her own arrangements with Catholic Charities and was installed on the upper floor early enough, before anyone detected her shame, with the understanding of complete confidentiality. Even her family didn't know her situation. No one ever visited her. Maybe they thought she was touring Europe for the summer — the postcards sent, an elaborate scheme of cloak-and-dagger espionage pulled off with the help of a trusted cohort.

That's how it was, secrets and lies, one piled on top of the other. They were our black raincoats, worn to protect us from anyone who, with a flick of a finger, would destroy us, all the while with a smile smeared on their faces. Personally, my cover was that I was struck down with mono, the pestilent kissing disease. Nearly dead, I had to be sent away to recuperate. I never told my roommate my real story. I just kept quiet and sympathized with the unfairness of hers.

My job was to work in the laundry. Eight hours a day, five days a week, I stood on a concrete floor bent over a work table, folding surgical gowns and whatever else was piled there in need of orderliness. It's not bragging to say I did not complain, ever. It was what I owed, what I expected of myself. I would have swabbed the floors with a dishrag had they asked.

The more uncomfortable my punishment was, the more it cleansed me. The harder I worked, the more I endured, the more I earned the right to a new life. There is always a sizable chunk of time and suffering attached to purgatory. I wanted to make sure I left my confinement owing nothing. My slate wiped clean. All of my brother Jackie's juvenile records would be expunged when he reached adulthood. I needed that too. Another chance to be good. This time, I wouldn't blow it.

All day long, as I folded in silence, I fantasized about being free. Free. Never having to see *him* again. I daydreamed about laughing without the worry of his hands, back there, somewhere, waiting to make me dirty. I pictured the day I would walk out of the hospital in a new dress as a new girl. I imagined myself free, saw my feet sweeping light across the floor in a dance of buoyancy, surrounded by the shimmering glow of joy. I could barely wait to start over, be released from my past, my shame buried the minute I walked out the front door.

Every day in the laundry, I fantasized and daydreamed and smiled and clutched at Sister Social Worker's promises. As I sat quietly on my bed, ate the hospital food, and waddled down the halls, wherever I was, wherever I went, I composed and embellished my dream of a brand-new, freshly minted life and planned it as my future. And gripped it so tightly to my chest as I fell into exhausted sleep at night that my hands were still clenched into aching fists when I woke in the morning.

My blood boiled with belief in Sister Social Worker's promises. My trust in my mother was what I inhaled. My past would be buried, and yes, I would wear white at my wedding. My mother said it. It was true. My mistake would be erased as if it never happened. I would not fail them. I worked without complaint. That was my part. I did my penance and dreamed of one day.

A few weeks in, an entourage stumbled into our room hauling three suitcases and a needlepoint bag of essentials, and emitting a loud argument that surely had been running since their car pulled into the visitors' parking lot. At the center of the shouting match of parents, assorted friends, and relatives, including the boyfriend and a social worker looking like she hadn't had time to run a comb through her hair in a week, was a skeleton of a girl with raven hair and a small bulge. She was having none of their nonsense and was shouting right back at them.

I kept my head down, buried in my magazine, but was transfixed by her bravado. She argued. She yelled. She didn't seem to give a damn what any one of them was trying to tell her. Instantly, she was my hero. They argued about everything. She wanted to get married. She wasn't going to stay here. She would do what she damn well pleased. But she could scream, shout, stamp her feet, hurl her clothes to the floor and stomp on them for all they cared. There was one thing she could not overcome: her age. Fifteen.

So in truth, her anger was simply a hopeless display. She was here to stay. What her anger hid from her, what she couldn't see as she stormed about, was that they — that large, Italian, volatile clan — were trying to love her. Desperately trying to bring her senses back into order. Frantic for her to see reason. No one threatened to smack her across her smart mouth. Or ridiculed her frustration. They were trying to get her to see reason. The family had hopes for this young girl, and having a baby at fifteen was not one of them.

Everyone shouted at once: *you're too young; you have to go to college; you'll get married someday, but not now; you don't know what you're getting yourself into; please, please listen.* But the raven-haired skeleton girl just spit fire. I liked listening to them. They loved one another. And they loved her. No matter how loud they got, no one crossed the line. Love was the undertone even in their anger. She was part of them; maybe she was daddy's little girl, or the pride and joy of their clan. I don't know, but they were not going to let her fade away into her mistake. They were fighting for her. For her future.

But when the social worker pushed official forms into the girl's hands, she said something that chased the high heat of summer off my skin. A small piece of advice that would seem a minor footnote to anyone who took her security for granted. A warning laser-focused on the future handed to the girl almost as an afterthought.

Passing skeleton girl a pen, the social worker said, "Don't use your real name. Make one up. Otherwise they'll be able to track you down." That messy-haired woman's casual remark raked icy fear down my back as I saw myself sitting at Catholic Charities in that vinyl chair, hands shaking, signing my full name, then printing it so it would be readable on all those official forms. And *his* name printed in bold black ink on the line below. In my obedience, my stupid naiveté, I'd made a terrible, irreversible mistake. And no one, not even my mother, had stopped me.

The nun charged with looking after wayward girls was elderly and frail, and short enough to earn a few *ahhhhs* when folks first saw her. She looked like a doll fashioned from dried-up apples, wrinkled and weathered to the color of late-autumn mushrooms. I had anticipated the Sister Social Worker type — the kind you see in grade B movies about orphan girls who are beaten by a nine-foot Mother Superior wearing a stiff habit; nuns who get their kicks out of shoving girls' faces into the food that the good sisters of the kitchen slaved over but that the girls refused to eat because it tasted like dog food. Tiny Sister, though, was bathed in quiet most of the time, floating in and out of her office next to our room, peeking in occasionally. But her sternness surfaced when she insisted I go to confession and confess my sin of getting pregnant out of wedlock. I could not wiggle my way out of it.

~ ~ ~

If my room is quiet, this chapel is a tomb. I can hear him in there, sitting in the dark, waiting, the rustling of his cassock, the scrape of his shoes back and forth across the floor. His breath puffs out in short pants. It must be the heat that makes him restless. Maybe it is the anticipation of a juicy confession. More likely, boredom.

I despise confession and never make a good one. I have my standard list of sins; they're the same every time I go. I was unkind; I got angry; I took the Lord's name in vain. That kind of stuff. I make my penance — always a couple of Hail Marys and one or two Our Fathers — and bolt.

Confession is just another form of Catholic torture that only the old ladies who stand in line mumbling and clacking rosaries take seriously. How many sins could those widows have left in them, anyway? What do they do all week that they have to confess every Saturday at three? But I wish those old ladies were here now to buffer me, give me some extra time, before I have to lug myself through the door where the brooding Jesus dangles on the crucifix.

I am shivering as I sweat, kneeling in the pew, trying not to smell the pinching scent of incense that lingers too close and heavy. I feel wetness just above my lip. Beneath my arms, itchy droplets are starting to form. And damp stickiness between my legs. I am panting, but I'm trying not to. Sister has ordered me to confession, and I am to confess all the sins of my condition. If I don't confess, then my freedom, my future as a regular girl, will be withdrawn. She did not tell me this; it was hidden in her words, in the tone of her voice, how she stared at me without blinking. It was buried in her smile that wasn't quite a smile, but rather a tight line drawn across her face. I am an expert at detecting unspoken threats.

I hate the good father. I hate that he is a prince and that I am a slut and I have to bare myself, strip off the last pieces of my skin before him. I could engulf this room with my tears—helpless, useless, furious tears that simmer away just out of sight. But I don't cry anymore. I have nothing left inside except darkness. No tears. No dignity. I am below the floor I walk on, below the smelly ooze that inhabits the mattresses I cowered upon. I am nothing. I am shame.

It is torment every time I have to leave the safety of my room and the two others who look like me. None of us ever speak of what grows inside our bodies. None of us exist below our necks; we are skilled pretenders. Even though I feel naked all the time with my swollen, distorted body on constant display—one enormous, blinking neon arrow announcing my disgrace—I am still startled when others remind me of the shame I carry.

I have not ventured outside the hospital since the night the three of us went for a walk in the warm night. We heard the music blasting before any of us actually saw the car full of teenage boys pull up. *Oooooh, look what you did. Got caught, huh?* they yelled, hanging out the windows, throwing us the finger. *You oughta learn to keep your legs closed, you stupid cunts.*

For the first time in my life, I said the word no decent girl would ever utter. Not only did I say it, but I bellowed it like a loudmouthed broad. *Fuck you! Fuck you!* But it didn't help. No matter how much I want to be, I am no motorcycle chick. I am damaged goods and shamed beyond all repair.

But being it and suffering for it are not enough. Knowing what I am and being too spineless to defend myself are not enough. It's never enough for a religion that needs its revenge against the flesh. Now I have to force it out of my mouth without choking—slash myself further with my own words, say them loud and clear. Let my misery become music to God's ears. But I feel like the crazy hollow-eyed suspect admitting to crimes she didn't remember committing just to get the interrogators to shut up so she can get some peace.

So I have to slink into the confessional and admit my condition—as if the good father couldn't see it rising on my body—and all the sins that got me this way. Claim myself as a whore to gain God's forgiveness. Is he in the dark salivating, the priest? Is God hovering just to the left of the good father's shoulder, smirking, rubbing His golden hands together, thrilled with this win, the prize of me condemning myself? It feels something like being shoved into a pool of diarrhea for the enjoyment of others and being coerced into giving a grinning, blow-by-blow, stink-by-stink account for the really big laugh. But isn't that what I've been doing since John J. Allen first sent me to the store to beg for imaginary items and then forced me to detail my embarrassment before his friends? Didn't he train me to humiliate myself and smile while doing it? Wasn't my degradation the big payoff? Can I expect any less from the priests? The nuns? My mother? From God Himself?

One last time, I rehearse the words that feel skinned of meaning, that seem to bleed a stranger's blood. He claimed his rights to my body, and I never argued. What remains is only fault. And it belongs to me. I push myself up and drag my bulk into the confessional with the intent to make a good confession about what I am, to ensure my freedom. But when I open my mouth, nothing comes out. The speech I rehearsed, full of self-recrimination, won't budge. All I can whisper to the silhouette beyond the screen is, *I am not married. I am having a baby.*

The good father recites his holy mumbo jumbo, the same slur of prayers I've heard since I was seven, while I make a fine Act of Contrition. Then he gives me penance in the form of a few Hail Marys and a couple of Our Fathers, and I leave. But I am not forgiven: I know this as I recite the familiar lines and bless myself with the sign of the cross. Even as I genuflect and bow my head toward the tabernacle, and leave the tomb-like silence behind, I know I will never be forgiven. It is not possible. All I want is for this to be over. I go back to the safety of my room, curl on my bed, and demolish an entire package of Oreos.

CHAPTER 10

The Lies of Promises

Pain stabbed my midsection with all the vengeance of a crazed thrill seeker, my body's last personal attempt, it seemed, to defeat me. But I was ecstatic and welcomed its punishment, its power of purification. I had to walk straight through this final cruelty — the last licks of a spiteful God — with dignity and composure if I was to win forgiveness. And I would do that, because just beyond its horizon, I spotted the peeking daylight of my new life, and in all my bulk and ache, I could have spun joyful cartwheels down the hall. My two friends, bearing their own anguish, gathered around me with sweet, tender concern. "This isn't going to be fun," I said to them as I gripped the wall in support. But I was euphoric, and despite the convulsions clamping my middle, I could not stop smiling.

Only a thin shaft of lamplight from the hallway disturbed the dark in the room where I lay in total silence, drawn up on my side, clenching the cold bedrail. It seems I should have called out for my mother, cried for her reassuring hand on my forehead. Pleaded for her to curl up beside me and hold me through the terrifying final act of my ordeal. Far down below where I stored my tears, I craved her voice whispering encouragement, gently guiding me down a soothing path as pain gorged on me in the solitary darkness. But I never expected her to be by my side, and she wasn't. I accepted my debt of sin, and the agony of labor was the last, most horrible payment that would finally expunge my offenses and ensure me a new life. So I wanted to be there alone in the dark with the strange and frightening noises just beyond the door, unfamiliar faces, and the poke and prod of brusque hands, enduring labor in complete silence. It was, after all, the last of what I owed. Maybe my mother at home sleeping in her bed knew that.

When the resident, dressed in surgical blue, strapped a gas mask to my face, I did exactly what my mother had told me in her spare pieces of advice and guzzled my way into unconsciousness. When I woke, I was flabby-bellied and empty. Tentative and scared, I ran my hand down over the thin cotton gown, touching my stomach again and again, making sure *it* was gone — making sure it wasn't just a dream. It had been nearly two years since I owned my own body, and touching the soft, doughy flesh, knowing it no longer belonged to him or his implant, gave rise to such peace that I felt as if I glowed in the arc of a gentle light.

All the prayers I'd known since childhood swirled inside my head, and I recited each one over and over — *Our Father, Who art in heaven, hallowed be Thy name; Hail Mary, full of grace, the Lord is with you; Oh my God, I am heartily sorry for having offended Thee; Glory be to God the Father; Amen, Amen, Amen* — an endless wave of gratitude mumbled silently as I kept my hands on my belly, making sure. Just making sure. Making sure that it was over. That I belonged once again to myself. That I had served my penance. That God would not ask me for any more. *Thank you. Thank you, Jesus. Thank you.* Every breath I inhaled. *Thank you.* Every time I looked out the window at the sunshine. *Thank you.* Every time I touched my belly. *Thank you, Jesus. Thank you. Thank you.*

But it was anger I elicited — palpable, corporal anger. Frozen on the faces of the hospital staff. Squinted, hardened eyes zeroing in to mine. Reminding me. Taunting me still. Looks accusing me. A fast girl. A spoiled prima donna, putting the kid on the auction block like that. They're all alike, *those girls, those selfish sluts.* As if all that existed of my circumstance was their opinion. The anger was static, raising the hairs on my arms, riding on the glances into my room. *She's one of them.* Coded in the mandatory touches. Jarring and frightening me into the stillness of my fear, making me afraid to move too quickly, to utter the wrong words. Afraid I would trigger an attack.

Why were they so mad at me? Was it the shameless relief coursing through my bones, soothing me with its balm, radiating from me like a halo? The joy I couldn't contain when I smiled that stuck in their throats like an insult to humanity? Did they need to knock me down a few pegs, wipe that irrepressible beam from my lips? Make sure I remembered what I was?

The nurse who was assigned to me smelled of cloves and rubbing alcohol and stained her cheeks cherry and her mouth fire engine red. In her fresh whites and stiff cap, propped just so on top of a long, tightly curled bob, she gave the impression of goodwill. But when she grabbed my arm to take my pulse, she raised her drawn-on eyebrows into two perfect arches and dug her fingers hard into the hollow of my left wrist.

"You know," she said after she finished her notations, bobbling her head in the self-satisfied way someone does just at the verge of unleashing a good tongue-lashing, "I see girls like you every day. You never learn. None of you. Never. You'll be back here, just like the others. Every day it's like a revolving door around here with girls like you. And you're just like the rest; you'll be back here too. I don't know what it's going to take for you girls to learn." She shook her head, the disgust in her eyes, in the harshness of her touch, as primal as the need to swat a mosquito.

I sat on the bed wide-eyed and speechless. Motionless before her — just as I always was when facing an attacker. My arm limp in her cold grip, her venom lumping in my throat. I willed myself into a speck no larger than the dust motes floating across the sunrays pouring in the window, and listened as she berated me, mangled my joy with her hostility. Was it my face bleached of all color against the white sheets, my body wilted with fatigue, that gave her the courage to hurl acid into my wounds, only barely beginning to heal? Something was wrong, really wrong. I felt it in my gut, now flat, delivered of its disease.

But they said, I argued with myself. Sister Social Worker. My mother. They promised me freedom, forgiveness. They said I would have a fresh, new, clean life. I gave Sister *his* name as my guarantee. I did everything everyone asked of me. I took all the blame for everything. I worked in their laundry. I never complained. Not about the hours on my feet or the ache in my back. Not about the ice block of terror that sat heavy in my chest. I never said a word or even scowled when John J. Allen ridiculed me about missing home, teased me until I wanted to cry when he and my mother came to visit. I just smiled. Obedience was part of my penance; complaining diluted it. So I kept myself smiling, agreeable.

I obeyed when Tiny Sister made me confess the sin that had found its way between my legs and crept into my belly. I did it. I did it because it was supposed to earn me a new life. Everyone agreed. I signed my name to Sister Social Worker's official forms. Labor was supposed to be my final trial, and I endured its ravages without a whimper, without even asking for so much as a glass of ice. I worked my way out of purgatory. I was supposed to start fresh. Today. Right now. I was supposed to be untarnished. No one said anything about backsies. I believed that everyone understood the rules and would stick to them as I had. They were supposed to let me go, my sins forgiven, vanished as if they'd never occurred. It was time for my reward. I earned it. No one, not even God, could claim anything different.

But there it was, slashing at me from the inside, a truth as vicious as the violence *he* had threatened against me. The reality was in Nurse Gulch's eyes, in her grip, in the loathing tone of her lecture, in the screeches of the maniacal demon so familiar to me taunting me now: *You may have done hard time, girlie. He may be gone, the swelling that his crud planted in you gone. You can ignore it, turn your attention away from the horror, look sweetly into the future, but you will never, ever escape.* But I couldn't listen. Nurse Gulch was just a bad vision. She couldn't predict the future. I stayed quiet and listened to her, listened to her hatred of me as her angry words unhinged my joy. This couldn't be true.

Except for Tiny Sister, all the nuns seemed attached to stilts the way they towered high above me with their power and authority. They all looked alike, faces pinched into early old age by stiff wimples and stern features. Sister White Habit swished into my room all cloth and clicking rosary beads, medieval-looking in the rigid hood fastened to her head. She was there on business; I could tell from the clipboard and the curt set of her mouth. I didn't know she was going to ambush me.

I was eyes-squeezed-shut, arms-locked-over-my-head frantic not to know what had been delivered from me. My body had betrayed me, tilled its moist earth, and hosted an invader. Forced me to bear the unbearable. Refused me the courage to rid myself of it, of myself. I had wanted it aborted, and this birth was no more to me than a late-term abortion. How I envied the girls who had found their way to the creepy subhumans lurking in the gloom, scalpels unsterilized but at least sharpened. And the girls who'd found the courage to sink a blade deep enough into their arteries to promise final oblivion. It was over for them. It was not over for me. It would never be over for me. Sister White Habit would see to that. She stood tall, her lips pursed, and announced as if her news were welcomed, *She's going to a good home.*

Right there in that hospital bed, I wanted to rock and lurch, bang my head against the rails. I didn't want to know. I didn't want to know. And now she'd told me, seared it into my brain where it would never leave me — more and more manifestation of *him.* Throwing *him* right beside me on that hospital bed where I was supposed to be, at last, clean. Her words slathered me again with his filth, once more dripped his crud on top of me, trapped me inside his foulness, drowned me all over again in his oily slime. With his dirt-encrusted hands he had strangled the life from me, as surely as if he'd squeezed his fingers around my neck. And I wish he had.

My body, now stretched and used, raked with fiery marks, was ruined. He'd stolen my name — Kathy — that I once thought so cute and bouncy, and turned it into a shameful smear that made me cringe every time I heard it. He had taken over my life and wasn't stopping. It would never stop. For the rest of my life he would somehow keep forcing his way into me, over and over. Again and again. A horror movie on endless replay.

I was so scared. So scared. Panic lashed and hacked at me, ranting and raving like a mute lunatic. I battled to be polite before Sister White Habit. But I could picture myself plunging backwards in a blaze of screams, engulfed in a frenzy of madness that would have Sister White Habit dropping her clipboard and running, shrieking for the orderlies who would haul me off to the psych ward where I belonged. Couldn't anyone, *anyone* see that I could not, I just could not, endure any more of *him*? I could not amass any more memories that would devour what little of myself I had left.

Inside my noiseless screams arose the wild cries of the banshee, accusing me, ridiculing me: *slut, whore, liar,* it screeched. Mocking my despair, my stupidity for believing in the dream of freedom now so hopelessly beyond my reach. Maybe that out-of-control inner tirade was the God of Retribution.

Or the devil. Standing so indifferently beside my bed, Sister White Habit was both as she forced me, face first, once again onto those mattresses with their ooze, their stink, and behaving as if I should be thankful for my good fortune. *She's going to a good home.*

I fought not to double over in that hospital bed before the virginal Bride of Christ, defeated, crazed with confusion. Why did she have to tell me? Why couldn't she just leave me alone? What reaction did Sister expect to extort from me after she announced the particulars from the delivery room? A big hooray? Blathering boo-hoos? Would an abortionist cock his head, plaster on a condescending grin, and chat with me about what he had vacuumed from my womb? Without asking, an abortionist would know about violation of the worst kind, the defilement that happens between a girl's legs, wouldn't he? It would be there, so easily spotted right in her eyes — desperate, festering pain clouding the color. Time and time again the abortionist would recognize violation in all its sinister costumes, hear screams so fierce that they had long been converted into petrified silence. He would see facts and go about his business fixing them, forgoing pointless niceties.

Everything was there for Sister White Habit just waiting to be read. Sister saw what was written on her clipboard, but she did not see me. Perhaps Sister White Habit would recognize big-event brutality, the kind that leaves contusions and yawning wounds in need of sutures. Blatant proof for the blind. But she knew nothing of the sly, covert slam of a penis against fresh tissue, a collision of grunts and rustles and anguish that left bruises on soft flesh and gaping wounds on the spirit. The abortionist would. He wouldn't doll up the horror with a sappy heart-to-heart. He'd just roll up his sleeves and get to work.

The clock on the wall above Sister's head made a tick, tick, whiz sound as it clicked off seconds, minutes, hours. In less than twenty-four hours, I'd be home. My parents were due tomorrow early, at nine o'clock. Grasping hold of this vision, I inhaled short, choppy breaths. Tomorrow I was walking away, free. Nobody was going to stop me. Not now. By this time tomorrow I would be free. I would clench my fists and get through this, just like I'd endured what *he* did to me. Waited patiently until it was over. I could do this, though I could barely manage the pretense of good manners as I lifted

my gaze and stared at Sister, blank-faced. Not even John J. Allen could have coerced a smile from me. Sister had more for me, though. And had I been given a choice, I would have chosen a scalding bucket of road tar dumped over my head, topped off with a cluster of sharp-toothed quills.

BIRTH MOTHER. My stomach churned in spasms, racing bile to my throat when that depiction of me fell from her lips, dousing me in thick, permanent stink, singeing that symbol of unbearable disgrace directly into my skin. I could almost smell the char from the branding iron. Hear the sizzling hiss. *Oh my God. Oh my God.* Yoked always with humiliation. No, I couldn't think about it. I had to think about tomorrow. *Remember tomorrow,* I kept repeating, struggling to breathe. But she'd marked me as surely as if she'd tattooed it on my forehead.

BIRTH MOTHER. Oh my God. Oh my God. He had destroyed my name, and now Sister White Habit smeared it further by tacking the contents of his vile insides onto it. *MOTHER?* I wanted to screech. I was no more *mother* to what had grown inside me than I was mother to the offal and splatters that crawled on the mattresses *he* used me on. *Oh my God. Kathy Allen, Birth Mother. Kathy Allen, Biological Mother. Kathy Allen, Unwed Mother.* I was never to be rid of *him.* Never. Or of *it. Oh my God.*

For the rest of my life I would be forced to bear this stigma. It was not going quietly away like my mother said. Like Sister Social Worker promised. This scandal would follow me down the halls at school — be there, just waiting to lunge forth on my future wedding day. Haunt me when I shopped for groceries. Waiting. Always waiting. Then one day when I finally convinced myself that I was safe, it would blow out of its pit and do what it had been waiting to do all along — destroy me.

How I kept myself upright and appearing sane before Sister White Habit with the tonnage of that panic bursting inside my chest, I don't know. There was nothing for me to do except silently stare straight ahead or jump up and down on the bed in a blinding rage. I chose silence. Stony silence. In her blundering arrogance, Sister White Habit thought I gave a damn about what she was telling me, or at least thought I should. Maybe she couldn't believe that I didn't give a shit. Maybe all the girls she dealt with were mired in teenage love and loss. I stared at her, refusing comment. Maybe she'd never seen a girl like me. Numb with relief. Joyous to be rid of *it*.

Maybe all the girls like me met their saviors in a backstreet alley, inside a deserted storefront set up just for the occasion of messy, human butchery. I'd waited too long to tell my mother. If only I hadn't waited. If only I hadn't. The back-alley abortionist understood; he didn't ask questions or serve his moral judgment. Or get all gooey with sentiment. Just took the money and went about his craft. Gave the girl her life back. Or killed her. Whichever came first. Not that the girl cared which way it went. Someone that desperate would take her chances. Someone like me. If only I'd had the courage to tell earlier. If only.

~ ~ ~

They are late. Nine a.m. sharp. That's when they were due. Now the clock is creeping toward eleven. At first light I jumped out of bed, showered, and wiggled into nylons, and for the first time in months, pulled a regular dress over my head. Not that it fit that well, but it had a waist and a belt and just buttoning it was a celebration. After I fixed my hair and blotted some excess lipstick, I slid my feet into the black flats I had worn to a dance a very, very long time ago, and well before nine, planted myself in the vinyl chair opposite the bed to wait. And wait.

I am too jittery to read and can barely sit still as I try not to stare at the minute hand chugging by, second by second. I busy myself smoothing imaginary wrinkles from my dress and glancing into the hallway that bustles with activity, hoping to catch a glimpse of my mother and father racing down the hall to my room. As much as I want to hold on to my excitement at leaving, anger coils up my spine each time I look at the clock. Maybe they decided to make a day of picking me up — a regular pleasure outing away from the house and kids. Go out for pancakes and hot coffee at a diner along the way. Laugh over cigarette and pipe smoke, John J. Allen flirting with the aged waitress, making her feel pretty once again, despite her varicose veins and rump that's grown to portions known only to God. Maybe John J. Allen is meandering in the slow lane, enjoying the turnpike through rolled-down windows, admiring the landscape, both of them crinkling their noses at the smell of the refineries as they inhale the stink into their lungs like salt air from the shore.

By the time they stroll into the room, I am a trapped animal desperate to bolt. When John J. Allen sees me primped and ready, my fist gripping the handle on my suitcase, he can't resist. He reads hunger in my eyes and knows how to play it. Nothing about me escapes his mockery. Today is no different. And so I smile as he ridicules my eagerness to leave: *You must really be ready to come home. I've never known you to be on time for anything.* On and on. I cannot climb above his ridicule, not today. And once again, the screams that seem always lodged in my throat pulse and push, and the blood that bathes me in hotness and rushes to my brain seems a gusher about to blow.

This is hate, raw and unconfined, and I dig for the control not to wish him dead. But there is not one ounce of charity coursing anywhere through my body, and I would cheer to see him drop like a sack of rocks right at my feet as, in a singsong tone, he mocks my letters home, calling them *so pitiful...tsk, tsk, tsk... So, you're even gonna eat pork roll now, huh?"* he says.

He is referring to my hatred of the pink mystery sausage prized by Trentonians that gags me, and how, diminished and lonely in a scrawling letter home, I swore that I even missed that. He is heartless. And I am helpless. So I gulp and swallow the hulking, panting sobs that want to shudder and jolt from my mouth, and squeeze back the tears that won't clear from my eyes.

I'm going home.

I force a smile.

I'm going home.

The main doors to the hospital swing open and I step into dazzling sunlight. It is as if I have never before seen such radiance, never been embraced by such brilliance, such warmth. It pours over me. And it feels like love. Cotton-ball clouds, perfect for imagining shapes, float against a sky so turquoise that it seems painted in oil. I lower my head as if I am watching my steps, but I don't want John J. Allen to see the joy that reverberates from me like tremors. The air is heady with the fragrance of roses and lilacs, though there is not a flower in sight. If I were by myself, I would collapse to the pavement and kiss the ground beneath my shoes, its pebbles and dirt, bury my face in the dying greenery lining the walkway.

Never have I tasted such freedom. Such relief. Grief is no match for such joy, and all that was falls away. Events, tormentors, despair, evaporate in the bliss of this brand-new day. Can a girl actually be reborn? No one can see, but I am a balloon bouncing along, colorful, laughing, soaring with the kites that dance on the wind, tails weaving and waving in freedom. I am free. My sins forgiven. I feel this deep in my bones.

I will keep nothing of the past. Nothing. It is gone. In this moment, I bury it so far down that it does not even take up space as a memory. I do not care what they call me. How they threaten me. I do not even care what was done to me. It is over. I will not think about it. I will not speak about it. I am finished with it. At long, long last my ordeal is over and I am here now. I do not look back at the hospital. Yesterday does not concern me. I have been given back my life.

CHAPTER 11

The Darkest Secret and More Evil Deeds

It never happened. IT NEVER HAPPENED. I would entertain no other notion—not in my mind, not in the leering, questioning stares of gossipers who were lying in wait, teeth bared, readying for the kill. What happened to me over the last two years was nobody's business. *Nobody's!* It belonged solely to me, and I decided it didn't happen. I didn't bobble. I didn't waver. Somewhere in the mystery of my DNA, bedrock genes prowled waiting for such an opportunity to be invoked, and this was it.

And as if I were chiseled out of stone from a quarry on a mountainside, I was cold and stoic, unyielding about the years that had annihilated all that was good. It was a detachment so complete, so absolute, that I never shed a tear of anger or sorrow over any of it or even once replayed a single event in my head. And except for the two occasions I approached my mother with a question, I never spoke of it. Not to anyone. Ever. That was my power, and I grabbed it whether anyone liked it or not. It's called survival.

My parents sold 14 Beaumont Road. For me, they said. So I could get a fresh start—somewhere far away from my past. I believed them. I hated the neat yellow house with the lattice of red roses meandering around the front door as if inside lived a family named Happy. Let the misery imbedded in those walls stay put; we were moving on, and I was drop-to-my-knees grateful to be going where my name would not have a ring to it. Where faces were bright and friendly. I didn't want to suffer any more smiles with malice snaking beneath them. I was desperate to let down my guard and blend into normal, not constantly be waiting, waiting for the ambush.

I wanted to stop scanning every interaction for danger. I needed anonymity. I needed to be safe. I needed to find the girl I used to know. That is what my parents were promising. They were sacrificing everything to give me a second chance. Giving me all I needed for a fresh start. I was weepy and tearful at their generosity, at their love for me. Because I did not deserve such indescribable kindness. Not after what I had done. They would never regret this sacrifice; I swore this to them in solemn words. I would make everything up to them. Everything. Never again would I fall from their grace. *I hope not,* they said in unison. *We think you've learned your lesson.* And so I clung to their pledges as I would last bits of ebbing oxygen and slowly began planning my sun-drenched future, dreaming of all the pleasures a brand-new start would buy. Until I realized it was all just another lie.

~ ~ ~

I am sitting at a long lunch table, watching through a hank of hair that I have discreetly pulled in front of my eyes. John J. Allen has just completed filling out official forms with lies as to why I am starting school a month late and other necessary deceptions and has kissed me on the cheek saying, *Have a good day, honey,* in the meaningless way a reigning personage might turn away a shiftless stranger. Boys in black suits are carrying a makeshift coffin down the center aisle, a lone drummer beating cadence behind the procession. Members of the football team, I suppose, vowing to kill the opponents this Saturday.

Groups of kids, some of their faces familiar, are gathered in tight cliques around the hundred or so tables, crowding the cafeteria, and their laughter charges the air with fanatical energy. Except for me, my table is empty. The incessant drone of the funeral march thumps hollow inside my chest. There is plenty of room; nothing much lives there except fear and anger. The swell of joy at regaining my freedom has long vanished. Gone like a vaporous dream.

It is the first day of my senior year in high school, barely a week since I set foot into my new life, and I am anchored to the bottom of something broken inside me, shoehorned into clothes that don't fit. My blouse pulls and separates at the buttons, fashioning gaping peepholes no safety pins could close. Last year's pleated skirt won't fasten for the tire of blubber encircling my waist. I long for the security of my black trench coat.

It was supposed to be different, this new start. Full of energy and optimism. Focused on all the benefits life has to offer and the heights of accomplishment I can achieve through meticulous study, even if it is only in the secretarial course. I dreamed of a vast and incalculable distance from the gloom of my past, maybe even a move to another state. Complete and absolute anonymity in which I could perform magic and bring myself back to goodness. Instead, my parents have plunked me into the archrival school of the one I had left in shame, separated by scarcely four miles. So close I could pedal my bike back and forth between the two high schools several times and still have the better part of a day left over to waste. I can't swallow past the lump wedged high in my throat.

~ ~ ~

"Not there!" I bellowed. "Anywhere but there! Everybody knows everybody."

Both of them stared at me through the haze of blue-white vapor putt-putting from John J. Allen's pipe and curling off my mother's stubbed Raleigh. I was part of the smoke John J. Allen dismissed with a wave of his hand. I could have kicked myself crippled for my stupidity in buying John J. Allen's professions about the big life-changing move that was now turning out to be no more than a simple change of houses in the same school district, where kids attended one high school or the other and rumors sailed with zipline speed between the two. I'd already gone to one; now I would be going to the other.

I was born stupid — there was no other explanation for my failure to grasp the reality that my father's convincing bluster is never more than performance art, my mother his compliant fan. We are a family bound by deception, by secrets. It is our legacy; it is the route we follow. With the Allens, talk has no heart; it is all insincere prattle, adjusted for the moment. Dates and names are fluid, events and promises altered to suit circumstances. Wasn't I proof?

Long before John J. Allen fell hard for the porcelain beauty of my mother, I was fatherless, existing with my own surname, living with my mother and her family—grandparents, a great-grandparent or two, aunts and uncles, and a cousin here and there running in and out. It's documented in plenty of black-and-whites—a chubby baby with lots of smiles around her. And except for no father anywhere in sight, I belonged to a regular family. I was loved. Then along came John J. Allen with his good looks and war injury, and what was common fact—my single mother raising me, her daughter—got altered, along with the first two years of my life, and a dastardly, not very hush-hush secret took hold and began growing. My parents' wedding date—the fullest, truest expression of their newly minted love—got erased and replaced with a date two years prior, as John J. Allen slipped into the open slot of biological father, contending that the life before him did not exist.

"But Dad," I pleaded once again. "Everybody knows everybody."

"Everybody, huh?" he laughed. It was the same old smirk. My mother's same old detached expression. "If you believe that, I've got a bridge to sell you." Putt, putt, putt.

"But you said! You said!" I cried, glancing from smirk to blank look and back again. "You promised we were moving far away. I can't go to that school! They'll know me there."

Begging. Crying. Reasoning. All a waste of time; I saw the high relief of indifference sculpted onto their faces. If I possessed Jackie's constitution, I would have lunged at them, clamped my hands around their necks, and shaken until their eyes connected with the despair in my own. Squeezed hard and long enough until they at least owned up to their promises, now blithely ignored. Who was I kidding? Nothing could penetrate their sympathies. Lies underpinned my parents' lives, fixing them forever on a glacial landscape long-distanced from the warmth of their own hearts.

All things difficult were effortlessly slicked away by John J. Allen's glib banter and nonchalant smile and undeclared changes of intention. A big *oh, well* was implied in the aloof raise of John J. Allen's eyebrows, in the vacancy of emotion from both of my parents as they watched me grovel for compassion. In the Allen fatherland, betrayal was as routine as meatless Fridays, promises as weightless as the smoke coiling and looping now on the air currents in the stark living room at 14 Beaumont Road.

I could not look at my father, at the pipe resting so peacefully in his mouth, his eyes bearing a sort of glee I could not comprehend; I could no longer swallow his fluent cruelty. And though to my parents truth was a personal enemy to be banished, a mutineer capable of exposing fear and opening wounds, a tyrant proffering harsh judgments against them, it sprawled before them despite their efforts to discard it. They were using my private horror as a convenient excuse to do exactly what suited them. A neatly packaged justification — *we're doing it for you, Kathleen* — to spend money they didn't have to get the hell out of Beaumont Road with its newsy neighbors and unspeakable memories echoing through the rooms. Move to save face, to keep up the charade that the Allen family with the happy-go-lucky John J. at its helm was not imploding. Distance from my past was never on the agenda; getting out was.

So, their impassioned assurances that had propped me up, those visions of buoyant hope that spun dreams, evaporated like pipe smoke as if they had never been dangled in front of my face. Instead, without the bother of offering an excuse, my parents dropped me into the core of my fear, where I knew that sooner or later the dignity I was trying to restore would be once again torn from me. My alarm stood untouched by their concern, no more than an annoying interference to their otherwise blissful future. We could have been actors in a movie lolling about in a Victorian parlor, them peering at me through handheld monocles, drawing in smoke from extended cigarette holders and blowing threadlike streams up toward the coffered ceiling.

I half expected them to utter a few tsk-tsks and shake their heads over my hyperactive imagination. But it wasn't fiction; what they were intending to do to me was reality. And though I felt disloyal and ungrateful even thinking it, and despite my sweeping love for my mother, I realized with a clarity born from experience that my parents were abandoning me. Just as they had abandoned Jackie. The only difference was that they had thrown me a line of lip service, and I was still hanging on to them with hope. Jackie had given up long ago.

That loose and spinning knowledge of the ease with which they were deserting me fueled my anger, as helpless and raw as ever, into a freewheeling wail with no place to shriek as it swelled and reddened into a fireball, fighting and battling to explode, pushing to burst into a zillion sparks and flames, but dared do no more than sputter. Lit up with fury that I could barely contain, I gulped and clenched my mouth into a stripe of rigid muscles, because if I foolishly let one sound escape, the viciousness of my wrath would thrust outward and destroy the only life I knew. But that did not stop me from imploring God to tell me just how many times I had to wish John J. Allen dead before it finally came true.

~ ~ ~

Through my veil of hair I glance around this room that stinks of Clorox and corned beef boiling in a bath of vinegar and peppercorns. If it weren't for the throng and I were in this canyon-sized lunchroom by myself, the fear beating tempo against my ribs would echo louder than the drum that jackass is pounding. There is so much I hate, and at the moment it is this crowd of kids who act like they have nothing more to be concerned about than a football game and the brand name sewn into their crewneck sweaters. I despise myself for offering a feeble smile as the cavalcade marches past just a few feet from me. What I want to do is glare and jerk myself about-face, fling my spite at them by way of rejection.

I wish I were mean with a streak as wide as John J. Allen's, as explosive as Jackie's, all tied up with a hair-trigger temper. Wish I had the courage to be rude and callous, to strike first. If I were the daughter of a bitch instead of a wounded puppet, broad, nervous swathes would be cut for me as I sashayed down the hall and the whispers would be *just stay out of her way* instead of *I heard she's a slut*. My eyes would shoot daggers, not be misted over with fear. And nobody would dare cross me, because they knew revenge would be quick and ruthless. I'd master the art of being ungrateful, banishing pathetic terms like *please* and *thank you* from my vocabulary, replacing them with one single phrase: *go to hell*.

If I could, I'd figure out a way to hack my heart out of my chest so the pain that lives there and radiates from it like throbbing liquid would just stop. That would be the best part; my meanness would cure this hurting that chases through me constantly and won't leave. But wishes are just that, and I am cursed with good manners and damned by too many soft spots.

In a few minutes the first bell will ring and I will make my way to my homeroom, where I will be introduced as the new girl. I don't want the teacher to reveal my name. But she will. She will say, *Class, please say hello to Kathy Allen*. That is where it will all begin. I am about to be born again fresh bait. And I wish I could slide beneath the table and become part of the crumbs and scuff marks, because I cannot bear it. This despair ripping me with its razor claws is bested only by my loathing for my father and his cold, simulated smile that shoved me forward into this hazard. The bell rings, and I lift myself from the chair and tag along behind the swarm, heading into the hallways. I find my homeroom and take a seat in the back. And then the teacher says it. *Kathy Allen*. And I know it is only a matter of time.

~ ~ ~

And it didn't take long.

Trauma had changed me, whether I liked it or not. Despite my outgoing, happy appearance and my ability to make friends quickly, no one saw the heart full of pain I lugged around those school halls — dread over what was creeping toward me like an invasion of cancer waiting to strike once again. But if I allowed myself to collapse into the fear that outlined me with its trembling silhouette, despair would devour me whole and there would be no way back, ever. I would be gone, completely, trapped forever on those filthy mattresses, enduring over and over the violation of *his* greasy hands and the rape of more than just my body. *He*, all he had done to me, would destroy the rest of my life.

I was all I had, and that had to be good enough. There was no mercy to throw myself upon, no outreached hands supporting me. No one waiting with kind eyes and a sympathetic shoulder to soothe away my woes. Disclosure of my secret would be lethal, would slam me right back to his world and its raging horror, and I knew I would not be able to withstand its onslaught. It had taken all my energy to survive the past two years.

Now I was using all the might I had left to keep my dignity while striving to stay balanced, pushing one foot in front of the other, forcing myself into composure I did not feel while shame rode on my back like a decaying, scaly tuber.

I may have looked like any teenage girl, but I felt like a humpback fretting over hiding her deformity. Who could know what it is like to cart around such panic with a smile? To battle constantly to keep the warped, animated defect hidden from view even as it pushes and strains and grows more and more disfiguring? What does a newly deformed person do except die or learn to live within the limitations of the bend and buckle of her body?

No, it didn't take long. Within two weeks, gossip rolled off the tongues of my new friends with wide-eyed surprise. *Jeez, guess what I heard about you. It's not true, is it?* Each time I had to level a denial that was only half believed, my gut leeched acid that blistered me from the inside out and skewered my spirit right through its shaky center. The stories that took hold there were just as merciless as before — somebody knew somebody that had seen Kathy Allen's kid in the maternity ward at a local hospital; it was a boy. An endless stream of implausible facts with me at its center. Whenever a rumor stormed from the gutter and caught up with me, I forced a blank-faced stare or an innocent, confused gaze, denying everything to those scandalmongers, willing myself to hold the charade despite the race of my heart jamming my chest and my body heating like a furnace on full blast, and revealed not a blush, not a hint of anguish. I bled only in private.

I'm not sure when compassion was created, but I can attest to the fact that it was after the sixties. Looking back now, I wonder where I got the strength to manage the relentless ambushes. In a momentary collapse of poise when the gossip so overwhelmed me with its ruthlessness that I could barely face my days, I finally forced myself to swallow the embarrassment that inflamed my cheeks and drove me into stuttering, and I sought my mother's advice. I watched her eyes shadow in awkwardness, her body tense and recoil, if only slightly, as I stood before her shamed and contrite and whispered my question. *Mom, what should I do?*

Maybe panic lived inside her always as it did me, urging her to scream, to flee, or at its most lethal, to fall into paralysis, a sacrificial numbness of inaction. I saw all this in her eyes, felt it issuing from her like heavy perfume as I waited for her to answer. In those few moments of unnerving silence, I dropped my eyes and noticed, as I had since I was a child, the thick, paled slash marks slicing her wrist. There were grim, untold secrets living within those scars, telltale cords of pain that haunted me despite my mother's innocuous tale of how they came to be.

At that moment, I understood what a mistake I'd made in asking my mother for help; she did not want to hear about this. Whatever her reasons were, she could not risk touching my torment. Nowhere within her entire body existed words of guidance or comfort, or the strength to gather me into her arms and soothe away my anguish. Words of support or solace did not belong to her, as if the act of consolation were the sole property of others, a skill to which she was not privy.

What she knew were clichés. The one-size-fits-all advice. *Tomorrow is another day; troubles don't last* — bland and mistaken counsel for a kid stumbling down a cliff blindfolded. "Hold your head high," she managed, avoiding my eyes. "If they're talking about you, at least they're leaving someone else alone." She was not about to visit the realities of the life that she and John J. Allen had created. It was as if none of it had anything whatsoever to do with her. Burnt pot roast, fallen cakes, dust on the end tables were her problems — tendable, solvable problems, even blamable at times. *You kids keep running like that, you're going to make the cake fall.* Looking at her was like looking at a scared rabbit too frightened to move. My mother was paralyzed in the face of my situation and its aftermath, and all she could offer were feeble sayings found in any woman's magazine. It wasn't as if I didn't know I was on my own. I just thought that if I tried one last time, maybe things would be different. They weren't.

So, I forced myself strong, conducting my new life like a series of adages, clichés similar to my mother's advice but reinforced with action: *live or die; sink or swim; when life hands you lemons* — those kinds of annoying one-liners you wish you never had to hear again but that come with a rigorous dose of truth. What happened to me on those vile mattresses crawling with *his* vermin while I cowered in a place beyond the darkness was nobody's business. And I was not about to provide anybody with the ammunition to kill me all over again. No one was going to steal my life away from me, not if I could help it. I had given to my situation all I was ever going to give. I didn't give a damn about telling its truth. But they tried. All of them.

When my new best friend made her arms into a swaying cradle and mouthed *I didn't know you had a baby* across study hall from me, I screwed my face into a quizzical look like I thought she was crazy and just shrugged. In the Middle Ages, fine citizens turned public hangings into a festival. It was a big time when the neck snapped and the body dropped and that old corpse started doing the jig inches above the ground. Those death spasms gave the horde the cheering moment they'd been waiting all day for. The Dance.

And that is what I saw in everyone's eyes, in their claws. The mob, friends and enemies, wanted to watch a dead girl dance. I guarded myself always — watching, listening. Cruel intentions rested in the slight flattening of a smile. In the eyes that betrayed a snap of coldness. In the buttery tone of voice chilled by a smidgen of arrogance. They wanted me to lie down beneath their feet so they could trample me with their loafers and black flats, then huddle together afterward and feast on the satisfaction that only someone else's blood can provide. My squeezed-out confession would make terrific party talk, hours of *well, did you know this?*

A new friend, who had obviously heard the rumors, cornered me in the girls' bathroom. Looking as docile as the cream cashmere sweater she wore, she smacked her lips and stuffed Revlon's Bubblegum Pink back into her patent-leather purse. Looking at me, she purred, *I wonder what it's like to be pregnant*, the smile on her face gooey as honey.

Being traumatized is like being driven psychic: you learn to read people without having to worry about figuring out tarot cards or crystal balls. Her coyness was all an act, and not a very good one. Never missing a beat, I leaned in close and in a doe-eyed, conspiratorial singsong answered, *I don't know, but it must be scary.*

She peered at me for longer than was comfortable — I never broke eye contact — then finally shrugged, disappointed, I guess, that I didn't fall for her not-so-innocent question. *Yeah, you're probably right.* Fate had its comeuppance, though. In a few years Lynn wouldn't be wearing the fine sweater her daddy's business afforded her. She'd be buck naked, dabbling in porn flicks — the kind where the actors all wear Lone Ranger masks. Talk about secrets.

Scavengers, that's how I saw the kids at my new school — no different from the kids I'd left behind. Face it, that's how I saw everyone. I envisioned *everybody* eager to gorge in a feeding frenzy where they would joyfully rip my arms from their sockets, my legs from their joints, tear sweetmeat flesh from my ribs. And I wasn't wrong. A good scandal creates monsters even out of people who should know better. A relative who knew firsthand of my nightmare and had initially offered help and support in the end threatened to ruin me by exposing my secret. No, a crowbar could not have pried my story from me. But it was a strange and private war that I waged in those classrooms and study halls as I battled for my dignity, for the right to my privacy, against all who wanted to wrench it away from me.

I shouldn't be here. I should have known better than to place myself in this kind of jeopardy. We are at a basketball game, my girlfriend and I. The Big One. The Rivalry. I should have known better than to come here. I know that I am not like everyone else. I am not free to walk anywhere I want. I have to take precautions, have to watch my step. But I have allowed the excitement of the pep rallies to seduce me, to lure me away from my good sense, and for this night I make believe I am a normal girl.

The gym of this new school is hot and steamy with sweat and the humid breath of so many fans who've come to holler and root. The drum major and the cheerleaders stir the crowd into a furor of stomping bleachers, shouting, and screaming. I am yelling, pumping my arms, seemingly as if I am in full spirit. But in truth, I am trolling, monitoring my surroundings, ensuring my safety like I always do, when I spot "him" in the bleachers directly across the court from me.

The pandemonium rises — a cacophony of voices and methodic beats of the drums and hundreds of stamping feet all unite into a pulsating, synthesized warning of danger. And like an unexpected smash to the head, panic attacks me, and all the bits and pieces that have begun to heal under the tender mercies of emerging close friendships explode into wet, strangling sobs that rack my body with spasms. I cannot stop. I am blubbering, streaming mucus, shaking so violently that my teeth

165

are chattering. Right in front of an entire gymnasium I have become unglued, my body daring in its defiance, refusing my control, and I am mortified with shame and embarrassment.

"What's the matter with you?" Sharon asks, her eyes wide with disbelief.

And the words gush out, words I do not want to say gush from me in a stream of toddler hysteria. "He's here. He's here," I gurgle over and over.

"Who? Who's here?" Sharon asks, confused, swinging her head back and forth.

"He's here. He's here. Over there. Over there."

"Who? Who?" She's almost in a panic. "Who's here?"

"Him. Him," I keep repeating. "He's here."

My friend does not know what to do. I do not know what to do. I'm trapped. The game is not over, and my father is not here to pick us up yet. I can't walk down the bleachers now. He will see me, and he'll follow me. And then he'll steal me again. Sharon is frowning at me, like I'm a spoiled brat just wanting attention. But I have to disappear. I have to. And I'm so sorry that I've ruined her night with this messy display.

I'm trying, trying to calm down. I have to. I sink onto the bleacher, duck behind the kids in front of me, gulp deep breaths, and hunker down inside my sweater, hiding my face as well as I can. And when we leave in a pointed rush at the end of the game, I am a hawk, watching, watching, trying to contain myself. Sharon will not forget this, and the next time she eats dinner at my house, she will pull this incident out in front of John J. Allen and my entire family and laugh about how I got hysterical over some nameless kid in the bleachers.

To earn money, I took an evening job as a telephone solicitor at a one-man insurance agency. My father dropped me off, and the agent was to bring me home after work. It was my first night, and I was alone in the dimly lit office with a slovenly pig of a man, slick and overly friendly. Smiling politely, I tried to ignore him without seeming rude, dialing and dialing the phone to keep myself busy, earning ten cents a call, and distanced from his big mouth that he never shut.

The drive home was long and achingly slow as he toyed with me in his suave little game of hunter and prey — contrived talk and inappropriate comments I didn't know how to respond to. Each time he spoke, each time he slowed the car to a near crawl, I felt my panic rising. Long before the turn to my street, I gave him plenty of warning. *It's coming up.* Then, *The next street, turn right.* After that, *Get ready to turn right.* Then finally, *Turn here! Stop! Stop! You're going to miss it. Turn here! Turn here!*

But he ignored me, and his voice, shrill and unnatural, reveled with startling amusement as he laughed, saying, "What'd ya say? What'd ya say? Turn where? Turn where?" And kept driving straight, picking up speed, barreling down the highway toward stretches of farmers' fields and uncut darkness.

Go back! Go back! Stop! Stop! I screamed and screamed.

I screamed hard enough to upchuck blood, had there been any left in my body. Screamed until my heart threatened to crash-land onto my lap in a mottled clump of purple veins and dying beats. Maybe my guardian angel kicked Insurance Man hard in his fat ass, or maybe he realized that despite my compliant demeanor, I wasn't going anywhere without a vicious fight, because he finally got the message and swerved the car around and drove me home in blessed silence.

I never went back. John J. Allen retrieved the few dollars I had made that night, but he never challenged the creep. Despite his bravado with fools and the powerless, at his core, John J. Allen was a coward.

The few dates I had didn't go well. When one boy tried to kiss me goodnight after a movie, panic gripped me so hard I could not contain the hysteria that exploded into wrenching sobs and bone-clanking shakes. He didn't say it, but he thought I was insane. And I was. On the next couple of dates with a mild-mannered, low-keyed kid and a couple he knew, I sat in tense silence, unable to find words to speak. Even with my unresponsive manner, or maybe because of it, he professed his love for me and penned lots of sappy love letters. I avoided him, and eventually he disappeared.

The only boys I was comfortable with wore white socks and madras shirts — clean boys I could flirt with in the safety of crowded school halls but not date because they already had their love interests. At dances, I surrounded myself with my new girlfriends, and though I longed to be asked to dance, I didn't know how to be with boys anymore. Where once

I danced with joyful abandon, now I felt like a clumsy galoot stuck to the sidelines, afraid to be conspicuous. When a young man asked me to be his date for the entire three-day senior class trip, I lacked the courage to refuse, even though I knew I would not spend one minute with him. Somehow I managed to pawn him off on a girlfriend, who was crazy enough to take me up on it. Prom time came and went. Though I was asked, and the boy in his sweet generosity even offered to buy me a dress, I felt I didn't deserve to go and didn't want to bother working up the courage to ask permission from my parents.

In a sad and weird surrender to my fate — the despicable secretarial job loomed — I did what I had promised myself and knuckled down at school, and earned honors. This, of course, became grounds for caustic revelry at the dinner table, with John J. Allen leading the charge. *How many teachers did you have to bribe? You better check; there's been a terrible mistake.*

My stupidity was great fodder for my family, and except for my mother, they all worked the taunts the night I brought home my first string of good marks, each one trying to outdo the other. To their grave disappointment, I was becoming immune to living with sarcasm and didn't rise to the bait. And in a surprise turn, my mother piped in and said, *I'm proud of you.* Her sincere, kind favor during that testosterone-fueled free-for-all is something I still carry with me today.

Every now and again I babysat. Somewhere along the way, I'd used up my fury. The days of being responsible for my brothers were over. John J. Allen, though impossibly rigid and prone still to temper and so controlling that you could barely draw a breath in front of him without his permission, had softened somewhat toward me. The gossip had died down, and I was enjoying my new friends. Kindness was beginning to blossom in the spaces vacated by despair. Though I still didn't particularly like kids, I now was able to gently tend to them when they were under my care, somehow relating to their vulnerability.

It was strange, this new feeling of tenderness; an experience I had never known. I felt like I was growing a heart. So one warm spring evening after I tucked my charges into bed, I threw open the front door as if I were unbolting something deep within me and marveled at the bright golds and brilliant reds streaking through the fading light. Possibilities and a fresh sense of happiness flooded me, and suddenly my life felt doable. Misery seemed to be giving way to hope, birthing in its wake a sense of brightness. I was healing.

Across the road, down the street from where I stood, lived the boy who had gifted me with my first kiss. Being so close to *once upon a time* summoned such sweet memories — the flight and tumble of butterflies tickling me from the inside, the rustle of tall dry grasses, the rhythm of waves lapping onto the shore of that hidden cove by Gropp's Lake where we sat. Gazing into the falling darkness, I could almost hear the ripple and splash of water advancing and receding, feel the warmth of being tucked against someone safe. It was gentleness I craved, the muscled curve of a familiar, protective arm around my shoulders. Soft whispers of affection. The relaxed interlacing of fingers. The weave of shared smiles.

Ronnie was the first boy to tell me I had beautiful eyes. I stared at his house enfolded now in shadows, wishing I could see him again. Reasoning away flashes of that night in the schoolyard where in the darkness he'd pinned my arms behind my back and encouraged his friend to molest me, I told myself that the incident had happened a very long time ago, and he had apologized, made promises. Like a starstruck ingénue, I kept gazing at his house, convinced I could revisit the innocence of my first crush if just granted the chance.

And as if I had conjured him up from starlight and moonbeams, he came walking down the street. It had been so many years since I'd seen him, but I would have known him anywhere. "Ronnie?" I called, stepping out onto the porch beneath a shaft of yellow light. He looked up and didn't recognize me. "It's Kathy. Kathy Allen," I said, my heart swimming in my chest.

"Hey, how are you?" He strolled up the walk, heftier than I remembered, with a hint of a smirk in his smile I didn't recall. But this welcome, familiar face from the good part of my past melted away all the lingering strain of months and months of chiseling my way into the tight cliques of strangers. The ordeal of the last years dissolved, and in a flash of magic, I was the bubbly Kathy Allen once again, the Kathy of before, before the anguish.

After a few moments of idle chitchat that chased away the distance between then and now, I opened the door and invited him in. Unease and excitement blended into a rush of disbelief that, after all that had transpired, my first boyfriend, the one of my first awkward gentle kiss, was actually sitting beside me on the sofa. It seemed a new, safe beginning. When he put his arm around my shoulders, I curled up against his side as if I belonged there, as I had done long ago on the shore of Gropp's Lake. I rested into the nook of his male protection, thinking I was safe, thinking my life had come full circle, and at long last I was actually and truly getting the opportunity to start fresh. At that moment I was freed from the despair of all those horrid yesterdays.

My head was still floating in puffy clouds when Ronnie leaned in and kissed me. But it was not like on the little beach by the lake. It was rough and bruising. And I was startled. And before I had a chance to comprehend what was happening, he pushed me down onto the cushions and was on top of me, his hands raging and tearing at my body, at my clothes, tugging at the buttons on my blouse, yanking at the waistband on my slacks, wrenching me this way and that like I was a rag doll beneath his weight.

For a second I was dumbfounded, dazed, smothered under his bulk. Then I knew. I knew. I knew. I knew what he was doing. I knew what he was doing. And I exploded into liquid, molten rage. *This is not happening again. This will not happen again.* And I kicked and screamed and clawed and pounded my fists and ripped at his hair. My fingers were talons tearing at any bare skin I could reach. I was murderous and berserk, screeching, grabbling, kicking. A girl gone demonic. He would have to kill me, because I would not stop. And I did not stop until he jumped up and ran from the house, me screeching, "Get out! Get out!" right behind him.

Stupid, stupid, stupid girl. Stupid girl. Stunned and shaking, I straightened the sofa and sank down into the cushions, shocked. I dropped my head in my hands and rocked back and forth, back and forth. *Stupid, stupid, stupid girl.* The parents would come home and have no idea that their babysitter, the one in charge of their precious children, had almost been raped right on their couch where they snuggled with their boys to watch Ed Sullivan. By a neighborhood kid who probably cut their grass and served them Communion at Mass on Sundays. Where one of the little boys could have easily awakened and stumbled onto the sight. Almost raped by a kid she herself had let into the house. *Stupid, stupid girl.* What the hell was wrong with me?

I rocked and hated. Rocked and hated. Hated myself for my idiocy, for my goddamned daydreams. Hated the girl that kept falling and falling, tripping over her worthless hopes and sappy illusions. Part of my brain was missing; it had to be. The piece that stored memory. Otherwise, how could I keep forgetting what I knew? What I'd known for seven long years, since I was ten years old, the first time my father raced his big hands up and down the sore swellings of my miniature breasts — that I existed in two separate and distinct worlds. One regular one, the world of the girlish, happy Kathy Allen. The other, grim and ominous — the secret, isolated world of unnoticed abuse I was yanked into time and time again by backdoor violators: the smirking predators and grinning vultures disguised as family and friends, neighbors, acquaintances, employers. Authorized vermin who presumed liberty and plastered me with their vile. Not only protected by their titles — whether it was father, brother, boyfriend, uncle, whatever — but also safeguarded by my terror, by my voice frozen solid with fright and shame. It was a netherworld inhabited by sneaks, shits who understood the value of intimidation served up noiselessly or with an amazed look of innocence spread across their faces. Or like tonight, sensed weakness and read *willingness to be raped* into my friendliness.

From the outside, the world I lived in looked garden-variety ordinary. But it wasn't. In an instant it could and did spiral out of control, attack without warning. Personal danger lurked everywhere. In love letters. In my father's smirks. On the tongues of nuns. It was as if I were shadowed by cruelty.

And yet to speak it, I would be condemning myself as paranoid. Overreactive. Given to drama. What would I say? "Everybody's mean to me"? I could hear John J. Allen's comeback: "Everybody? Oooooh, poor Kathy Allen, everybody hates her." Or I could say, "A boy I know tried to rape me tonight." He'd look at me through the smog of pipe smoke and say, "Who else do you have to blame but yourself?" And my mother would add, "It's your own fault." If I could gather enough courage to defend myself, I might say, "I didn't ask to be raped." To which they both would shake their heads and counter, "What did you expect when you invited him in?"

I was so ashamed of myself; ashamed of my stupidity, my weakness. Ashamed of how much it all hurt. Ashamed that I could not stop the ambushes. That I didn't even know how I was causing them.

Yet as I rocked back and forth on that family sofa, still shaking from Ronnie's attack, a hesitant, watery notion, as pallid as first light creeping over a twisted wreckage, began stirring down near where my spirit lay in shambles. Slowly the despair shifted and a tepid awareness inched its way forward. I had fought for myself tonight. Hard. Ferociously hard. Battled fearlessly. Viciously, as I'd fought Jackie, ripping and tearing. The mania in me unleashed, ignoring my fear and shame. And I'd done the same with Fat Ass Insurance Man — not physically, but with my screams — and had it come to it, I would have fought him with the same bloody intensity. And when that boy had tried to kiss me on that date, my fight instincts took over, even if I looked crazy.

Somehow I was pulling on a strength I never knew I possessed. Meek, powerless me had fought back. And won. I'd fought. I'd fought. I stopped rocking and listened to my own words. I'd fought and won. I could hardly believe what I was hearing. Could hardly believe what it meant. Could John J. Allen be wrong? Could it be that I wasn't just a dizzy airhead with nothing between the ears? That somewhere I had strength? Could it be possible?

But all the good thoughts about myself could not change the reality of what had happened on the couch tonight, whether I had fought or not. Though the sofa now looked spotless and welcoming in its plushness, it was changed, tainted by violence, though no one except me would ever know. It became one more despicable event to add to my catalog of secrets. One more incident I would pretend did not happen. With a wide smile plastered on my face like it was a Christmas homecoming, I would welcome the parents back tonight, giving no hint of the scene that had defiled their living room. I'd tell them how good their children were, and the husband would take me home and I'd huddle silently, nearly frozen in the passenger seat, praying he would behave like a gentleman. Then I'd go upstairs to my bedroom and not say a word to anyone about my trip back into a recurring nightmare.

Whether I froze in the face of degradation or rallied against it, I lived always within the reach of its shadowed world, even as I put forth a beaming smile. It was a life I had no questions for, except one: why the hell did I always expect it to be different?

CHAPTER 12

Love at First Sight and Another Evil Deed

My brother Jackie's fight with life was escalating. John J. Allen's health was deteriorating. And I discovered love at first sight.

Love at first sight. Such a tattered sentiment — an overused fairy tale with a poor track record. It speaks of pining and the lovelorn. Who even uses terms like that anymore? And nobody actually believes in love at first sight anyway, thanks to the scientists with their theories on hormones and pheromones that have robbed love of its magic. Secretly, though, like the Santa Claus myth, everybody wishes it were true. Think about it: Where would romance novels be if we didn't at least have hope of being swept off our feet and carried off into the charmed forevermore?

But I like that this outdated saying has been discarded, thrown out along with saddle shoes and seamed stockings. Its worn-out reputation suits me. I like things ragged around the edges. Since it's outlived its usefulness, I now claim those snubbed four words as my very own, exclusively. Never have I swiped anything so grand. But don't fret — given the correct set of convincing circumstances, I'm willing to share. So yes, with a few concessions for exact timing, when I was seventeen years old, love at first sight came calling, along with a bonus feature — a spooky spiritual experience that more than makes up for the hiccup in timing.

Go ahead, snicker, because by the time I tell you the story, you'll also be rolling your eyes. And that's OK with me, because I would not want to be responsible for any kind of shift in a rigid belief system. Though, the way I look at it, if God speaks to the Pope and schizophrenics and an oddball assortment of true believers — including those bloated, crazy-eyed preachers hawking Him on TV — why not me? I don't know how the Pope does it, but I have a foolproof way of knowing it's God Himself, or at least one of His support staff. To my amazement — and yes, frequently to my profound disappointment — it works every time.

Spending time with my mother away from John J. Allen was like relaxing in the comfort of a swaying hammock. Without a hammer-wielding dictator present, ready to smash into the fun, laughing together was free and easy. We would lounge at the kitchen table, smoking cigarettes, counting Green Stamps from the A&P supermarket and Raleigh coupons saved from the back of her cigarette packs, and pore over catalogs of pots and pans and stainless flatware, choosing what to buy for my hope chest. I would call her Jane, my pet nickname for her that soon John J. Allen would ban, accusing me of calculated disrespect.

Those days when she let me play hooky from school and we warmed the kitchen with our closeness, I could love her without his envy looking to belittle it, and I think that during those private times, she loved me without worry. There is a natural high that comes from such intimacy — as addictive as an illicit drug, only more difficult to come by. How many times in your life do the stars align just so and you are granted the blessing of jitterbugging in the kitchen with your mom, rock and roll blasting from the AM radio?

If John J. Allen had seen us fearlessly wrestle each other to the floor giggling, what hair he had left on the top of his head would have exploded, igniting flames that would shoot straight from his nose and eyeballs, and he would have instantly banished me to my room, claiming that I was dishonoring my mother and yelling that he'd better never catch me laying a hand on her like that again. He would make me a criminal, and my mother wouldn't argue. John J. Allen could turn the joy of baking chocolate-chip cookies into an offensive pursuit.

When he wasn't there, my mother and I were girlfriends offering each other affectionate consolation as we puffed smoke rings around our heads. Surrounded by stamps and dog-eared catalogs and engulfed in drifting haze while the sun wiggled its way past the café curtains and sprawled just as it should across the trappings of our excitement — my mother so close our fingers touched as we pointed out prizes — I was embraced by perfect bliss. For those brief recesses, I was completely safe and protected from menace and risk in a home so unpredictable with its constantly shifting foundation that even an innocent comment could trigger John J. Allen's fury.

During those days stolen from real life, a couple of months before my high school graduation, with the house belonging just to my mom and me and our cigarettes and worth-real-money stamps, we were freed not only from the vigilant eyes of John J. Allen, but also from the troubling, destructive potency of hate — that ever-present undercurrent, the infection that was both destroying and at the same time supporting our frail family structure. Jackie had stepped up his delinquency, barging into very dangerous territory. He sniffed glue and ingested drugs right in the house, stumbled home high or drunk after committing one kind of illegal activity or other that might or might not land him on the pages of the local newspaper. Those fleeting hours in the kitchen with my mother offered a respite from the disorder of confusion and anger present in a house with an out-of-control teenager, where hate flickers like a pilot light primed for a match.

Jackie was an outcast in the family, a rallying cause to arms, a dumping ground for all anger, blocked from any love or compassion, damned to live forever on the outside of the circled wagons. He wasn't one of us; he was evil, single-handedly responsible for trying to tarnish our family name. Without him, we laughed. Sat around the scarred kitchen table polished to high shine and told jokes. More truthfully, John J. Allen told jokes. OK, the jokes were at someone else's expense; you should know by now whose. But I laughed along with the rest, tolerated his humor; it was easier than the alternative.

Besides, Jackie's demise was my rising star. His troubles became an opportunity for me to shine, to prove my goodness by condemning him and supporting my parents. Who wouldn't love a daughter who kept nodding her head in agreement and saying, "That's horrible. I can't believe he would do that to you." From the height of that lofty position, I found it easy to scorn my brother. We all did. His unconscionable deeds secured our personal status as righteous and noble. But sometimes when I looked into Jackie's eyes, I swear I saw such loneliness and pain, such desperation for acceptance, that I was overcome with pity. But in a family that blames all their misfortunes on one individual, if you're not that person, you're grateful for the hell you're spared.

So we became a mob incited by our own wrath, and in our eyes, Jackie had no humanity. Whether the mob is gathered on a rain-slicked street or in a kitchen with its scent of fresh-brewed coffee, there is no sympathy or reason, no witness to the target's anguish; there is only belief. I believed Jackie was evil. And so did everyone else. His aberrant behavior reinforced my mother and John J. Allen as the innocent victims of their son, a rabid juvenile delinquent. Pat and Jack collected all the sympathy votes.

Who could not feel sorry for the good-hearted Jack, his body racked by diabetes, the joke teller who drew everyone into his friendly bubble? Or for my mother, patient and long-suffering, an immaculate housekeeper who baked killer cakes? How had this misery befallen these two good people? No one acknowledged the ugly parts of the past. None of us, neither the perpetrators nor the beneficiaries, admitted its truth — the beatings, cruelties, and mistreatments — or allowed room for the notion of pain in all its full-blown enormity trolling the shadows, having nothing else to do except wreak havoc.

In a family of secret keepers, the past is a very delicate affair of selecting and discarding. Truth has no value. To speak candidly would be disloyal, would cause our parents incalculable hurt. Might even mean our own dismissal from favor. Blame was our easy way out. It saved the bother of looking within; you didn't own up to anything if you didn't have to. Anyway, Jackie was the premier troublemaker; there was nobody better at creating aggravation. Everything bad was his fault. He was born trouble; my mother knew this when she saw his pointed head jutting out of the baby-blue receiving blanket. His lazy eye and flappy ears sealed the deal.

So with Jackie's declaration of war on the world, my mother and John J. Allen donned brave faces and trudged through the familiar territory of having such unfairness invade an otherwise happy family. Hate and rejection were stoked by tales of Jackie's despicable wrongdoings. With each telling, I resented him more. No one spoke in his defense. What was there to defend? He made everybody miserable; he always had. The only option was hate, his expulsion from compassion. Back then, beatings and relentless hostility had no impact on a little boy now grown into an enraged young man. Besides, he brought it all on himself.

Real life did not intrude on the delicate spirit of fun that my mother and I created in the quiet house that was free, if only temporarily, from the threats of John J. Allen and Jackie's unhinged anger. As we did every time we were alone, we planned a really fabulous lunch — hoagies, Tastykakes, and Coke. My mother dug in her purse and counted out a couple of dollars worth of change from the wallet I once pinched nickels and dimes from. It was money she'd scraped and gathered. In a house of seven with the breadwinner a public servant, there was little extra. Whatever was left over at the end of the month was firmly ensconced in John J. Allen's pants pocket. And nobody, not even my mother, had access to it. So, change jingling in my coat, I walked the mile or so to the 7-Eleven to collect our spoils.

With my history, I should have been scared of the car slow-driving behind me as I meandered along the sidewalk. But I wasn't. When I glanced around and thought I saw an old man behind the wheel, I shot him the dirtiest look possible. Twice more he circled the block in his turquoise cruiser, slowing each time to take a look. And each time, I glowered at him, annoyed because he was disrupting my concentration and I was trying to decide what kind of Tastykakes I should choose. My mother wanted the Tandy Kakes, small rounds of vanilla cake smeared with peanut butter and enrobed in chocolate. So delicious, but not very filling. I was seriously considering the standard pack of three hefty chocolate cupcakes, because I could make them last a really long time by eating the icing off first. But I couldn't focus with the big blue dawdling in my peripheral vision.

How could I have ever known that truancy, Tastykakes, and a freshly washed Dodge would conspire on that ordinary morning to transform my life?

It turned out that the old man in the car lived down the street and around the corner, right next door to my best friend, Janet. And he wasn't an old man after all, but barely a year out of high school. I'm not sure how I missed him, because Janet's house was my second home. But she never even mentioned the cute guy living in the split-level next to hers — probably because she didn't think Phil was cute, owning to the fact that she'd known him since he was in grade school. I guess she looked at him more or less like a creepy brother, and nobody I ever knew thought of their brothers as dating material. Despite Janet's *ewwww, why-do-you-want-to-meet-Phil?* attitude, I wrangled an introduction, and soon he would be whisking me off for our first date in that big boat of a car with the push-button dash.

My heart does a little flip-flop as I watch Phil stroll up the walkway wearing an ironed plaid shirt and pressed slacks. He stops, stoops down, and offers a cookie to our dog, Tami, who greets him with such enthusiasm that I think her tail is going to spin off her back end like a detached propeller. It is April—the twenty-first, to be exact—and the evening air is still and unseasonably warm for early spring. Looking at him as he rises and smiles at me, I push open the storm door and stand aside, waiting for him to reach the steps. I know what he will smell like—soap and aftershave. His fingernails will be clean. All this I can see in his posture, the way he carries himself. In his half grin. How his hair is combed.

He is yards away from me; I have yet even to touch his hand when I am struck with a sensation so strong that it has shape and form and could be plucked from the space between us and read like an announcement. It engulfs me in pure and absolute knowledge, a clarity so keen I can feel its radiance pouring over me and filtering into my pores like bright sunshine. I am going to marry him. I'm going to marry this guy Phil.

Not maybe. This is not a starstruck, romanticized flight of teenage whimsy. I'm going to marry him; I know this without doubt, without hesitation. Without question. This is fact, as real as Tami's frenzied barking, as tangible as my hand, bitten fingernails and all, propping open the door. For a few seconds as Phil walks toward me, I revel in this forecast, in its heat. It is the summer sun rising after a bleak, cold winter, how it floats across your skin and melts into your blood, making you want to dance in its warmth.

Many, many years into the future, when my duct-taped and nailed-shut past tears loose and explodes out of the sewer and into our lives, and despair shatters me into so many pieces that I do not think I will recover, I will look at Phil and ask, "What if I die from this? What if this is the end for us?" He will get up and kneel before me and gather my hands in his. "I'm not going to let you go," he will say. "I will never leave you. When we die, I will find you. I promise you, I will find you."

Of course, standing in the threshold watching him walk toward me that first night, tailed by Tami and her commotion, I didn't know the specifics of our future. All I knew was the truth of its certainty, and that premonition, its absoluteness, made me want to erupt into hysterical giggles. It's not every day I get a direct hotline communication from the heavens; understand, it was extremely challenging for me to retain my composure. If I knew Phil, I would have grabbed his hand laughing and squealed, "Guess what!" But of course, I didn't know him at all. That was our first date. We'd barely shared conversation.

This is my love-at-first-sight tale. There I stood glitter-sprayed with stardust that no one could see but me. It is a foolish fairy tale created for violins and harps, suited for *oh, really?* skepticism. That's what I love about it. It sounds so fake. But this love–at-first-sight story is mine, not Phil's. He had no idea I'd just received an urgent memo from the Big Buddy Up There who was supposed to be locked up inside the tabernacle at Saint Gregory the Great Roman Catholic Church just the other side of Route 33, a mile or so down the road. The church where we would eventually marry.

We go to the drive-in and see Hush…Hush, Sweet Charlotte *and smoke cigarettes and share buttered popcorn. And talk through most of the movie. He makes sure I understand that he is dating other girls. I can barely keep a straight face and don't say what I'm thinking — that the whole "dating other girls" thing is not going to last long. Before he kisses me good night, I know he will ask me for another date. And he does. "Just so you know," he says, "I have other dates lined up." A prom, he tells me, and a weekend in New York where he and his buddies plan to carouse and hit a lot of nightspots and maybe meet girls. Oh, Lord, let me not laugh at his innocent unawareness; I do respect his sincerity, though. In truth, we are already a couple; Phil just doesn't understand this yet.*

But my mother does. The next morning when I come downstairs for breakfast, she looks at me and says, "You're going to marry him." "I know," I say. "I know." That's the thing about my real and true spiritual messages: there is always, always confirmation. It is never forced; it just appears. I had to laugh. What else could I do?

Phil's presence had a lifting effect on my family, including John J. Allen, whose good spirits transformed our house into a comedy club when Phil visited. The sounds of joking and making fun amplified the family closeness we all wanted to believe in — that we wanted Phil to see. So everybody faked it. Not that anyone admitted that. It felt so genuine, the truth so drab. The charade was a glow that pulled all of us forward into the brightly lit kitchen, around the table, elbow to elbow, smile to smile. All except Jackie, who wasn't about to play his part in the illusion.

Easygoing and confident, the last of six kids living at home, Phil slipped easily into the framed glossy that concealed the reality of life at the Allens'. Where our house was noisy and raucous, heaving with laughter — at least when Phil was there — his house was heavy with quiet, the masked anger so palpable that it seemed a flesh-and-blood presence given to constant brooding. His dad had apparently taken a domestic vow of silence. Except for grunts and one-word answers, Mr. Foley rarely spoke at home, but at work and in his other life — the mystery one he silently disappeared into every night after dinner — Denny was everybody's best friend.

As soon as he finished his meal, consumed without a sound except for chewing and swallowing, Mr. Foley would push back from the table, walk three feet to the closet, put on his coat and hat, and walk out the front door without a single word falling from his lips. And nobody ever said, "That's a damn ignorant thing to do." Or, "What kind of bug crawled up his ass?" Not a mention, as if it were the most natural thing in the world for a man to show such contempt for his wife who home-cooked his meat-and-potato meals seven days a week, and for whatever other family members were present still forking up the last bits of dinner. Which got me contemplating fathers.

How is it that without even asking, they con us into granting them absolution for their mean and nasty behavior? Forget about an apology. No kid would ever get away with the shenanigans fathers pull, and no father would have the least bit of a problem calling him on it if he tried. In the Allen family, John J. Allen's belt had settled a lot of scores, and that was after sworn repentance. And I'd like to know precisely how fathers managed to wiggle their way into the Ten Commandments anyhow — at number four, no less. You know the one: "Honor thy father and mother." I'll concede to honoring the mother part. But jeez, knighting unrestrained testosterone, giving it top billing in the family? Every man I've ever known has had trouble controlling the he-man bluster that one hormone spawns.

OK, giving God the benefit of the doubt, maybe He yielded to a bit of arm twisting and had to make a few olive-branch concessions to Moses when they were working it all out. *Look, I'll make it a really big sin for kids to badmouth their folks if you'll concede the top spot to me without argument.* That kind of thing. But where did that leave us, the kids, having to ignore a parent's bad behavior while at the same time putting up with it because even mentioning it is considered high sacrilege, scored with a big black checkmark on the transgression side of the ledger? Someday I'm going to have a little sit-down with God and ask him to explain exactly why that *poor* John J. Allen — just because he had five kids and a wife to support and that high-pressure job to manage — and why that *good* man Denny Foley — just because he put food on the table every day and faithfully ushered at church every Sunday and tended to women fainting in the pews — didn't have to bother playing nice at home. And I won't settle for anything less than the whole thing being scratched from the Top Ten. So there. Let the lightning strike.

Dads notwithstanding, Phil and I started building our history, creating our own lightning. Those nighttime drag races, blasting down deserted country roads at over 100 miles an hour, the Dodge shuddering and quaking as I hung on for dear life to whatever I could grab hold of — which most times was Phil's neck — screeching *go, go* until we blew past the competition for the win, were crazy exciting. How none of us ended up on the side of the street in a pile of smoking scrap metal is a celestial mystery.

Then there were the beach parties. Since we were east coasters, nobody owned woodies, but that didn't stop us from tying surfboards onto the roofs of rickety coupes and balloons to the antennas and speeding down the highway to the shore in dozen-car-strong motorcades of rumbling glass packs and chewed-up mufflers. My task was to lay on the horn every few miles or so, pulling all the others into a racket of clashing honks and earsplitting blares. Is it any great wonder why people hate teenagers?

Since Phil was from Brooklyn, he took me on tours of all his old New York haunts — Bergen Beach, where he once lived and still had friends; Coney Island, where he introduced me to cheesesteaks and we rode the wooden roller coaster and the Steeplechase. We'd end up at the Pizza King, a deafening, dimly lit joint crowded with teenagers old enough to drink, where we danced and chased mediocre Italian food with gin and tonics and whiskey sours. My curfew was midnight, but we always saved time to visit Crematory Hill, a backdrop for a horror movie if there ever was one, or squeezed into the car lineup by the Delaware River to watch the submarine races — teenage code for *going parking*, which was code for *making out*. Steamy windows, acrid smoke pulled deep into our lungs and blown out in thick streams, and long, long talks about our future. And soon we were planning a life together.

I never thought about my past. But it worked its way into a malevolent force, lurking, waiting for the right moment to ambush.

Every day at noon I unchained myself from my desk at the Department of Education and escaped downtown, sometimes with a group, sometimes by myself. No need to complain about how much I deplored office work and felt forced into obedience. Given a choice at least, I would have worked in the musty basement of the NJ State Museum cataloging bones and broken pieces of pottery. That is where I should have ended up. It was the last remaining job on the Civil Service list when my name, with the lowest score, finally came up. Nobody wanted me. Nobody wanted *it*. It would have been a perfect match. It's the one I coveted. But John J. Allen had other ideas and some big-shot contacts.

So I ended up surrounded by marble and glass and by people who were as sterile and polite as magazine advertisements, in a prime position that should have gone to a girl with skills — someone with a bend toward subservience who wouldn't take offense at being asked to sit and take dictation. Or, God forbid, read it back. Or — are you kidding — type it up without errors. My typing and shorthand skills were flawless, executed with speed and accuracy — in my head, of course. Unfortunately, my hands refused to perform on demand. By the end of the day, my wastebasket overflowed with crumbled letterhead ruined by eraser holes, my steno pad filled with squiggled muddle that no amount of staring would ever decipher.

What I did do with swiftness and precision, though, was stuff envelopes. So, oftentimes I was relegated to the back room with the part-timers. Weathered Trenton women with hard-luck stories they wheezed out between phlegmy coughs and serious drags on Lucky Strikes and Camels. But I fooled around too much with those behind-the-scenes sub-workers, and one day I scrawled *TEE HEE* across a college scholarship rejection letter just before stuffing it into an envelope.

Nobody could believe I did that. It was a callous and thoughtless way to instigate some laughter that felt spiteful and somehow seemed rooted in the bitter college toe-to-toe I'd had with John J. Allen at 14 Beaumont Road. And I've carried the guilt over that single act of insensitivity for my entire life. I have no excuse, except to say that joking had no boundaries where I came from and that there was little I wouldn't do to make time in that cheerless, stuffy office go faster.

But each day when noon finally rolled around, it was as if a guard had unlocked my cell. I bolted into freedom.

I was by myself on the day my past decided to employ some low torture. Half a block away, in the midst of the lunchtime crowd as throngs of people milled about, I spied *him* angled against a brick wall, one thick thigh crossed over the other. Trauma is its own brand of higher learning, and it had imprinted me with stern protective instincts. Ever see a cat spook over nothing, perking her ears over something you can't see? Or a hawk, circling and circling, looking, watching? A bloodhound with her nose pressed into the air, sniffing? Because, I swear, before I even laid one eye on him, I sensed his advent, smelled his stench wafting toward me amidst all the cologne and aftershave and fresh roasted peanuts — that oily slick of grime and last month's sweat. A swift struggle for a gasp of high-noon heat and suddenly I saw his face, disembodied, rocketing at me, dark and humorless, eyes shifting right and left.

Vanished are the years distancing me from those cold, purple-shadowed eyes, from his omnipresence. And he is here, after all this time, his hands slathering me with filth and stink, pushing, shoving, making me do what I don't want to do. He whispers in my ear. I hear his words, not from long ago, but spoken at this very moment. I smell his breath, stale with smoke and stinking of matter lodged between his teeth. "It's your duty," he says. I know what he is talking about. He's talking about the stiffness between his legs. "You're going to be my wife. It's your duty."

Dug up from piles of buried trash is the threat that underlies all he does to me. The knife poised in my fear, pointing at my privates, what he will do to any girl if the need arises. It is happening now. Again. Right here on the streets of this capital city, where uniformed police patrol every corner but cannot safeguard me. No one can see what I know. Then for all eyes to witness, he climbs on top of me and I slither away like a terrified snake into my own darkness while submitting like a beaten animal.

No, no, no. No! He is nowhere near me. He has not seen me. I'm too far away, part of the crowd walking into town for lunch and window-shopping. But panic takes its own directive and blasts through me, spinning me around on my two-inch heels, pumping my legs into action. Purse flying off my shoulder, arms like pistons shooting forward and then back, propelling me forward, heels pelting the sidewalk with rapid-fire click, click, clicks. Legs sprinting, vaulting, inflamed by terror, the fire of it sizzling at my back, chasing me, for a quarter mile, a half mile, more. I go full speed, faster than I have ever run in my life. In spike heels, tearing down State Street, nonstop. Running. Running. Racing for my life. I see no one. Not the onlookers who must think me berserk. Not the snarled traffic. Not the blur of scenery, trees, buildings, flags, flowers in manicured beds. Just me. My legs. My crazy arms. My heart, my lungs, bellowing. My purse thumping against my side. And him at my back.

I do not stop until I reach the steps of the State building where I work. There is no need to look back. I know he has not followed. He didn't even see me. But that does not mean I am safe. I am never safe. I am always on the brink of being seized and towed back into the gutter, by him, by what he did to me, by my failures. There is barely one thin line separating me from emotional catastrophe; this is how fear works. So I run and hide from him, from my disgrace.

Often I wonder about the women in my family. My grandmother who ran away from her husband and children. Aunt Nellie, protecting herself inside that ratty black coat. My mother, holed up behind her silence. All those women, hiding, running from something. Did they, too, touch raw fear? Did they find their once-immaculate hands flailing inside the heart of a pulsing, heaving cesspool? Like I did? Am I carrying forth their strange legacy, running, hiding, cowering, always looking over my shoulder for the phantoms chasing me?

There is not a day that passes, ever, that I am not reminded of what I am, of what I became underneath him. Even my name. I can barely tolerate *Kathy*; it feels always like a slur spit out of the corner of someone's mouth. But match it up with *Allen* and it is no longer a name, but a stain that plagues me with disgrace. Every time someone utters *Kathy Allen*, disgust stabs me with a quick reminder of just what I am, lest I forget. Every time — without fail. It's a permanent souvenir, a small keepsake I never have to dust.

Are the mute women in my family familiar with such keepsakes? Do these kindred women know well the terrain of ordinary days, but they don't tell? What god-awful power strikes women voiceless? Women who deliberately withhold from a girl the answers of how it is every day, every day, to live surrounded by the malice of co-workers. Friends. Relatives. The odd neighbor who thinks it is her mission to convict the unchaste. Why don't these life-bruised old women speak? Tell a girl how to be, what to do, when she is openly yet secretly condemned?

"It's not possible to get pregnant from rape," he says.

"They get in trouble, go away, have the kid, and come back acting like they're virgins," she says.

"Tramps deserve everything they get," they say.

Even though I have driven out the memories, refuse to let them anywhere near me, I still know what happened, and I wear that knowledge and its blame like a thick coat of soot I cannot remove. I cower and cringe and hide inside my protective darkness while words of the respectable crawl across my skin like fire ants laying down bites that will throb for days, months — a lifetime — and warp the picture frame I have tried to construct.

I love these people who say these things. It is myself I hate. And what he lodged inside me that ravaged me like a fatal disease that failed to deliver on its promise. I have begged God for the courage to butcher myself into unrecognizable slabs. I know I am condemned for what he did to me, for my inability to fight. And for the rest of my life I will curse myself because I didn't have the guts to rip it, to rip him, out of my body with the power of my bare, infuriated hands.

I want these people — they're good people, aren't they? — who say the worst things to love me back. Even though I know they will spit in my face and turn and march away if they find out my truth. So sometimes I join the fray and become like them — guttersnipes — and jump on the hearts of living-dead girls and call them whores and sluts, and condemn them with the same venom I use to condemn myself. I draw on my mother's words — "If they're talking about you, they're leaving someone else alone" — as license and stand on the broken spirits of innocent girls just so I can reach air that will not choke me when I try to breathe. Because now it is not me they are gossiping about. As a guttersnipe, I get to attack first, using my dripping fangs as defense, thwarting any scavenger who might catch a whiff of the stink trailing my mortal sin. For the mere cost of kicking a corpse, I can buy a few sacred moments of safety. It is another way I make myself ugly.

So it is that the same fear that fights to consume me also keeps me standing upright and moving forward. I will not fall back. No matter what, I will not return to that filth. I do what I know how to do. I pretend. And hide. And smile. And when insults and condemnations batter me, I do not let it show. Ever. Just like the other women hiding in plain sight inside my own family, I suppose.

I pull a tissue from my purse and dab it over my cheeks to check the sweat and pale-peach foundation and rose blush melting down my face. No, I'm not safe. Nor will I be. That's the way it is now. I take my precautions and protect myself the best way I know how. Tonight I'll see Phil, and maybe we'll go bowling and out for ice cream after. I will never mention a thing about what happened this lunch hour.

I take a deep breath to slow the commotion inside me, smooth my wild hair, climb the stairs, and walk into the air conditioning as if I have been out for a lovely afternoon stroll.

Phil and I began talking about marriage. And wouldn't you know it, there was God, drawn and dark, scored with a perpetual scowl, His yawning mouth charging me with blame, anointing me with fresh guilt, as if the old stuff had worn off. Maybe you have to be Catholic to understand this. Guilt is not just reserved for something you did wrong. It covers what you did not do and should have done, along with what someone thought you should do. What's more, guilt covers the dubious act you fantasized about carrying out but didn't—but you might as well have, because you're credited with the sin anyway. Then there is guilt assigned to actions committed against you, because it was your fault and you know it.

Back then, Guilt posing as God had this great scam going, masquerading as my conscience. It lorded all manner of stuff over my head, terrifying me with its power. God? Guilt? At eighteen, I saw no difference. I only knew God was constantly yelling at me. And let me tell you, the Catholic God has a temper, even uses His own name in vain. Yes, even says *goddamnit.* I was convinced of it. How else was He to get His anger across? I believed that if I got too comfortable, God would don his velvet robes and cashmere slippers and swoop down and slap that self-satisfied smile off my face. God didn't want happy. He wanted blood.

So, when Phil talked about selling his surfboard to finance a diamond engagement ring, I heard God's sniggering, mocking reprimands, warning me it was time for me to stop imagining myself kind and loving—time to expose my real self: a monstrosity. *You'd better tell him. You'd better tell him,* the voice sneered. God's a lot to stand up to. Let's face it, He has a reputation for casting folks into the fire. But since I had already been to hell and I knew firsthand what lived there, I was determined not to fall for His tactics quite so easily.

Though for the first time since deliverance from my ordeal, I began to waver and wobble, allowing myself to be swallowed up in doubt. Truthfully, I didn't deserve this joy and probably hadn't worked off my penance after all. Maybe all along I was really supposed to destroy myself to pay for my mortal sins. Confused, I asked my mother, my stand-in for Jesus, for advice. "Should I tell him, Mom? I think I have to." It was the second of the two questions I ever asked her about the fallout from my situation. Cold fear constricted her eyes; I could almost see it ride up and down her spine. "No," my mother warned. "He'll never marry you. No man will."

Not that I believed her conviction. Phil had this maturity about him, sort of like he was an old soul on another go-round, if you buy that sort of thing. Maybe that's why I mistook him for a codger tooling about in his blue Dodge that day. But still, the thought of confessing my story to him struck me with such cold terror that I froze solid in its shadow.

Coming clean about my story, about what I had done, would once again strip me right down to my dirty skin smeared with the worst sins a girl could commit. I could not bear to have anyone see me so naked, so shamed, while I was being forced to display a bright-red sign calling myself a slut, a whore. And worse. Having Phil know, having to confess to him — to anyone — would shove me back to *him* and all that degradation. Because through words, it would all become real once again.

But that wasn't the worst part. All during those acts of abuse, I survived by crawling far away, deep into my solitary darkness, shunting myself from reality, removed from my skin. And had I been able to keep those horrors hidden from peering eyes, tucked neatly away, I could have managed them privately, maybe indefinitely. Survived as I had learned to by becoming numb, all inside me deadened. But then my body betrayed me in the most hideous way possible and fostered a seed. Beyond the squalor of the mattresses, beyond the strangling humiliation, the pregnancy was by far the worst part — a permanent, public disgrace forever stigmatizing me as a gutter whore. Pregnancy. That was my blackest secret. Despicable and excruciating. Unspeakable. My hatred for that visibly displayed deformity was so fierce, so palpable, that I would choose self-butchery over having it revealed.

If I was coerced into admitting the truth of all I had done — all he had done and how *he* had mutated and embedded himself inside me only to slither out from that most shameful part of my body as indelible proof of my disgrace — the me I had finally found again would blow apart and I would, just as I had on those mattresses, cease to exist. And there would be no coming back, not a second time. Confession would be summoning *him*, and once beckoned, *he* and all that happened in *his* vile world would stay permanently, and I would never be free. I needed to be safe — from *him*, from the nightmare. I was all I had to protect myself; it was always that way.

Phil did love me; I knew that. But his love would not be enough. My self-loathing was a spreading disease, and given half a chance, it would devour me whole as once it had already done. I would not be able to convince myself that Phil could know about this ugliness and not be repulsed.

And not turn away. Everyone else had. It would be there in Phil's eyes, imprinted on his memory forever. "Is this your first child?" someone will eventually ask us when they see us holding hands, me in maternity clothes, and I will glance at Phil and see a fleeting shadow in his look. And there it will be, my past alive and well, contaminating our present. It would be *his* maggot hands not just all over me, but all over Phil, and our child, our marriage.

And just as on Sister Social Worker's official forms where she printed *his* name below mine and where it will stay forever, he would be a part of our everyday lives as surely as if *he* had planted his reeking-of-shit ass on our sofa. No, I could not manage that horror and its life-threatening consequences if it were loosened from its pit. Already I could feel myself breaking under the weight of just the thought. My past was a monster. If it were given life again, I would never escape its clutches.

OK, enough of that. Decision made. Guilt be damned. My past had to stay contained, stay buried right where I had put it. I refused to willingly face the torment of its disclosure. I'd temporarily weakened after I'd read all the sappy letters to Dear Abby and her insipid warnings to fallen girls to reveal all sins to their fiancés. But advice columnists, like everyone I knew, understood nothing of true darkness, the kind that will not recede in the light. No, I could not and would not suffer the broadcast of my slide into hell. Not for anyone. Not even for Phil. If I wanted to destroy myself, there were easier, quicker methods. I was in love, deeply in love. I was not going to share the gloriousness of that blessing with the filth from my past. My past was gone, I tell you; it was gone. And I meant it.

The black crepe shadowing the weeks to our wedding had nothing to do with my past. Or Jackie's shenanigans that had me belting him over the head with a bicycle pump. Not even the religious debates that Phil and my mother regularly engaged in that got her so stinkin' mad she'd want to throw pots at his head. Nothing even of John J. Allen's manufacture. Or our honeymoon plans going askew because of a mix-up in reservations. Or my aunt's lesbian lover's threats to doom our wedding by outing my shame. Ordinary life as I came to expect it had nothing to do with the cloud hovering over the countdown to our wedding day. It was a simple, evil slant of the moon that fractured the veneer of the make-believe happy Allen family.

My mouth is open, contorted as I struggle to scream. But no sound comes out. Nothing. I thrash side to side, throwing my body this way and that, but I am not moving. I am steeped in quicksand. My legs, my arms, weighted with thick sleep. Unmovable. Leaden. I feel the heaviness of hands all over my chest, rushing, kneading. But I can't react. It is as if I am in a drugged stupor, trapped in a slow-motion world. There are no images, only swampy darkness and the compression on my chest. I've been here before. Paralyzed inside this bodily turmoil that I cannot identify.

Suddenly, I realize I am having the nightmare, the same nightmare I've had three nights in a row. But these nightmares are different from any nightmares I've ever had. These feel real. There are no disjointed images spooling off into frightening nonsense. Only body disturbance. The sense of being assaulted. Panic ignites a force inside me and pushes me up, up toward the surface, propelling me through my sleep coma, up through the bog. I push and dig my way through the mire like I'm buried alive, panicked. Starved for air, I suck in a ragged breath as my eyes fly wide open. Oh my God. There are hands on me. Actual hands. This is not a dream. A shadowed figure is bending over me, his hands roaming, kneading my breasts.

I can't breathe. I can't breathe. But I do. I gulp a huge breath and force out a shriek that scares even me. The dark figure bolts from my room, slamming the door behind him. My heart is a jackhammer inside my chest, pounding, pounding against my ribs, its racket deafening as I jump from my bed and race downstairs to my parents' room. "One of the boys was in my room," I scream. John J. Allen bolts out of bed, confused, and rushes up the stairs, me following. He pushes open the door to the boys' bedroom, right across the hall from my own. But they are all asleep. Soundly. One is faking. Maybe they all are. Maybe they've taken turns at my bedside with their adolescent bear paws.

When John J. Allen calls out to them, not one moves. Sleeping like babies. John J. Allen tries to rouse them, and maybe they look at him in a daze, but no one seems coherent. Nothing will be done. No questions asked. John J. Allen gently closes the door to the boys' room, and I go quietly back to bed. I listen to my heartbeat fade to a near stop and feel my fear and anger melting away in the stillness.

I am not afraid of any of my brothers. Not even Jackie, who is half the time addled by drugs and anger. I could kill any one of them in a fury. I can kill, because the wellspring of my rage is far greater than their size and bulk and their willingness to batter me with their fists. Yes, even in a family with fluid boundaries, there lingers one or two fixed, if unspoken, principles. My brothers can sexually molest me, but they won't hit me. And I could with immunity beat any one of them until they sputter their last breath. But I dare not speak EVER of a family member's hands on my breasts.

It does not seem the least bit odd to muse about a killing. My mother as she snoozes peacefully next to my father in their double bed is not that many years away from attempting to kill her abusive second husband. All that saves her from a murder charge and spending her golden years in a barred cell is what Phil will eventually term "your mother's dumb luck." Rather than confront the bastard, who deserved a killing anyway, or call the cops, my mother will mix a cocktail of hooch and sleeping pills and feed it to him, even as he questions the residue clinging to the sides of the tumbler. Only her lack of chemical understanding and the fact that the drunkard is so permanently marinated in liquor that nothing short of several blows to the noggin with a really big ax would take him out spares both of them.

His eventual legitimate death from a brain tumor should grant her a peaceful existence, but another refugee from normal life will elbow his way into her bed. We will come to find out that this subhuman is no stranger to law enforcement and that several of the dustups involved minor girls and sex. Not that these vices will matter to my mother; it will be Mr. Todd's recklessness in toying with her concealed rage that will lead her to some very calculated, thoughtful plans to smother him as he sleeps rather than risk embarrassment for both of them by banishing him from her house.

"Mom," I will say to her when she reveals her scheme, "you can't go around trying to murder people just because you don't like them." I will have sprouted hairy zits on my face; I will know this by the way she'll stare at me. "Who would ever suspect a little old lady?" she will say. "Besides, I can't hurt his feelings and ask him to leave."

Looking at her in that moment, I will know that I have lived forever in the Allen wonderland of absurdity. My only response will be bulging eyes and a shrug. In our family, the idea of killing is easier than making a scene with an untidy confrontation.

Mr. Todd will take his chances and continue exploiting my mother's wrath because he's dense and a fool and thinks it is funny to keep provoking her. He will laugh as he goads her into slapping an old lady in the grocery store, and he will not suspect that it is more than just amusing misbehavior hidden by meticulously coiffed hair and the lovely pinks and violets of her clothing. Maybe it will be the rosary beads she prays and the Holy Communion she receives at every Mass that will deceive him into believing she is harmless. Or the home cooking and loans of money.

I know my mother, and there are no guarantees of what she will or won't do after her wrath does that quiet explosion thing. But once my mother starts contemplating jamming a pillow into your sleeping face, it's time to leave. Only you'll have to make that call before you end up stiff, your face mottled purple, because she'll never let on what she's plotting.

That's the stock I'm spawned from — frightened enraged women who will go to radical lengths not to create a scene, will quietly endure depraved abuse and hide their rage lest it mess up the freshly vacuumed carpet. Then like a buried land mine, it detonates someday, somehow. That's half of my genetic material. The other half could be rapist blood, for all I know.

I am furious now that my rage is skulking away like a licked animal. But it's a fury I cannot feel, only appeal to as I watch it glance back briefly in that dreary, colorless manner it has as it slinks into the dark.

I want my rage to stay. I need its power, its potent energy. I need to wring somebody's neck for what they have done to me in the dark. I must scream into my brothers' faces. Force a confrontation. I must do these things. Get retribution. Get even. Get something for the use of my breasts, goddamnit. "You're my only defense," I want to cry, exasperated as if I'm being deserted by a loved one. That rage, my one security, is melting away like an ice cube on a sizzling sidewalk, leaving me abandoned with this impotent steel fist lodged inside my chest and a voice silenced beneath its weight. It is only triggered rage that can drive my violence. When my wrath fades back into its pit, I become once again a coward, on my way to becoming a nonchalant victim — one of those bullied souls who lie by smiling and laughing off cruelties.

I am not a good sport when it comes to being abused and brutalized. I am hardly a good sport about anything. I just pretend, as John J. Allen has trained me. In truth, I am defeated by fear and self-loathing; it's just packaged with a hollow smile. Laughing after you fall down a cliff is one thing; dignity during rape, making a joke about being molested — well, that's not natural. There is no such thing as a blasé victim, all warm and fuzzy about accepting God's will. Instant forgiveness is a big lie too. And maybe the weirdest is no reaction at all. That is where I am right now, frozen into calmness as if I am channeling Immaculate Mary. But eventually, someone or something will pay. That's the odd thing about rage: you never know where it will crash-land.

I think about Jackie. He is the face of impounded rage unleashed on the entire world outside our door. By proxy, he is paying back John J. Allen big time. Rape. Child abduction and things I cannot even bear to face. There is no terror more exquisite than hearing the screams of your four-year-old and turning to see her grabbed off her tricycle and hustled off by a street monster named John J. Allen, Jr. You will never know such intense relief or be so faint with gratefulness as when she is snatched back into safety before he gets very far. That's what Jackie creates now: pain. And lots of it.

I am annoying the hell out of myself with these distractions. But that is what cowards do. And we are a family of cowards. Cowards and liars, pretending to be brave and virtuous. We believe in truth, justice, and the American way — the appearance of it, anyhow. But in reality, each one of us, including my parents, is broken, some of us beyond repair. And so, we disengage. Bypass what is real. We inoculate ourselves from pain, even against our own.

Without anger, I have no emotion; I am frozen solid, completely stunned, dumbfounded and numb with grief that will not rise, so I force myself to think. To touch the underbelly of what has happened in this room. To think of myself sleeping in my bed, dreaming of my upcoming wedding, when one of my brothers slithers to my bedside where I am completely and chillingly vulnerable and unprotected. Slowly, I unfurl into wide-eyed shock as thoughts and images worse than nightmares knock around in my head. I repeat the phrase over and over again: *sexually assaulted while I slept, by one of my own brothers*. Three times, at least. I can't get over it. Time enough between assaults to have shared several meals with him and his phony good manners. I passed him the milk, maybe the salt, the platter of roast beef so he could have seconds. I sat with him watching television. Shared some laughs, surely.

Then off to bed, my room across from his, from theirs. And he waited. And waited, diddling with his hard-on, thinking about what he was going to do to me. Then, following the throb of his craving, he rose from his bed; sneaked out the door as if he were going to go to the bathroom but instead crept across the short hallway, careful to avoid the creaking floorboards; and slipped, unnoticed, into my bedroom.

Protected by night shadows, my brother stood over me and pulled back the blanket, gently so I wouldn't wake. How long did he stare at me? Did he pull up my nightgown to glimpse me naked, outlined in the moonlight? Was his first touch of my bare breasts tentative, or did he grab them hard right away, praying to God that I wouldn't wake as he tried not to pant while he rubbed his foul hands all over me and maybe even jerked off in the process, letting his come spurt into his pajama bottoms, sticking the flannel to the hair on his legs, all within a few feet of my Chantilly-lace wedding gown hanging on my closet door. Several times he assaulted me. While I slept tormented by bizarre nightmares that were really alarms sounding deep within my body.

This brother's face will smile innocently from our wedding pictures that will be snapped in less than a month's time. Forevermore. This brother will kiss our future children on the forehead. Maybe even become a godfather to our firstborn, or secondborn. If we have four children, there will be enough honors to go all the way around. This man-boy who has plastered his hands onto my breasts. In the dark. Long after midnight. He will smile always as if he is harmless. He will make believe. And it's all a sham. He will be tomorrow morning as he was yesterday morning. Smiling. Benign. Drinking a glass of milk. Swiping a few cookies from the cupboard as he heads out the door and into his day, his sexual aggression satiated.

And he will, for his entire life, carry with him this cancerous secret of what he did. Always. Though he may bury and deny his deeds, the memory lives in his hands. The mind may forbid recollection, but the body never forgets. And I, too, am once again penalized right along with him. The consequence for the victim is always life without parole, and already I'm serving several sentences. That's just the way it is. I will never, ever know who has done this. Jackie is the obvious culprit. But I am not convinced. There are good reasons that it could be any one of the four.

There is a grief so profound that it is known only by its silence. It defies weeping and hand wringing. It does not rage. It hunkers down and lives inside its private world that just happens to be your soul. I stare toward my wedding dress that looks like ethereal mist suspended in the falling moonlight, not believing this has happened. I am about to be married, for God's sake. I simply and utterly cannot believe it. That one of my brothers has sexually assaulted me. Several times. Breached the sanctity of my room, of my body, of my role as sister, one step down only from his mother, and did the unthinkable while I slept, vulnerable and unprotected. Were it not for my own eyes and the shock that ended in a bloodcurdling scream now imprinted into memory, I would call my own self a slanderer of the worst kind. One who kills another with ugly, traitorous thoughts and despicable lies.

I may have little psychological understanding as I lie in my bed, but I understand practicality. What has happened to me in this room over the past three nights is not to be spoken about. To make a fuss would be viciously disloyal. John J. Allen could beat little boys until their screams hurl outside into the summer night, but this cannot ever be acknowledged. My father could squash and crush my budding breasts with his large hands under the guise of tickling, but I dare not mention it. Ever. Alluding to such an occurrence is an act of treason. Speak of it and I will be branded a traitor — a betrayer of the family and its dignity, accused of defaming its good name. Worse, dubbed an evil liar. Banished. Forever. *Can you believe what she accused her father of?* (Insert brother, uncle, boyfriend, neighbor, boss.) *What a lying bitch. She deserves to go straight to hell. Oh, that poor man. After all he's done for her. Even if he did do it, so what? She should've kept her mouth shut.*

Servitude to the mirage. Not just in our family; I know this. As I've seen it, family loyalty trumps violence every time. I may have witnessed my friend Margaret get thrown against a wall by her drunken sailor father, but she never confirms it, nor do I embarrass her with questions. The incident remained as if it went unseen. What happens in the family stays within the family. Always. I resent this allegiance that gives brothers and fathers and twisted sisters an enormous playground. But really, who cares? Even if the dirty boys did set up that impressive little domestic system themselves, so what?

Everybody despises victims anyway. I do. I'm at the top of my own list. It's my weakness, the flabby tail tucked between my legs. My eyes always begging, pleading, *please, don't hurt me,* when I ought to be raising my fists and landing powerful head blows. And the screams, Jesus, victims' screams, outdone only by tears, pumped upwards from their bottomless font of pain. How many times in life do normal people scream? Not an *eek there's a mouse* scream, but lung-ripping, born-from-the-pit-of-despair screams? In my nineteen years, how many times? How many?

Count them, damnit! a voice commands, then counters, *Can't, can you? I didn't think so. All those dramatic, pitiful screams. And oh so useless. Poor, pathetic you. You want somebody, anybody, to hear, don't you?* Then the voice continues: *Ahhhh, you want everybody to stop being pissed at you because of somebody else's obscene behavior. Is that it? Well, let me spell this out. No one is going to give up a comfy arrangement simply because of a little funny business. For your information, sister, the messenger is killed all the time. And nobody, nobody listens to screams or tears. It's words, tootsie; they're what count. And most of the time, nobody, listens to them anyway. Not that you would actually speak. You won't.*

I hunker further down into the blankets, damning the voice, vowing that this time it'll be different. This time I'll speak, and I'll keep right on speaking until my voice wears out. Until somebody listens, sit-down-and-look-me-in-the-eye listens. I'm telling. This time, I'm telling. A sigh rattles from of my mouth and heats my cocoon a bit. I'm a fool. And a puny one, at that. The voice is right. I've seen it written in faces a hundred times over, and I've obeyed every time: *Just get ahold of yourself,* the looks convey. *It's not as you say. Don't tell me. Don't tell me. Don't tell me.*

I cannot sleep. The icy, eerie calmness is slackening—not giving way to rage, as I want, but to a stomach-plunging freefall, a nosedive into hopelessness. And although I do not ever review the past, I am a prisoner of the phantoms rampaging there, haunting me as they flaunt their victories. I don't understand what I have done. Or why I am a laboratory experiment for up-and-coming predators, that long list that continues to grow and now, besides all the other demons, includes a mystery brother. The angry voice that chides me is right. This grief that snarls and twists within understands its place; it will remain mute, out of sight of memory, contained, flash-frozen like the other anguish. What happened in the dark in my bedroom over the last three nights will remain unchallenged. By me. By my parents. It is unimportant.

My mother and father will not mention it; they will make believe I did not come bursting into their room screaming; they will easily ignore that one of their sons committed unconscionable acts while everyone, including me, slept. The sun will rise. The family will go about its business as usual. My father will smile and kiss my mother good-bye. I will walk to the corner where John J. Allen's colleague will pick me up and drive me to the Department of Education, where I take dictation I cannot read back and erase large holes into expensive bond paper, and as he shifts gears and steps on the brakes, this man with a red crew cut and weak chin will tell me the details of the sex he had with his wife the night before. I will stare straight ahead at the bumper-to-bumper traffic and smile on cue so as not to make the degenerate feel bad. I am a coward. And I hate all men except Phil.

Listening to the ticking and tapping of the water heater working the perimeter of my room and the squeaks as the floors settle down in this house so hushed now with petrified silence, I push my fist into my mouth to stop myself from screaming loud, pitiful, useless screams. I am deluged with so much unspent frustration that I could hammer my head against the wall until it bursts like a rotted watermelon. But that wouldn't be enough. If I had courage, I would grab the heaviest carving knife I could find and jam it into my wrist and yank and tug, twisting and stabbing through bone and arteries and slippery blood until the blade comes out the other side. It would feel so good. The bliss of spending this reservoir of unfocused fury would send me into such euphoria that even Jackie with all the shit he pumps into his arms would never be able to match.

How many times before have I felt like this? Times I've wanted to hurt, and hurt and hurt — someone, anyone. It does not matter who. Me. The mailman. John J. Allen. All that matters is that I expel my pain. A volcano wants to blow. Steam must vent. I feel like a pressure cooker about to spew the beef stew all over the damn walls. But I know there is nothing I can do. Nothing I will do — not speak or even cry. Because there are no tears; they're stalled somewhere out of sight.

Coiled under cotton sheeting and a wool blanket, still wearing the nightgown that now bears strange fingerprints, I know, as I have always known with a clarity more earned than mystical, that there is no retribution for the assailants in my world. I am simply community property, fair game. Somewhere exists a predator's handbook listing the names of all girls — the fearful, shy ones, the girls too embarrassed to complain — inscribed boldly in red. Yet another list where my last name, beginning with A, is printed at the top. This must be true; I have no other explanation for all the male hands that have assaulted me. Abuse, sexual or otherwise, is a fact I have accepted just like the weather. There is nothing to be done about it; there never has been.

And though tomorrow I will tell Phil of the incidents in my bedroom, I will convey them from a place of remoteness, disengaged from the shock, the agony of their truth. I will shrug my shoulders and roll my eyes as if I am merely annoyed at the nonsense; I will make the facts seem unimportant. Once again make the violation of my body no more than a minor bother. Even mentioning these things to Phil seems an act of disloyalty far worse than what was done to me, because in reality I am embarrassed for the brother who sneaked into my room and sexually attacked me. Should he be confronted or even questioned, I would not be able to witness his shame.

Already after my fantasy of self-destruction, I am sliding down back into artificial composure, and by tomorrow I will be entirely paralyzed by fear, both physically and emotionally. An obstruction so mammoth, I will choose, as usual, to abandon myself in favor of the predator. This, I think, is why the voice is so angry. I abandon myself over and over again. In the heat of rage and panic, I can kick and claw and draw blood. In its aftermath, in the settled quiet, I am motionless. Struck silent, wanting only to slink away unseen. I am, once again, a prized victim. Complying with the aggressor.

Let's face it, by morning my trailer-park drama will be the last thing on my parents' minds as they hustle about to get six people up and out the door. If I hold my breath, ignore the nausea rumbling not so far down, and dare make a stink about what my brother did to me just hours before — well, I would ruin everybody's day. Mine included. Not to mention the damper that tattling would put on our wedding, which is bearing down very quickly. But these are smokescreens, I must confess, quaint diversions that allow me to evade what is true: that I simply don't have the guts for a confrontation. I'm a weakling, a teenage milquetoast. I don't have the nerve to stand up for myself. To ruin the dinner my mother has cooked. Or make worse the day my father has endured at work. Or embarrass anyone, including the molester, by making waves.

In the background, I hear the angry voice rumbling. *Oh, no, we wouldn't want to embarrass a molester, or a rapist, would we?*

But the voice does not understand. The courage to speak does not exist inside me. I know. I've looked. I don't have the nerve to let my tear bag show so that John J. Allen can take his potshots. Or shame myself by saying awkward words out loud. Or refer to sinful body parts. Yes, our bodies are corrupt: the likes of Sister Thomas Marie declared this, warning us as students to disrobe only in the dark so as to never catch sight of our nakedness. It is the sixties and we are years away from uttering the word *bra* publicly, never mind *breast* and *vagina* — even to possess such parts is considered shameful, at least in my house. Lucy and Desi do not sleep in the same bed, so how she got pregnant remains an unspoken mystery.

We are, all of us, to be eunuchs, to live cardboard lives. How then could I possibly divulge that one of the boys touched me? Because then my father would ask where. And what would I say? The word *breasts* to my father? I can't. I can't. What happened to me is so embarrassing. And so personal. I can do nothing but resign myself and stay in line. Honor all gag orders. Keeping secrets and smiling while doing so is easier than telling the truth. Truth destroys. Generation after generation has reinforced this. Hiding. Lying. Smiling. It's family tradition.

~ ~ ~

~ ~ ~

Tomorrow after work when Phil and I steal a few moments alone, I will tell him what happened. About swimming through the sludge. The shadowed figure. The heaviness of hands on my breasts. But I will tell it in such a way that I will set off no alarms. And neither of us — me at nineteen, Phil to celebrate his twenty-first birthday on our wedding day — will understand the ways of agony and secrets and how, when forced underground, they only play dead.

CHAPTER 13

Jackie and John J. Allen

Jackie was the only one home the night I stopped by my parents' house for a visit while Phil was working. Shortly before he disappeared into the wallows from where he would never return, Jackie and I had the last — more accurately, the only — real conversation we ever shared. My mother prized her "front room," as we called it back then — the low pile carpet scored by frequent vacuuming, upholstery hand-smoothed of wrinkles, tables mirror-shined. Basically a showroom that no one ever used. She wasn't home, so that's where we sat, me in a patchwork rocking chair, Jackie crossed-legged on the floor a few feet from me.

I would never admit it, ever, but he was good-looking in a James Dean kind of way — casual in how he held his shoulders and in the way his hair lazed toward his eyes. And I'd never noticed, but his head had grown to accept his ears. For that hour or so, we were brother and sister, suspended above the past, protected, at least for that brief time, from the future. It was a lone bubble of strange love, an easy intimacy of small talk that had no life beyond the delicate boundaries of that specific time and place with its tang of our mom's favorite fragrances, Pledge and Windex.

Had you peered in the picture window through the ruffled café curtains, you would have seen us laughing, getting a kick out of each other. How such sweetness wedged its way into two hearts so solidified with mutual hate, I will never understand. But it was genuine — a passing glimpse into how things could be if they weren't the way they were. We appeared normal. In an unspoken pact, we skirted the common ground of our individual plagues, which by now were so immeasurably vast that they completely defied coherent description anyway, and we reminisced about innocuous stuff — old loves, the safe ones; the interminable family car trips.

Poked fun at John J. Allen's toupee that looked more like a pile of bad knots than any hair we'd ever seen.

In the midst of that odd scene, before our sibling goodwill vanished and once again we took up our roles as adversaries, Jackie raised his head and looked at me, his eyes still crinkled by a fading smile, and revealed a scandal-sized secret as disturbing as the one I had discovered in my mother's closet so many years earlier. That secret I'd dared never speak of and never told a soul until Phil: that John J. Allen was not my father. As Jackie spoke, I froze mid-rock, my head pitched forward, my eyes surely popping, making me kin to a bulldog straining at the leash.

"Dad's got another family," he said casually, as if he were chatting about matching socks. "A wife and two kids. I've met all of them. He got divorced so he could marry mom."

I reared back in my chair and stared at him, stunned.

"What?" I stammered. "What?"

"It's true. A wife and two kids. I'm telling you the truth."

But in the Allen family the truth was never the truth. It was guarded, shaded, twisted to fit. The real truths — dire secrets too painful to acknowledge — were buried, left to kick furiously at the dirt covering their graves. More likely than not, what was voiced as fact across the kitchen table or during a swirl of ill-mannered banter was just a convoluted batch of lies and wishes. Believing could be a costly mistake, as risky as relying on the wind. Jackie was a practiced liar, charming and sweet-talking when he chose to be. That's the only compliment I ever heard him receive. You know the lines: he could sell snow to an Eskimo, shit to an outhouse.

So, could he possibly be telling the truth now? John J. Allen, divorced? An ex-wife and two kids? Jesus, Mary, and Joseph, did it ever end? How did he unearth all this, anyway? And why would he even know to look for a backstory to our family history? Was he taking me into his confidence or handing me a line of bull? Never had I heard even a whisper of a spare family sequestered somewhere on the back roads of New Jersey. Good God, I knew so little about this family.

Had it not been for a nagging mystery that Jackie's claim instantly solved, a peculiar reoccurrence that had troubled me ever since childhood,

I would not have given his bizarre story a second thought. My mother, a devout and devoted Catholic, never ever received Holy Communion.

Every Catholic of age is obligated under pain of sin and excommunication to receive this sacrament once or twice a year. It's a big deal, a very big deal. If you're Catholic, you understand this. If you're not, you're going to have to trust me. No practicing Catholic ever fools around with this duty. It could mean the difference between heaven and hell.

At every Mass I have ever attended with my mother, present time included, I held my breath, eying her, hoping, praying that she would rise and inch her way to the Communion rail like the rest of the faithful. At first, I was terrified that she would die with a black soul; then, as I got older, I tacked embarrassment onto my dread, because she seemed to be the only one in the church besides little kids who didn't receive, and who wants a sinning mother?

I prayed rosaries; beseeched St. Jude, the patron saint of the impossible; begged the souls in purgatory to inspire her to receive, at least on my wedding day. She didn't. One time before I understood the ways of secrets, I asked her why. "Because your father's not Catholic," she answered. Seemed logical at the time, until I found out it couldn't be true. You can take the Holy Eucharist if your spouse isn't Catholic. But not if your spouse is divorced. That makes you an unmarried woman in the eyes of the Church, living in sin with a man it does not recognize as your husband, toting five little bastards to Mass, committing for all the world to see, one of the unpardonables — adultery. Uh-oh.

I gulped, making one of those undignified noises reserved for corny slapstick, and stared at Jackie, who was simply gazing back at me, watching my confusion. Listen, God might yak on and on about truth, but He has His exceptions. And nosing around in your parents' private business is one of them. I'm sure of it, because at that very moment, as I was about to ask Jackie for all the gory details, God himself roared in my ear: *Tit for tat, tootsie.* And I knew instantly what He meant. I mess around in my parents' secrets and He would see to it that somebody messed around in mine.

In those years, the God I knew was ruthless and maddening, having something to say about every damn thing — John J. Allen but wearing a mink cape and packing a cattle prod. I thought about what I would lose if my secrets were bared, about how my life would die in so many ways. I was married. We were planning to have children. We wanted to buy a house. All of it would be crushed if my own past was exposed. Truth seeking in my family was a crime, a damnable one. I didn't need to see blood to know that I was cut. So I changed the subject, allowing that mystery, that opportunity for understanding, to suffocate beneath my fear.

I like to think I hugged Jackie good-bye that evening, but I don't remember. Over the years I'd offered him some kindnesses, but very few. I hope I left him with at least a good memory; we would never create any others worth saving. You know how his story ends. What he left me with, though, was something astonishing that would not manifest itself for many years. And when it did, it would arrive quietly, without fanfare, and its force would nearly knock me to my knees.

~ ~ ~

John J. Allen did not live a long life. In the few years before he died of congestive heart failure at forty-eight, there was a sweetness about him. Mellowed, perhaps, by the Florida sun and long walks on St. Pete's Beach, holding hands with my mother. Jackie was gone, immersed in his misery somewhere in the United States — no one knew or cared where. The other three boys were grown and self-supporting, two married off. My father cared deeply for Phil and loved and doted on our two little girls, and that counted for something.

I never gave the dark years so much as a backward glance, never pulled them up for a mulling-over. That past was not worth my time and attention. So it wasn't forgiveness that warmed me to John J. Allen. I simply responded to the genuine love he offered. He had grown a heart. His flesh-and-blood heart was failing, but he had found an authentic one. Somehow, I think he finally became the man he always wanted to be. Though he died with the whys of his cruelties intact, his callous deeds disregarded, he passed away surrounded by the kind of love he had been unable to give for most of his life. I wonder if he understood this supreme blessing.

But where John J. Allen discovered his heart, my mother lost hers after his death, and I don't think she ever found it again. Stuck in a netherworld fantasy somewhere between Disneyland and the Waltons, I figured my mother would pack up her things, leave Florida, and come live with Phil and me and our girls. We could be best friends again, like those times in the kitchen dancing to rock and roll and counting Green Stamps. And how the five of us would laugh! I could actually hear the upcoming echoes trolling through the rooms in our home. We'd make dinner together and maybe someday open up a craft shop selling brilliantly colored ribbons and fancy baubles.

I adored the life I created in my head. I thought that's what my mother wanted too: a happy home and a close-knit family to go along with the Holy Communion she'd been receiving every Sunday and Holy Day of Obligation since John J. Allen's death. How little I understood about the pull of grief. I wanted her, but she needed something else, and she took to garish makeup and hanging out with shady characters who frequented questionable establishments. The absolute shock of her change from mom to barfly made me frantic. Imagine the Blessed Mother hiding booze in the folds of her blue frock, tossing back several fingers worth when no one was looking.

There is something brutally distasteful about seeing your own mother plastered. And though I didn't challenge her, my immaturity, fear, and crushing disappointment collided and spawned a hard-edged anger that spiked the tone of my voice whenever I heard that high-pitched squeal pushing out disjointed nonsense that had become her new manner of speaking. Back then in my twenties, when I knew everything, I believed that family love and my personal will could stop her self-destruction — turn her away from the hidden gin, from the men that pawed at her, from her own bottomless desolation. I failed every time.

So, I grieved the loss of both my parents. Within nine months my mother married a well-paid Merchant Marine captain, who also happened to be an abusive alcoholic. John J. Allen had left debt, and the small amount of insurance money was hardly enough for my mother to live on. It had been years since she'd worked outside the home, and Drunken Sea Captain's money offered a powerful security blanket, even if it did come with bulky, tangled strings. Financial comfort came with a high price, and along with my mother, we all paid handsomely as her life spiraled into crisis after crisis, which she dragged us into time and again.

~ ~ ~

Phil never believed that John J. Allen was not my father. He believed that I believed it. But that's the way it was with John J. Allen: nobody noticed the shady side of his sunny smile. Maybe all the years Phil spent as a cop made him skeptical about my little forage into my mother's closet and the discovery of the letters that I could not produce. And after all, as evidence of my delusion, we did have my birth certificate with John J. Allen's name listed as my father. Like that couldn't have been doctored. Honestly? I've always been completely apathetic about who fathered me. I much prefer the fantasy of a tidy conception without the assistance of all that slobbering and heavy breathing. It was only validation that mattered. That little nod of reassurance that I indeed saw what I know I saw.

I could ask her, you know. Burrow deep into my mother's sad secrets with my want; hammer her, oh so gently, with the sins of her past. Force her to step to the edge of her own dark pit and look down. I could go over to her apartment right now, ring the doorbell, and say, "Hi, Mom. Do you mind if we have a little chat?" Bomb dropping is best done delicately.

Knowing myself, I would have to glance away from my mom's eyes turned rheumy in these last few years, because danger is telegraphed and fear would widen her eyes just a bit, and I would be in jeopardy of losing my courage to compassion. I would be on a mission; I could not afford sentimentality.

Then over tea — hers hot, mine iced — I could say, "Who is my father? I know it's not Dad." Now, you know I am completely justified in this. It passes for acceptable nowadays, rattling the skeletons flinching inside another woman's vagina. I would not, though, divulge that I've known about John J. Allen since I was ten; I think that would be overkill, and even bloodsuckers have their limits. Just the same, I must insist that my mother comprehend that at any moment I could contract a deadly ailment from the paternal side of me, and my family practitioner, the one who bombards me with tests each time the moon turns blue and I drag myself to his office for a flu shot, needs this history of mine. So he can…so he can…do more of whatever it is he does.

If my mother showed the least bit of reluctance, I would be prepared. "For God's sake, Mom," I would say. "Your secret could mean my agonizing death from cancer, heart disease, middle-age-tub-of-lard syndrome." She's Catholic. Guilt always works. Though again, I would have to shift my gaze, ignoring the little wells of moisture building up in her eyes. Maybe I'd wiggle a little bit, too, because there would be dread in the intake and exhale of her breath alongside the steam from Earl Grey, and that would make me uncomfortable. But I could push and push, use the power of my entitlement from my very safe perch of her sins, until she revealed her truths, all of them. She would finally break. Then I would know. Through her tears I would earn my salvation. My medical one, at least. Plus, I would confirm my hazy facts.

Still, I would probably feel bad about my willingness and capacity to punish. That's the part I don't like but have known about since I swung a belt across the behinds of my younger brothers — how easy it is for me to step over the line and justify my cruelty. The real thing that would bother me, though, is what would I do with all the torn-off pieces of my mother after I'd coerced her into tattling on herself? I mean, I would try to console her, tell her how brave she was in finally telling the truth. That might work. Or try to pump her up by telling her that finally her honesty has liberated her. Assure her that in time she will come to thank me for granting her this benefaction of the soul.

Who am I kidding? The reality is not so admirable; it simmers in the dark, not wanting to be seen. In fact, I won't want to clean up the mess I've made of her; I'll just want to walk away, blissfully satisfied with my plunder. So, I would try to convince myself that my mother is better off for our little chat; she'll get over the shock and truly, truly, she'll be unchained from the burdens of her secrets. I will defend the hell out of my higher purpose — that my doctor will be happy. Plus, I'll confirm that those unbearable minutes spent in her closet reading letters were real. And my mother would now be free to fly. See? We both win. You know how the refrain goes: it's a win-win situation.

For once everyone would be on my side. Everybody would say to me: *She should've told you a long time ago. She had no right to keep such a secret. You have every right in the world to know who your biological father is. It's about time she stepped up to the plate and did what was right by you. You deserve it, after all.* Finally I'd get the sympathy votes. I would be the injured party. Me! Me! Me! The only thing is, I haven't quite worked out yet how I could leave that little apartment without feeling like a rat that has just finished feasting on living flesh.

Call me crazy, but there's an upside to not knowing whose sperm made the swim. I take wicked pleasure in having drama and mystery surround my birth; it is a gorgeously wrapped gift that stays perpetually exquisite, untarnished by reality. Nothing on the inside of the package could equal the beauty of its exterior. If I have a mind to, I can ponder and choose at will any heritage I wish. Italian. British. Or, I don't know — Polish, for the cheese–and–potato pierogies. Play with virgin-birth imagery, something like being plucked from the stem of a sunflower. All very mythical-like — pure, luscious fantasy. The truth is not nearly so pretty. It never is.

The men my mother chose to love had broad, well-developed mean streaks; chances are, the male who is the other half of me was no big prize. Somewhere there probably lives a toothless old derelict munching on the miseries of his life, surrounded by a litter of hunchback relatives, one of them an 800-pound Twinkie-eater needing money for gastric bypass. No, spare me legions of fake relatives waging a campaign for love and togetherness because of a few spurts of sperm juice. Nobody need ever show up at my door uninvited.

But it was never the toothless old man who may or may not be a rapist barging into my life that I had to worry about. Or even the demon from all those years ago. It was someone else. Someone looking to settle a score.

I hope you never have the misfortune of being hunted down and stalked by a stranger. Never experience that kind of fright, the piercing cold that slithers along your spine and clamps down on your insides and shakes. The hopelessness that makes you utter useless prayers. And the overpowering shock of the ambush — that single swing of the ax that shatters life as you know it. I hope you never come to know firsthand this law of nature: that you are just one malevolent person away from hell.

CHAPTER 14

Hunted Down

We're heading out for shopping, the three of us — Phil and I and my mother, who is visiting from Florida. Used to be the five of us when our girls were little, traipsing about days before Christmas, enjoying my mother's fleeting goodwill. But our daughters are grown and married now, and our once-exclusive holiday celebrations have shifted into subdivisions of time and additional extended-family members — meaning our daughters' in-laws are now factored into the equation.

I read lots of magazines and am envious of the standing-by-the-roaring-fire family get-together articles that seem to spell Christmas for those lucky enough to have a riverstone hearth and people who actually want to lounge next to it and drink hot toddies and eggnog while warbling about peace on earth. So, in rooms that echo a little too much this time of the year, I decide to fill them and throw a feast for my own extended family. My youngest brother and his wife are coming up from South Carolina, and the-next-to-the-youngest brother and his family from close by whom we never ever see are coming as well. So tonight, the Allen family, which is not really a family, is having a sort of holiday reunion. Baked ham, lasagna, the works. This morning the three of us are on our way to score a few last-minute gifts and frivolous extras for the banquet.

No wine, though. Nobody drinks. *Lips that touch wine will never touch mine,* my next-to-the-youngest brother is rumored to have vowed to his wife. Since I know so little about him, I don't know this to be true. We've shared no personal conversations over the years, given that any necessary family communication is conducted through his wife. But it makes for a cute story. So despite the once-a-year, freshly baked apple cream pie waiting at home along with tins of homemade cookies, we're off to buy a few fancy provisions for the spread. Not that any of these people are fancy, but it is Christmas, after all.

First stop is the post office. No mail delivery yet deep in the Jersey Pines. It's a fading ritual living out its last days. Phil hands me the mail and I am fiddling through a small pile of cards when I come across an envelope addressed to me. With its innocuous Burlington City return address, it hints at an invitation to a charity function. Not that I ever attend elaborate events. I do what most loners do: shun gatherings of strangers. And all gatherings are of strangers, whether the faces are familiar or not. *Recluse.* The term is flush with comfort. If you do not understand this — how a heart can beat stronger within the province of solitude — you, then, would welcome a coveted invitation to a ball. This is what I think is in the envelope.

We are talking, the three of us. It's always a good time with my mom before Christmas. The holiday serves as a great distraction that keeps us busy and focused. Energized with mission and anticipation, my mother is diverted from the anger that she normally feeds and nurtures like a favored companion. Little escapes her wrath, which eventually winds its way to me. But for now, the three of us are enthusiastic with plans for tonight. If apple pie is in the picture, all is right with the world.

We are talking about that pie sitting in the refrigerator at home and how we should just buy one from the bakery for tonight and eat ours for lunch when I casually tear open the envelope and drop my eyes to the typewritten letter. *Catholic Charities,* the letterhead reads. It is not an invitation to a ball. *An interested party is trying to contact Kathleen Barbara Allen Foley,* it shouts, and instantly I am windless, boot-kicked in the stomach by an attacker jumping from the bushes. This can't be real. This can't be. My throat squeezes tight and cuts off all air. *Oh my God.* My next breath is stalled somewhere in my lungs, pushing upward against the constriction of sinew, trying to burst out into a shrill wheezing cough that I will not be able to stop. It will be a croupy, panicked gasp for breath that will have Phil startled and reaching for me, leaving my mother confused. And will without delay lead directly to the degrading shame that is now sitting in my lap.

No! No! Don't you dare make a sound. The warning comes from everywhere.

Don't you dare. Not one peep. Stay quiet. Act normal, goddamnit! But I am in freefall. A dizzying, tumbling dive that will have me spewing breakfast all over myself if I don't stop. But I can't stop. I am in a wild corkscrew descent. There is nothing to grasp hold of. Nothing. I am plunging through endless space. Chatter swirls about my head. Phil laughs at something my mother has said. I glance quickly over at him. He is solid. Real. I could reach out and touch him and know this. But I am whirling and spiraling in a world that has suddenly come unglued.

Panic jams and wedges itself inside me like plates of cement; its heaviness pulls at me like steel fingers urging me to let go — how yawning depths might entice the drowning. Winter freeze crusts the walks and blacktopped streets, settles in cracks on the windshield, but I am perspiring. If Phil looks at me, he will see beads forming on my forehead. My sunglasses are steaming up, for God's sake. He will ask me, *What's the matter?* Tell me that I look pale. *OhmyGodOhmyGodOhmyGod.* Every nerve is firing, urging me to rock and sway back and forth in my seat like a woman in the throes of insanity.

This fear has form; it is sackcloth and ashes and pus-draining sores. It is as real as a figure standing before me, brandishing a stiff, diseased penis. I ignore it all and quickly stuff the letter into my purse with hands that are floppy and disconnected. I tug and pull up a smile — from where, I do not know — and offer a few words that to my ear sound almost normal.

For the entire day, I stand behind myself, watching and directing my actions, making sure I act naturally. But every few minutes I remember that letter rotting the insides of my handbag and I have to steady myself, because I keep hurling down a vertical drop that has no bottom. When finally we get home, I rush upstairs and bury the letter in my closet beneath a stash of papers, out of sight, where, unless I die before I can tend to it, no one will look. I want to tear it into tiny shreds and flush it down the toilet where it belongs. No, not my toilet. It could be traced! I might drop a few telltale pieces and Phil could find them and ask, *What's this?* Or it could form a clog and backwash, still decipherable, right back onto the bathroom floor.

What, am I nuts? I can't destroy it anyway. I *have* to respond. I read the goddamn thing, and I swear, embedded in the Catholic Charities' wording is an *or else* penalty. Any delay might instigate a severe consequence. And when Catholic authorities dole out punishment, it is always harsh. I'm not even Catholic anymore and they're still lording their God Power over me.

Oh Lord, how am I going to keep myself under control tonight when I feel like I'm strapped onto a nonstop roller coaster and could vomit at any second? And what about tomorrow? Or Christmas Day? Sweat is dripping from me. I'm trapped inside a growing nightmare, and there is no waking up. I try to think. *Just think!* Not responding immediately is chancing disaster. But what choice do I have? None. It's Christmas. People are coming. I have food to cook. A table to set. *Oh Jesus! Jesus! What the hell am I going to do?* I need time. I need everyone to go away, but this house won't be empty for days. My mother's here. Phil's off. It will be days, maybe a week, more. And...*oh my God*...the social worker and this mysterious person who has arisen from the dark like a pestilent contagion could find their way to our home. Could end up on our doorstep.

I have to get ahold of myself. I have to. I can do this. Deep breaths. Fresh lipstick. A comb through my hair. A few sweeps of blush. Done. OK. I can do this. I won't think about that letter contaminating all it touches, leaking out its disease into our bedroom so beautiful with plump comforters and downy pillows and scented with lavender candles and vanilla bean potpourri. This is our home, carved out of the forest. Love lives here. This is where our souls rest. I will tend to the letter in time. I will type back a response and advise this Catholic social worker that Kathleen Foley is not interested in any kind of contact with this stranger. And will not be, ever. That is my answer, simple and clean. And this crisis will end there. And I will never think of it again. Ever. Just like before.

I am trying to convince myself of this. That this is simply a tying-up of leftover loose ends. It will all end neatly. But it is a colossal lie. I can feel the heartbeat of doom right inside my chest. I know this is only the beginning. When I beg God for help, I know there is nothing He can do. Something horrible is bounding toward me. And will not be stopped. I know this as I try to convince myself otherwise, as I say to myself, *Everything is going to be fine.* But right now I need this lie. Or else I will be a puddle on the floor.

For reasons known only to her, and in a complete departure from tradition, my mother is not helping out with this dinner or interacting with anyone. She is lingering by herself near the wall in the kitchen as if she is stuck to the floor, a wallflower scared of the people surrounding her. Phil is slicing meat. I am running back and forth between the oven and the dining room, and in the family room seven people are amusing themselves, and I feel like I am failing as a hostess. I need her to do something. Either lend a hand with the food or help entertain our guests. It does not seem too much to ask.

My blood is on low simmer. "Mom," I say, "would you ask everyone what they want to drink?"

She looks at me as if I have demanded all the money stashed in her wallet. "They don't care what they drink. Give them whatever you want," she answers, rooted in place, refusing to budge. It is a simple request that just requires her to open her mouth and speak. "Mom, just ask them, please," I say. My impatience is a serrated knife sawing against my nerves; I have no energy to disguise it. She just shrugs and does not move. Does not make a sound. It is her family in the next room, for God's sake. All I want to know is what I should pour into the glasses. But she will not budge. So I do.

The fear and anger that has all day been collecting inside me like stagnant pools of toxin has corroded my endurance. I march over to her, grab her by the shoulders, spin her around, duck down behind her back, and make believe she is a puppet. "Everyone, everyone!" I call in a squeaky little-girl voice, pretending I am her. "What do you want to drink?" The family all laughs. My mother is stiff, rigid. *Can't she take a joke? Jesus.* I laugh too, because really it's funny. So damn funny. But at the dinner that is supposed to be a cheery holiday reconnection, the table groaning with all manner of tasty comforts, my mother does not speak and barely eats a thing. It is as if she wills herself invisible. I think she is acting like this to spite me.

Yet somewhere beyond the leak of poisons, a truth nudges me, vying for my attention. A truth that I do not want to hear, that insists on reminding me that I am stronger than my mother and I have abused that power. What I did to her held no humor, only hostility. The prize of my little stunt was her humiliation. But I refuse to listen. Instead, I hold onto my frustration.

She could have avoided all of this if only she had conducted herself properly, unselfishly. It is her fault that I lost control.

My youngest brother and his wife take my mother out for the day. At least that is the plan. After yesterday and last night, I am desperate for the respite. I can't get that letter out of my mind. Nor can I stop this falling-down-an-elevator-shaft sensation, and the feeling of melted wax surging inside my chest every time my heart beats. Beat. Fiery ooze. Beat. Fiery ooze. I flinch each time I feel that hot, waxy seepage rolling all the way to my throat, then receding, only to return seconds later. And the nonstop tumbling, tumbling. It is all making me sick to my stomach. I am trying not to be frantic, working to keep myself normal, but I'm a mess.

The three of them return early, expecting lunch. The refrigerator is stuffed with leftovers, but the effort to lug it all out and set it on the table seems an enormous task. Just the chore of walking across the floor is overwhelming, and tears feel as if they will break at any moment. Upstairs, the letter lurks like a guillotine: that thought swoops in with each intake of stale air. That letter is a real being with its own evil heart. I am more terrified of it than I have ever been of anything in my life. I wish the evil would just kill me and get it over with, rather than forcing me through this slow, agonizing death.

Over lunch that tastes of dry tinder, my mother and brother unleash anger that has, evidently, been seething since last night, when my nephew had the nerve to bring his Puerto Rican fiancée to the gathering. Stoking each other's flames until both of them resemble spoiled brats beating up on the town retard, they spew out insults like *dirty spic, trash*. The fiancée has black hair and olive skin and a sweetheart demeanor. Phil and I thought she was lovely, but when we mention this, my mother and brother become louder, angrier, if that is possible. I can't imagine where this viciousness is coming from, why it is perverting our kitchen, our home. Or what the hell I was thinking when I decided to have this loving family reunion.

Night finally gathers up the daylight. In only an hour or so, I can inconspicuously excuse myself and head up to our sanctuary, where I can inhale lavender and boil my skin off with a hot shower. I will not think about the horror lying in wait in my closet. I won't. Except for the fright tingling my nerves, I am calm, mellow, fiddling around at the antique oak desk in the kitchen, my mother next to me fussing about something or other, when I explode so suddenly it seems it is not me yelling, carrying on like a deranged psychotic. And I aim it all at my mother. Who provoked it. By being impossible. By not cooperating. By smothering me. By standing too close to me. By breathing. *I can't take it anymore! I can't take it anymore!* I shout over and over as loud as I can push my voice.

I am bellowing; it is a plea emanating from a place unnatural. This anger from nowhere, from everywhere, swallows up all available oxygen. It crashes into walls and bounces back. Never in all my adult life have I lashed out at my mother, no matter how angry I've become. And now I have scared her, really scared her. I see it in her eyes, the fear. The tears welling up. She is shrinking, folding up into herself right before me. It is the worst thing I have ever done to her. I am a heartless bitch. But my anger won't relent. I storm away and up to our room, leaving her stranded, alone without support.

Phil follows me. He knows I do not express myself ever in a torrent of screams and stomps — excluding, of course, a donut incident years ago. "What just happened?" he asks.

Fury has stolen my breath. I heave and heave, trying to snatch it back. "She's always pushing me. Always. She never stops. Never." He looks at me, confused. "That's just your mother," he says.

I hate that he is so goddamn calm. Can't he see what she puts me through? How impossible she is? "What's going on?" he pleads and tries to touch my arm. I wrench away. "It's her! It's her!" I cry. He doesn't argue, just looks at me for a few seconds, unsure — maybe of what I will do next, maybe of what he should do — and says, "I'm going back downstairs." I nod, pissed because…because… I don't know why I'm so pissed. I just am.

Smile, smile. Kiss, kiss. Although I am besieged by guilt and remorse for the behavior that spikes into me like barbed wire, I do not apologize to my mother. Apologizing is, as it always is for me inside the Allen sphere, treacherous. An apology can quickly morph into a portal to personal danger. Suddenly you can become a big fat target accused of all manner of selfish, inconsiderate, malicious misbehaviors that fault you for the misery in someone's life. Remember Jackie? And how he alone ruined everything in the Allen family? Nothing much has changed in that department: my mother is always on the lookout to blame someone else for her problems.

So, I do what the Allens always do: make believe nothing happened. Except for my youngest brother, who reprimanded me shortly after my melee by saying, *She's your mother.* Twice he said it without knowing what the hell he was talking about. I decide I will never forgive him for that snide remark. It feels good to have a focus for my rage. It gives it reason to be. Also, I decide, this is my last family reunion. Done.

Smile, smile. Kiss, kiss. And everyone is gone. And I know what I have to do. Only how? I pull the letter out of hiding. It is weighted with filth, and the shame of what is inside blisters my hands. *Don't make me touch it! Don't make me look!* Panic swells inside me, grows fat nursing on my ballooning fear, and I do not know what is restraining me from running around the house panting and screaming. But I force myself to stay composed. I can't answer in longhand. I can't. I can't. That's hacking off pieces of myself and handing them over to the rapist. And I can't use the computer. Even if I delete it, it might be retrieved. An official could march into our home, snatch the hard drive, somehow find my confession, and say, *Aha!* And wouldn't it be possible for Phil to accidentally come across a deleted file? I've heard those warnings on television. *Don't leave a trail,* they say. *It can be traced right back to you.*

My heart is ducking and punching, enmeshed in a boxing match; the brawl is loud, violent. *Goddamnit,* I yell at myself. *Stop it! Stop it! Get ahold of yourself.* The typewriter I drag out of the basement is layered in gummy dust, its best days gone, but it's the only thing I can think of to use. But now I remember. Haven't letters sent by mysterious stalkers to their victims been traced back to a bum typewriter and its one stuck key? What I type on this derelict contraption can be tracked back to me. *Oh God!* I don't know what to do. Reasoning has taken flight, and all I know is that I must keep my secret, I must stay hidden.

That my shame has already been disclosed, that I've already been found, is something I simply cannot face. To accept that my buried secret has been unearthed, brought back to life, its decaying bones glued together with my putrid flesh, means all I have been since that time so long ago is meaningless: I will have to admit that I am no more than a dirty street whore and that I am as good as gone from the life Phil and I have created. At this moment, nothing exists except high alert and the dread that chases the blood through my veins so fast that I can feel its race making me frantic to escape detection.

There is no other choice but this typewriter. So I dash out a brief letter that seems more like a news release. *Kathleen Foley requests NO CONTACT. There are no medical anomalies to report.* I am emphatic. It is final. The answer is NO. I type my name. I yank out the ribbon, which I fear someone, somehow, will read, and it will be discovered that I have authored this letter. I get in the car and drive twenty-five miles, and I slide the envelope into a mailbox that will not bear our local postmark. This resurrected filth cannot touch our home, our family. And I have to get it far, far away from me. When I drop it in the postbox, I pray that this is the end. I know it is not.

Part of my daily routine now is to rush to the post office before Phil can get there. Each time I enter the door, my knees turn to water and nausea courses through me as if I am fighting a bout of food poisoning. It happens this way every time. Every day of the week, even on Saturdays, when I cannot find an excuse to go myself, I wait at home or sit in the car, watching, waiting for Phil, fighting back my stomach that wants to hurl through my mouth. It will be this way for ten months, six days a week. Every single time.

The reply is swift. A counter-punch that lands point blank on my jaw. No discreet return address this time. Catholic Charities ridicules me boldly from the left-hand corner of the envelope. When I pull it from the post office box, I think I will collapse to the floor. All I can manage is a shaken prayer of thanks that I intercepted it. Small favors are enormous now. I take none of them for granted. The letter is from the same social worker. And she is angry. My response meant nothing, she says, because I did not sign my name. I am to write her again and this time sign by my own hand. And the very least I owe this person wanting to contact me is my medical history. She lets me know that she is available to me if I need her counsel.

Am I supposed to thank her? Send her a small bouquet, perhaps daisies, for her kind willingness to support me with a cozy little chat? Would she listen calmly when I shriek that I want to plant a gun on her temple and pull the trigger? I think madness is going to blow me into pieces. The person inciting this fury, this stranger spawned on a filthy mattress, is goddamn lucky to be drawing breath. I want to scream this at the postmistress who greets me with a smile and a wave. I want to run up to her, throw myself on her mercy, and spill all that is happening to me. *SHE is living and breathing because I did not have the goddamn courage to self-abort. Because I was too much of a goddamn coward to kill myself.* I want to fill this little town center with my rage.

I speed home, pull out the old typewriter, and with hands that now feel juiceless and rusted, type out a letter and again yank out the ribbon that bears witness to my shame. This time I sign my damn name, in writing, in blue ink, worrying what if only black ink is acceptable to the Catholic Charities bitch who has assumed authority over my past and now my future. I have no name for the fear that is expanding inside my body as I speed the twenty-five miles to mail my NO. This is the end of it. This is the end of it. It is a prayer I repeat a hundred times a day. A prayer that I do not for one minute believe.

Weeks, maybe a month passes. Always I am on the lookout for a Catholic Charities envelope. With time lapsing and no other angry missive from the social worker, I am still uneasy, just not as stiffly guarded. So no alarms trigger when I open an envelope without scrutiny. In fact, nothing happens, because I and all around me fall into soundless space — no heartbeat, no wind stirring the pine trees, no chattering voices of townies strolling in and out of the post office. Just staggering disbelief and a slow sense of dread swelling and breaking into a spill that will soon drag me beneath its undertow.

I stare into a handwritten epistle glutted with pleadings and professions of love. From a stranger. From, it feels like, the rapist himself. *The rapist.* I can smell the waft of his stink, hidden for so long, like an ancient disease reawakened. Cower at the ghost of his leering smirk, reaching across the years to mock me. This new stranger comes armed with distant, familiar assertions, unshakable beliefs. In her words, I hear again *his* threats that promise me I will never get away.

She *knows* I did not mean it when I said *no contact*. She just refuses to believe it, she says. When I get to know her, I will see how much I love her, how much she loves me — she is, after all, a very nice person. She has children, she writes — the loves of her life — so she *knows* how much I once loved her, how much I still must love her. I *have* to meet them, her children, she insists — they are beautiful: I will not be able to resist them. And as if she is offering me salvation from misery, she announces I can come to live with her anytime I want; she will never turn me away. Not ever. No matter what.

She confesses that to prove her love for me, she tracked down my wedding portrait from 1967 published in a newspaper, though the photo was too fuzzy to make out my features. And in her ramblings, she insists I recently visited the drive-thru of a fast-food chain near her house. It was me, she claims; the cashier assured her with a comment about how similar her laugh was to that of a previous customer, the woman who only seconds ago had driven away. In a fanatical race from a place I would never frequent, this stranger chased me through streets I have never been on, hunting down my car, pursuing me like prey.

Needles prick my spine one after the other as I gape at the brazen, inconceivable absurdity before me. I have to see how much I mean to her, the stranger writes, and she knows I love her, too. I *will* love her. She begs. She fantasizes. She is splaying herself open before me — for me, she stresses. She is risking humiliation, rejection, just for me. I must see this — how much she loves me. Admit how much I love her. The slick of fear that leaves a wet, damp chill glazing my skin is as cold as wintered seawater. I am dense and sluggish, poised inside a trance, the letter I hold a tumult of menace. Crated inside sturdy Birkenstocks, my feet are roughcast plaster, and only through a great push of energy can I depress the gas pedal and get the car up to five miles an hour.

Home is barely three miles away, but it is a long drive through the sludge of a rising, strangely drugged panic. A panic that gently pushes me aside and carefully evaluates my situation, its danger, and ever so prudently directs my actions. I am not to make mistakes, it cautions. I am to work slowly, cautiously, and leave no evidence. None. Its voice is calm, yet demanding. Encased still in a fog, I take scissors and shred the letter into narrow slivers, then cut those in half, then into snippets so tiny that no one could ever paste them back together, and tie it all inside a plastic bag.

It is late afternoon, and Phil is scheduled to work into the evening. I have time for the trip, the voice reasons, warning me that I have to protect myself, my family, from this scourge that has broken into our home. I must get the filth away. Far, far away, where its fingers cannot reach me, Phil, our family. My heart is a crazy person trying to escape a padded cell as it slams against my rib cage, but I am oddly calm. Despite feeling like a criminal who has stuffed a dead body into a footlocker and is now planning to drag it two states away to hurl it into a river, I feel guided by rational, logical thought. After all, I am not racing around in a wild frenzy. This is a good barometer that I am behaving as any normal adult would.

As I slide back behind the wheel and steer this speeding vehicle through curving, dusky back roads thirty-five miles — terror demanding an extra ten for more distance — to dispose of the already destroyed evidence of my greatest shame, never does it register that I am in the clutches of a strange and frightening breakdown. I am simply a creature hightailing it through the woods, trying to save its own life and the life of its loved ones. Those headlights in the rear-view mirror? That's the hunter. Surely you understand why I must keep running.

Prayers are no more than lip service to a God who has turned a deaf ear to me. Full-fleshed entreaties offer me no more than milliseconds of relief from the fear that lives now in my bloodstream. With every piercing ring of the phone, my heart stalls, then jumps into overdrive, kicking and whipping itself into a frenzy, so terrified am I that it will be the predator calling to reveal my disgrace. Every trip to the post office wrenches my stomach into spasms. My body is on alert, always, even if my mind is elsewhere.

Every Saturday I fall into inertia, unable to think or move without precise thought until Phil returns from getting the mail. I search his eyes, his demeanor, terrified of an ambush that I will not know how to handle. Not until I riffle through all the paper and chaff to confirm for myself that there is nothing do I sigh with semi-relief, because I still am not safe. Not with a working phone and steps leading to our front door. It is getting harder and harder to conceal my deer-caught-in-the-headlights look. Why, I wonder, am I not skinny? This level of stress has to burn a good number of extra calories. Then I remember. I'm feeding this constant anxiety with whatever I can get my hands on. There's always a place on my agenda for raw cookie dough.

Catatonic. No other word fits as I sit here impaled in the driver's seat. I have just returned from the post office, and I hold in my hands another letter from the stranger I now believe is a stalker. If I permit it, one minor step will send me flying off an emotional cliff and I will be unable to return. The urge to jump — more accurately, to allow myself to fall — is pushing me closer and closer to some ethereal edge I can't see but know is there. Where do you wind up, I wonder, when you finally let go? I picture myself trapped on a bleached, barren landscape, wandering aimlessly about, hearing voices calling me back but ignoring them in favor of staring into colorless space. I am beyond terror now. How much harder can my heart beat?

The hot melting ooze that sickens me already claims large parcels of every day. I lie numb inside an artificial casing, all that's left after the catastrophe, terror boiled down to its essence. That thought strikes me as kind of funny. It's as if I'm a concentrated version of terror — its purest form. *Parfum de Terreur.* The old me would run with this gallows humor; the new me screams that I should just shut the hell up, that there is barely any old me left to cling to.

I feel like a servant given a detestable task she knows better than to refuse as I slowly open the envelope and pull out the letter. A picture falls onto my lap. All I catch is dark hair before I flip it over so I won't have to look.

WHY WON'T YOU TALK TO ME? the stalker screeches in bold capital letters. *I DON'T TAKE NO FOR AN ANSWER.*

Look at these kids, she shouts, referring, I gather, to the photograph eating through my jeans like acid. *Look what you're missing.* All she needs is a chance, she cries. No, there is no limit to terror, as I've always believed; it can always intensify. Because at this moment my heart is hammering so hard it might rocket-blast out of my chest. It is *him* all over again, alive in the stalker's DNA. I hear *him* in her noise. The threats. The demands.

The entitlement. The refusal to listen to *no*. One day *he* was not in my life. The next day *he* was and refused to leave. It is all happening again.

With hands working double time, I stuff the photograph and the letter back into the envelope and run into the house. At the kitchen table I dash out a short, desperate note. *No Contact. Honor what you have, not what you don't have. Your children love you.* Something along those lines. Sticking it onto her envelope, I cram the whole mess into another envelope and race, once again, the thirty-five miles to drop it in a mailbox far from our home.

Sleep hypnotizes me on the drive back, sweet-talking me into closing my eyes, to coast into its peaceful silence. The pull of exhaustion is such a temptation. At a red light, I let my lids drift closed, and for just a second I savor the enticing, dizzying swirl of velvety weariness. But I snap my head back, open the windows, blare the radio, and keep driving. I am in deep, deep trouble, and having to smile through dinner is more than I can cope with. Claiming fatigue to Phil, I escape to an early shower, and while the heat and steam and the steady pounding of water envelop me, I slide quietly down the wall and onto the slippery floor, sobbing. I don't think I will ever be able to stop.

CHAPTER 15

It Was Rape

I don't know who is driving, but it can't be me. The hands clutching the steering wheel look like mine. There's my wedding band, the one-third-of-a-karat engagement diamond rising from the center, surrounded by dozens of smaller ones. On my right hand, the mother's ring that our daughters gave me — the semi-precious stones symbolizing our family: two daughters, two sons-in-law, two grandchildren, and space for two future angels.

So it must be me. But it's not. Because I'm suspended far above, sitting on a boulder of sorts, like I'm a Buddha or a yoga master. So high up that I could reach out and touch blue. But I don't. I am just staring straight ahead, still and quiet. Well, that's not exactly correct. Still and quiet sounds meditative, like I have chosen to contemplate my navel from this elevated position. No, I am frozen in place, unable to move, which is why I know it is not me driving the car.

"Are you going to be OK?" Kelly asked as I was leaving. I kissed her on the cheek and hugged her close. "I'll be fine," I answered. That was a lie, kind of. Because I could not figure out exactly what *fine* meant. I wasn't bleeding; that proved something. And though my legs were watery and seemed owned by a feeble old lady, I could walk without collapsing. OK, so my breath was spurting out in short, shallow pants that I was struggling to disguise, my lungs refusing to grant me a cleansing deep breath. But still, in the great scheme of all things, I was fine. If fine meant functional. So, I slid into the car, turned the key, and waved good-bye to my daughter and two grandchildren. Then someone else drove away.

The car moves forward. Then stops. Then starts again slowly. Then goes fast. It goes on and on like this. Gas pedal. Brake pedal. Low tinny music plays from a distant tunnel. I hear it, but the words don't make sense. Although they do wrap around me like an invisible blanket, and I imagine them protecting me from falling off this rock I am fused to. Gas pedal. Brake pedal. The person driving is doing all right. She knows the way. Forty miles to pick Phil up from work. He'll take over the driving then.

Or will he? Once he *finds out*, all bets are off. The driver does not think about this, but I do. I'm charged with thinking now. And since I'm all alone up here on this rock, I don't have much else to do except stare. So I begin to contemplate stuff. Not too much. The driver might overhear, and I don't want an accident to make things worse than they already are. And are about to be.

From my perch I glance down every now and then, and I can see by how white her knuckles are that she is gripping the steering wheel as if at any moment it is going to make a run for it. Maybe I'm wrong. Maybe she's trying to keep *herself* from making a run for it. Either way, that's the terror leaking out. Her life has crashed in around her these past two hours, and she cannot bear to think about it. In fact, she is refusing to think about it, which is why I'm stranded up here deflecting random thoughts. I let a few sneak through, though she just tosses them back my way. She's not even making plans about what she's going to tell Phil. All she is doing is gripping that damn wheel and pressing pedals.

That's it. There's nothing in her head except me, the truth teller. But she keeps forcing me away, probably because she already knows what I have to say: that life as she knows it is permanently, irrevocably altered. There's no pretty way to say this: she's been gutted. No different from those blowfish that John J. Allen used to slice open with the swift draw of a blade against their bellies, disgorging slimy, coiled intestines onto the wet sand. Who could forget those silent fish eyes bulging, the tiny gills fluttering, little mouths gasping, thinking they still had a chance at life when all the while their vitals lay in a gruesome, detached jumble nearby?

No, the driver does not want to hear more bad news from me about how in a very short time what remains of her ordered life is going to be annihilated. Completely destroyed. Shredded to bits. I am not being dramatic, just realistic. She's going down, way down. I wish she would listen to me. Prepare herself. Arm herself with a good speech. Erect a defense. Make some kind of strategy, for God's sake! It's urgent that she listen. But no, instead, she blanks everything out, including the truth that when Phil finds out that she is a slut, he will turn and walk away from her — or worse, he will demand that she go. The driver has to face this, has to make a plan. I know she knows this. I know she understands that no one can know this horrible story about her and not turn her away. Come on, it's written in her history. This is a justifiable deal-breaker.

Thirty years of marriage and this is how it will end. Their daughters will turn on her as well, and the grandchildren will disappear. The driver has to face it: it is over for her. Yet, no matter how loud I shout, she refuses to listen. So, I'm left to just doodle around up here with these certainties that she will not let in, counting the miles, distracting myself until the implosion. After which I will gently say, *I told you so.*

~ ~ ~

I love our daughter's home. It is small and quaint and decorated with lace and angels. Once a week I visit to spend time with her and to cuddle our grandchildren, a toddler and a baby. The baby is plump and smells of sweet lotion and sour spit-up. And the toddler is bright with energy and charming, endless demands. They are life's beating hearts, these children, the soul of all that is precious. Kelly and I are sitting at the kitchen table, its pine wood pockmarked and scratched with character. Phil and I rescued it from some estate sale or the other, and here it is with all its history, sitting in this kitchen catching the bright autumn sunshine pouring through the windows. We've just had lunch, and with both children sleeping, we are enjoying a quiet respite from the chaos. Or at least I am enjoying it. That is about to end.

"Mom, I have something I need to talk to you about," Kelly says. There is something chafing the usual easiness in her voice, a disquiet that I detect but can't quite catch. And as if I sense danger riding in unseen on the wind fanning through the screens, tiny alarms start to go off — beneath my arms, a slight ping of instant perspiration begins to itch; sweat collects quietly on my upper lip. Warnings. Am I sure? I'm safe here in my daughter's home. I am looking at Kelly, at her smile that looks apologetic, kind of like the I-wish-I-didn't-have-to-do-this-but-I-do kind of look that parents hand kids when the big punishment is about to be dispensed.

My pulse quickens; in fact, I can feel it beating against my neck. Yes, I am being warned. But what am I to do now? It's not like I can run from the house screeching, *No! No! No!* Whatever it is, it's coming. Right now. I go over a quick list. Cancer? A death warrant of some sort? Has she mulled over her childhood and decided I was the worst mother ever to walk the earth? There was that time I lobbed a plastic case of straight pins at her. She was only ten years old; what the hell was I thinking? And the time I hurled a box of Dunkin Donuts to the floor and stomped on each and every one individually. Full-blown PMS, but still. I need to burn for those two incidents. She's been scarred for life. I'll never see my grandchildren again. All this charges through my head in the millisecond before she continues.

Someone has contacted Carl about you. That is all I hear before I plummet into the abyss that opens up directly beneath my chair. It seems an amazing feat of human biology that you can actually plunge hundreds of feet while you are sitting perfectly still. Carl, our son-in-law, Kelly's husband, is an attorney. There is only one possible explanation why anyone has tracked him down flaunting my name. The Stalker, as I have come to term this person, has managed to do what nothing else, what no one else — not Guilt as God, not the advice-sayers, not the gossipmongers — has been able to do since the moment I walked out of that hospital all those years ago, when I swore I would never think about what had happened to me in those hideous, secret years of filth and vermin I had at last escaped.

The Stalker, with her diligence and tenacity, conforming to her warning to me that she would not take no for an answer, has exploded from the cesspool and crashed through the protective, loving shield I have surrounded myself with. She is running riot inside the cherished life I have created, spewing the vile from all those years ago once again onto me, and worse, onto my family. This is sewage gushing from a septic tank. An erupting volcano of oily waste, human and more. And I simply and utterly cannot draw a breath.

Kelly continues talking, quickly, tenderly, but I hear only snippets, little pieces of words and sentences cut out and dangled separately in front of me. They make sense. They don't make sense. I just stare at her while she talks, at her blue eyes rimmed by dark lashes, at the faintest sprinkling of freckles across her nose, thinking she is not to know this. This was never meant for her. Or her sister. Or Phil. Or anyone. I think she shows me an official paper. My hated maiden name, Kathleen Barbara Allen, typed on it. But I am not sure about this. Maybe I am hallucinating. Maybe somebody slipped me acid the night Phil and I went to that hole-in-the-wall bar in Trenton back in the seventies on one of our rare nights out and it's been dormant all these years and just now has decided to kick in. Or maybe I'm having a flashback to my tonsillectomy at eight years old when I was knocked out with ether and the world was one huge, pulsating head of broccoli, because this kitchen is inflating and deflating in weird, ordered sequences of rhythmic sonics — an iron lung from the polio days.

I can't even blink. I hold my breath and feel heat flame my cheeks and ride roughshod over my body. I am locked inside a furnace. No, I'm frozen solid, shackled inside a meat freezer right beside bloody, slaughtered carcasses. I can't feel my fingers. Or my toes. I can't breathe. How is it possible to freeze and go up in flames at the same time?

"You know what I'm talking about, Mom," Kelly says.

But how does she know that? Then I answer myself. *She knows it because your name is on the official paper, remember? Remember Sister Social Worker? Sister White Habit? Remember all the lies you didn't tell them? Remember how stupid you were? How naive? How trusting? Need I go on?*

"Yes," I whisper, and drop my eyes. Sixty seconds ago, back when life was warm and safe, I loved this table; now it is the most frightening spot in the world. There may as well be urban guerrillas surrounding it. "Yes, I know," I say.

Always, I work to contain my panic attacks, which are an embarrassing rupture in my otherwise normal appearance. These breaks in dignity sport their own agenda, constantly wanting to boil over into uncontrollable hysterics, which is their favored pastime. Sometimes they obey me, sometimes they don't. Slight matter, really, because there are too many times when bits of that heightened anxiety bubble and squeak past my carefully constructed shield, and there I am, performing abrupt reversals of polite conduct. For instance, spouting off inappropriate comments that have no business living outside my mouth, or bolting for the door with no more than a mumbled excuse that has nothing to do with what I'm really running from. It's all very messy. And what looks like wacky behavior is actually preemptive damage control.

The key word here is *control*: when I start acting weird, I'm about to lose it. So I have to go. No matter where I am. Either I leave or I blow. And igniting before an audience is not an option. I've been with my mother during her all-out attacks — crying and screaming, flailing at the danger only she can see. Lunging at me, trying to climb up my body as if somehow she can reach safety. There's little sympathy for that kind of craziness. Mostly what you engender is exasperation for not being able to restrain those emotions of yours.

And right now I am struggling, pushing against the combustion beckoning me. It would be so easy to let go. Instead I breathe myself into calmness. But I can feel myself slipping, and at any second, panic may up and carry me off, and there I will be, a woman possessed by imaginary entities, screaming and kicking in this cute, cozy kitchen, jerking against my chair, thrashing, slapping invisible filth off my skin, shrieking, "Get *him* off me! Get *him* off me!" Every single day in the hospital where I was confined all those years ago, as my shape grew more and more distorted, as the crud of *him* overtook every inch of me, when there was no place in my entire body *he* had not invaded, I wanted to thrust my fists hard toward the heavens and scream piercing, shrill bellows at the deaf ears of God, begging, "Get *him* out of me! Get *him* off me!" He had to listen; someone had to hear me. Someone had to scrape that growing thing from me. It had to let me go. It had to.

In those days saturated by the filth that had become the sum of me, I didn't know I could have reached out to an ally. That my brother Jackie could have shown me a way. Divulged what liberated him from his agony. What I could slip onto my tongue, or plunge into my veins. Had I known, it would have been so simple. Instead I obeyed, cowered inside myself. Allowed all of them to dictate my present, my future. *Chicken-livered*, John J. Allen used to call me; never was there a more fitting description. I never understood I had a choice. And it would have been so damn easy — one phone call and I could have taken charge. But it never even entered my mind.

If I'd had the smarts then, I would not be sitting here today, watching my life break apart into chunks, hacked to death by a foul resurrection. But everything's timing. What I could've done and didn't do was long, long ago. Now, today, there can be no musing about offing myself; you don't go and do that when you're surrounded by people you love. It's just not fair. I know what it's like to face that fear. My mother has planted it too many times. I was eighteen when she began those threats. Threatening to kill herself because of Jackie, me stumbling over myself to get home from work in time; making the threat when she was living in our home while our children slept peacefully upstairs, and then again, when she was twelve hundred miles away where we couldn't get to her. And so many times in between.

No, I cannot let myself fall into panic. Let me bite my lip. Grip the chair. Squeeze tight whatever I have to so I can stay composed, dignified. That is what I do now as Kelly starts talking about, I think, young love. How Carl's adopted sister found her birth parents. Happily ever after. That kind of thing. But I am somewhere else looking down at the blanched, stricken woman immobilized in the chair. In this dollhouse where babies play. Where there is love and all things are right side up. Until this moment. With life now dismembered, its order, its sense, its safety — gone. For good.

When I'm tooling along at seventy-five miles an hour on the turnpike, the danger of having an accident emerges from the fog of my daydreams every now and again. But a catastrophe in the sunny embrace of my daughter's kitchen? Where we've shared countless celebrations? Eaten too much cake? Laughed at the antics of the children? Ambushed? Here? Now? How could I have ever conceived it? But it is true. This is what the intruder has done — hacked and slashed machete-style into my life, the lives of my family, making dangerous my refuge and all the places I feel safe. And life will never be put to right again — not like it was; not the way we've created it. It will always limp, always. Because part of it is gone forever. Slash off your foot, and no matter how well fit the prosthesis, for the rest of your days, you will hobble. No matter what. We are all changed. As of this moment.

Callously. Unnecessarily. There is no return to what was.

Kelly is chatting about teenage romance and how times were different back then. Too secretive. Attitudes have changed, she says. Today there's no shame. I am just staring at her, staggered by what she is saying, unable to comprehend what she means. All I can manage is, "Dad doesn't know." I mumble this because, honest to God, I have no other words in my head. I am stunned into numbness. "Mom," she says, "Dad's not going to care. What would you do if it were Dad?" "Nothing," I say. "I wouldn't care." And I wouldn't. But this is different. This is different. I am trying, but I cannot pull the scattered pieces of myself together. My brain is not functioning. I am an animal trapped inside a whirling gizmo, spinning, spinning. All this time I kept it from them. All this time never a slip, not a hint. Nothing. I can barely move my lips, keep my eyes open.

Kelly is talking musically, as if sweetheart roses are rooted back there in the dark years where I come from. Back where the only thing that ever flourished was fear. She's like Phil, an optimist. They walk a different path, a path where things work out right. In the end, all is OK. That is not how it is for me. My past is always waiting, ready to pounce, to destroy. After all, that's what ugly is born to do. And today it has happened. Ugly has gotten its second chance.

I look at Kelly and think of how much courage it has taken for her to confront this, to look directly in my eyes and say the words. It may have cost her a sleepless night when she needs all her energy for her children and husband. It may have settled in her heart like a knot that could not be dislodged. A child has no business carting around this kind of burden on behalf of a parent. Cancer. Heart attack. Old age. Even divorce. OK. All this is allowable to some degree. But not this. Not this gore dredged up from another era. This was never ever to be her concern.

"Mom," she said only minutes ago, "I couldn't let this come between us. I had to tell you." There was no other way for her. The Stalker has seen to that. I finally claim that deep breath I need and look at her. When she was a baby, we could never venture out without people stopping us constantly to marvel at her beauty. She has only grown more so. And I detest that this horror is defiling her, her family, her lovely home.

It was rape, Kelly, I say in a voice that sounds stolen from a trance. The words are unplanned. I just opened my mouth to speak and out they fell, as if they had been waiting there all along. "It was rape," I repeat. And the banshee that for all these years has been pacing, straining against its chains, finally is freed and blasts from its pit, unleashing a long-awaited, glorious rant. *Liar! Liar! Liar!* it screeches. Once again it takes its rightful place in the spotlight. *You lying slut. Whore!* it screams. I hear the words clearly, as loudly as if I am screeching them myself. *What the hell do you think you're saying? It was your fault. And everybody knows it. Rape? Rape? Who the hell are you trying to kid? You put yourself in the gutter. You did it. Nobody else.*

It is there, all of it. The accusations. The vile. My mortal sins. The voice is relentless in its attack. I don't argue. I know it's right. "I have to tell Dad," I whisper. Kelly tries to reassure me. But her words are meaningless, as empty as withered husks. I know what I know. No one who knows about my filthy fall from grace will have anything to do with me ever again. Even Phil. Then Kelly says, "I didn't know it was rape, Mom." There is confusion in her voice, maybe an appeal to understand. Only I have no explanation. I have no proof, no reasoning that will make any sense or will matter.

"I'm not going back there," I say. Trembling rises from some dark and foreboding locus. "Not for anyone. I'm not going back there." Yet the second I utter these words, I know this is not true. I know that this is just the beginning of what retribution has in store for me. I know I am not going anywhere but back. That's how it works. My past has caught up with me, and it will do this time what it was not able to do before. Because this time I can't fight it. This time it will succeed.

~ ~ ~

Just as I am about to pull into the parking lot of my husband's place of work, I sever the ghostly thoughts that have been hovering around my head and poking me with barbs and curses since I left our daughter's house. At long last, I am officially empty headed, devoid of thoughts, random or otherwise. Right now I couldn't even conjure up a picture of a common household object. In fact, my brain has dissolved, fizzed right out of my head like so much carbonation. I jerk the wheel to the right and do the tight-squeeze thing, jockeying into the "compacts only" parking space right in front of the door to the main offices of the Arc, where Phil has worked as a facilities manager since retiring from the police force. Some years ago I worked for the same agency as a program director. It is only one of the thousands of ways we are connected. It think it is all about to end.

This is what it is like to be bloodless, I imagine, as I look toward the double doors and wait. Has it been only hours since I began life as a mechanical zombie? Motorized and automated? Heart vanished because I feel no beating inside my chest, only a frozen solid block? *I don't want to do this I don't want to do this I don't want to do this I don't want to do this. I can't. I can't. I can't.* Fright swells and batters me side to side, trying to unhinge my resolve, provoking me to explode, inciting my nausea to fire up and put on a show. But I am not going to crumple. I won't. I will stand up and do what it is I have to do. Phil deserves this. I will not run and hide from him. I won't play coy and dissolve into sobs. Not that there are any tears to be had — like everything else except the queasiness, they've hightailed it to safer ground. I will myself strong.

Phil pushes through the door and offers a wave. I roll down the window and look at him. *Something's happened*, I whisper, and quickly add, "The children are fine." His face pales to the color of ashy chalk, and in his eyes, I see controlled alarm. When he takes the wheel and looks at me for direction, I ask if we can go somewhere to talk. He does not hesitate and puts the car into gear and backs up. There are no words prancing around in my head, no coherent thoughts to pull from. The occasional screeching of the demon calling me slut and liar does not count. I am in a world of rote motion. Breathe. Sit still.

At this moment I have nothing to say. Certainly, I can't ask about his day. I hate when people do that. Strike fear in your heart with a shocking statement like, "I just had my leg amputated by a train, and oh, by the way, how was that movie you saw last week?" It's infuriating. So I am quiet, watching the road, the cars passing by as he eases into traffic and then steers into the parking lot of a derelict Acme with its scarred façade and clumps of weeds pushing out of the asphalt. He cuts the engine and turns toward me.

"What is it?" he asks, looking at me with so much worry I don't think I can stand it. And so I begin. First one word, then another. I string them together into a sentence. Then I assemble the sentences into a paragraph. And before you know it, I've executed myself.

CHAPTER 16

Lost in a Familiar Land

In stunted, faltering sentences delivered in a listless monotone — because at this moment, I cannot lift even my voice — I surrender a confession much like those I've seen on television, where after being tortured, the accused stares into the camera flat-eyed and emotionless, mouth moving independently of the truth, and rolls out strange words and phrases that may as well be in a foreign language. And submissively accepts all the blame.

Looking at Phil, I give him what I have not ever been able to bear knowing, much less acknowledge. "There was a person I was involved with. I couldn't get away from him. I needed rescue, but no one noticed. I got pregnant. And now that person" — I have no accurate language to explain that it was *the rapist* finally expelled from my body — "is after me."

Nor do I give details of that dark time, because I have none. Not yet. All those images, threats, cordoned off, sealed, frozen solid since 1964, where I had left them in my mad dash to freedom. Agony paused. Stayed, noiseless cries. The filth, minute flecks caught in a fixed, risen plume of noxious vapor. Glares, forevermore petrified on stone faces. Gossip, interrupted mid-sentence. The horror of my mother crying, "Not Kathleen. Not my daughter," on permanent hold. All the echoes silenced, buried beneath a landslide of terror and fright, stashed far, far away where memories wither into nonexistence.

"She won't take no for answer; she won't be satisfied until I have a relationship with her," I say to Phil, ending my confession in surroundings that seem fitting for such ugliness — the crumbling asphalt, the broken plate-glass windows of the abandoned grocery store boarded up and spray-painted with obscene graffiti. *Fuck you* seems a favorite expression. A bum slouched against the broken doorframe, guzzling from a pint hidden in a paper bag, is all that's needed to perfect this scene that looks like the first stages of hell.

Phil takes my hand and says things. Kind and loving words that I cannot comprehend. Words that have their place when, say, a finger is cut. Or when the flu turns a person weak and pallid. Comforting expressions of solace and assurance that would be expected if offered at a funeral. I have just admitted to committing the worst moral crime a girl could ever commit, and Phil is consoling me with the sincerity of his love. "This doesn't make any difference," he promises. "I love you. I love you." Over and over he repeats this: *I love you. I love you.* And he does.

We have loved and been devoted to each other for a long, long time — forever, it seems. When you see one, you see the other. We operate as a tag team. It has always been this way, since the beginning of our time together. As a couple, we've weathered the eruptions and firestorms and grave disappointments and griefs doled out to any long-term marriage. But not this. Not this. This transgression of mine is poised to destroy all we've built in our lives. So I'm confused. *You mean I can stay? I don't have to go?* I want to ask, but don't, because even in my state of bewilderment, these questions sound self-serving and offensive — an insult to our shared spirituality. My regular self — the part directed by my heart shored up by logic — understands this; at this moment, the mortally wounded soul that I have become knows nothing outside the throb of anguish.

So I talk, babble on in a flow of disconnected recitation. From the surge of prattle emerges the term *rape*. Just the word, nothing else. The grisly images struck deaf and dumb remain still crystallized, emitting only the shrill curses of the awakening dead. I swear to Phil that I will not go back there. Not for anyone. Ever. "Not even for you," I insist.

"You never have to go back there," he assures me.

"I'm not, Phil. I'm not going back there." I emphasize this lie as I lean against the seat and stare into the brokenness around us, clutching onto his hand, willing him to keep me from falling into the ugliness where the rapist lurks, tugging hard at my limbs, pulling me down toward his haunt. I will not, I cannot, look back. I am besieged with piercing terror at what lingers in the place where memories are forbidden.

"She's not going to stop," I finally say, draining my last restores of energy. "She won't take no for an answer."

It is so clear to me, the pathway so obvious. The decision has been wrenched from my will. And fate, God, or the devil will deliver me into the hands of this second-generation predator. My life, all that I have become since the misery of that time, vanishes, and these two generations of predators, materialized from the gloom, stand in joined forces. Once again I am owned property, coerced, threatened into obedience. At this very moment, nothing—not time, space, or a multitude of accomplishments over an entire lifespan—separates me from my fifteen-year-old self. The fear. The resignation. The futility of attempted escape. It is here and it is real, and I see no way of avoiding the clutches of this latest beast.

But Phil does, with simple, assured clarity. "Listen to me," he states, clearly, plainly, as if he is in uniform speaking to a dazed victim. "That is ridiculous. She has no rights to you." He sees what I do not, and I don't understand how he knows this truth. "She's not going to get to you. I won't let her. I promise you, this woman will not get to you." I understand English. I do. But I can't grasp what Phil is saying. He is speaking as if I have a choice. As if my will has value. I squint and stare at him, trying to visualize the words he is speaking. Struggling to believe their power, my right to the word *NO*.

Fuck You. Fuck You—the spray-painted profanities splashed across the crumbling Acme take on new, potent meaning. "She can go fuck herself," Phil states. His confidence amazes me; he is not the least bit scared of this person. "What she wants is not going to happen."

He repeats all this over and over again—how you repeat words to a child, hoping soon she will mimic them, knowing comprehension will take place later. I hang on to his declarations, pull them close, wrapping myself in their protection. I watch him, his eyes, for the fleeting suggestion of condemnation. Listen to the tone of his voice, instantly ready for a turn in tenor, a drift into mockery—John J. Allen's territory. An inflection of blame—the personal safety zone of cowardice from where my mother betrays others.

Phil is adamant. He is on my side. Wholly. Completely. Without question. Standing, unflinching, right alongside me in this fire that is just beginning its burn. And I don't know how to be, where to put my thoughts, even how to arrange them in this occurrence of strange happenings. This manifestation of love, this embodiment of his devotion to me.

Still there is more for me to do before this bloodbath of a day can end. It is a long drive to our youngest daughter's home in Pennsylvania. For over two hours, we wrestle rush-hour traffic to Kristi and her husband Mike's house in Hershey, with its freshly painted walls and its lawn carpeted in plush emerald swathes. A place I am about to soil with the filth of my history. In a room that will hint at potpourri and scented candles, I will have to degrade myself before them. A whore of a mother who must come clean. Publicly shamed and repentant for my fall from my family's image of me, now ruined far beyond repair. The hate I have for myself is outdone only by the loathing I harbor for this predator, who has seized for her own favor what the rapist seized for his personal gratification all those years ago.

But I have no choice—not a moral one, anyhow. We have to go, to relieve Kelly of any burden that is not hers to shoulder. It is my responsibility to speak the truth—the despicable, unfiltered truth. If I run from this, beg Kelly to keep this disgrace hidden from her sister, this sinister canker will swell and fester, and widen into an invincible distance that will never be able to be bridged between them. This secret that no one was supposed to unearth has the power to destroy. And it will do so. Anytime it pleases.

So, we drive and work at talking. About Phil's day. About the weather. About our grandbabies. But these wooden utterances of mine sound like gibberish thumped out by drumsticks beating the funeral march against a tree trunk. I force out a laugh every now and again. But it is fake and shrill, a pathetic attempt at scaring off the onrush of impending shame; a feeble effort at shoring up the cinders—all that is left of me after today's firestorm.

When we pull into their driveway, I see Kristi draw the curtain and peek out the window. They know we are coming, but they do not know why. The story was too enormous to spurt out over the phone. In one sound bite, how do you describe the ocean when you are drowning in its middle? Explain being lost on a road between here and there, stumbling along a flat, vacant landscape, with no beginning, no end? All I could say without cracking apart like a brittle egg unleashing moldering ash was, "Dad and I are coming up. There's something we have to tell you. Everybody's fine."

Within seconds we are standing in their kitchen. And as in my vision, I am fixed beneath the kitchen light that bores into me like the blinding laser from a naked bulb wired into the ceiling of an interrogation cell. It does not matter that I smell the floral sweetness of infused oils drifting on the currents of heat chasing away October's chill, or feel the hug of memories we've created in their home at the edge of a farmer's fields, with the distant wail of trains on their way to somewhere important. And the insistent brush of the grandcats Mittens and Melrose against my ankles, begging attention. It all falls away under that shaft of brightness, where I stand apart from the three of them — Phil, Kristi, and Mike — gathered in a semicircle facing me.

And I am struck with loneliness, at the oddness of this sensation, as if I am staring at pieces of myself that have been surgically removed from my ownership, and I am too shocked to react. It seems real, water, warm as a bath, creeping up my legs, my body, until I am engulfed, and faces, bloated and distorted, swim before me, viewed from my submerged house of all tortures. Fighting back groans, I am sickened to nausea that I have to pervert Kristi and Mike's home, our entire family, that we have attempted always to sanctify with love, with the vile I must now reveal.

But I do. I confess in horrible, degrading words. I strip myself of all my dignity before them. I am beyond humiliated. Beyond shame. I am destroyed as the rapist wanted, as this newly risen predator — this absolute stranger staking claim to the bruised and weeping tissue between my thighs — desires. Nothing, nothing can bring me back from this. Maybe after some sleep I will discover a hidden reserve and be able to harness a sliver of horsepower that I can use to playact. Pretend all is normal. Make believe I am still a living, breathing woman — a wife, a mom, a grandmother — even though I have been murdered.

Not tonight, though. This pain is a raw, moaning wound that washed away my spirit in huge viscous globs, leaving only those dusty cinders behind, and I am simply too dazed and limp to fashion a performance, even for my family. Not on this day, when all I understood to be my life has blown apart and left me lost even in the land of those I love.

CHAPTER 17

Horror Relived

In a panicked frenzy of wheezing and gasping, I bolt upright in bed, struggling for air that is barred from my throat constricted by spasms. Tears stream down my cheeks as I keep sucking at breath. It seems forever before I can force the tiniest stream of oxygen into my lungs that ultimately explodes into a surge of huge, fleshy sobs. I fumble for the bedside light and grab my journal. *The mattresses. The mattresses,* I scrawl across the page. I am back there: over thirty years have passed, and at this moment I am trapped and suffocating under *his* weight, pushed deep into a mattress with its pus and urine stains and splotches too disgusting to contemplate. Browned rings of dried blood? Encrusted ejaculate? And the curdled-spoiled-milk stink of limp clammy sheets exposing soiled ticking.

A place unfit for a dog. But I am here. And the rank vile is mauling me, devouring me. I am smeared with the crud and pulpy splatters lying beneath me. I am filthy everywhere. Inside. Outside. *He* is panting. Sweating *his* slime and stench on my clothes, on my skin, drilling it into my body. This is not a dream—it is a nightmare playing out in real time, and I am fighting for breath that now feels like hacked-off clots of air stuffed into my mouth. But how can this be happening? Has something in my mind snapped, launching me into madness? *I don't know what to do. I don't know what to do.*

Phil is sleeping in the back bedroom. Down the hallway, beyond closed doors, his snores are impressive feats of raucous grunts and snorts. I don't want to wake him. It's 3 A.M., and he has to get up for work in a few hours. But ripe, rotting garbage is shoving me back into my past, demanding I stay—where, it laughs, I've always belonged. *Once a slut, always a slut.* Vivid images casting their stink, and loud, screeching slurs of past gossipers have mobilized into an emotional onslaught; despite efforts to keep calm, my defense against this ambush is feeble. The scent of lavender and powdery roses that I have sprayed onto our linens do not shield me from feeling soiled, befouled with rancid mucus smeared everywhere on my body. Then and now are intertwined, as unearthly voices condemn me, mock me, repeating their old mantras: *It was your own fault. Your fault, nobody else's.*

I keep scrawling words across the pages of my journal, trying not to cry, trying to outwit the voices so relentless with their hatred as they tell me how filthy I am. How undeserving. How riddled with ugliness. I don't want to listen, but their accusations are louder than my written pleadings. *What do you think Phil's going to do when he finds out just how degraded you were? You think he's going to want you for his wife? For the mother of his children? Grandmother to those sweet babies? Somebody as filthy as you?* Something beyond fear, an instinct so primal that it erupts, pushes me out of bed and sends me scrambling barefoot down the hall. I am not running away. I am not slinking into the silent place to cower in fright. I am racing and stumbling toward safety — toward protection from the rapist. I am rushing for the help I never before knew how to find.

"Phil," I barely whisper. Instantly he is awake. "What's wrong?" he asks. "Come here." I crumple beside him into the warm bed, sobbing, gasping. "He used me in the most disgusting places. On filthy, dirty mattresses," I cry, curled up next to him, the agony of what I've just admitted a physical stab wound ablaze in my stomach. He pulls the thin blanket over my shoulders, wrapping me tight against him. "You're safe now," he whispers. "You're safe now." He's quiet, still, holding me as I sob. "I wish I could have helped you back then. I would do anything to make this go away." His voice is as hushed as the silent house beyond this room. But there is more besides relived horror that inhabits this dead time of night. There exists a certainty that has blossomed and now outlines me with its black aura, thick as ominous fog. I am so frightened to say the words, so terrified of their truth, of what looms within them.

"What if I become a monster?" I cry. But it's more of a halting plea for help. Because I know what has been unleashed, the savage menace of malignancy with its power of invasion and its capacity to infect all it touches with an ugliness that can never be overcome.

Phil has touched such hideousness. Plunged his hands deep into all the cancerous sores that an under-society can generate. You don't patrol unsparing city streets for twenty years and not see it, smell it, palpate it. Always, though, Phil scoured off the filth. Polished his boots to a high shine. Changed into a fresh uniform. Every day on the street spelled a new beginning. Phil never was the dirt that soiled him. Never had such filth invaded his body, swarmed every single cell until all that lived and breathed inside his skin was the festering squalor of a vile deviant. He's tackled them, cuffed them, thrown them behind iron bars. But he's never had a monster force its way into his very marrow and domineer with its depravity until all that lives behind his eyes is the monstrosity.

This is what I am terrified of. The escaped monster. The evil that surely is set to overtake me. That soon enough I will become as foul as my once-buried, unforgiven sins. I will become a spirit so dark, so contaminated, that it will blot out all light. My life as I know it will be extinguished, buried once again beneath a barrage of sewage spewed from my past.

In seconds it all flashes before my eyes, an old horror movie flickering on a wide screen. Once again I am cowering on the escalator at the World's Fair as grease-caked fingers rake across my exposed bottom. Slumped against the rain-slicked window in a car barreling toward Elkton, Maryland. Over and over again my mother's words replay: *Not Kathleen. Not my daughter.* And the mattresses, worse than any gutter. Lest I forget, there I am, hunch-shouldered, forced to stand, stripped naked before the gossipmongers as they rip and shred my dignity, term me *slut* and *whore*, defiling me with the dirtiest words possible: *Kathy Allen, pregnant.*

Then suddenly Sister Social Worker is here, mocking me for hiding in my raincoat. My black raincoat, the only thing that offers me protection. And the echoes of Sister White Habit searing me with the label *birth mother. Birth mother. Birth mother.* That gangrenous stigma disfigures me as much as any flesh-eating disease. Here in this room where I am supposed to be safe, Phil breathing quietly against my back and his hands stroking my hair, I hear it — the demon. Screeching that I am to blame for all that happened to me, taunting me with a truth so excruciating that it alone, *it brags*, has the power to destroy me. It is the monster that will devour me. The agonizing truth that I did not fight. That I obeyed like a beaten dog. That I put myself on those mattresses. That I did what *he* told me to do. That I never complained. That I kept smiling. And smiling. And smiling.

"What if I become a monster?" I say again, barely squeaking out the words. "What if the only thing that kept me from being one all these years was my secret? Its hold over me? What if I am really disgusting?"

"No. No," Phil whispers. "You are not what happened to you. You were a victim. A victim," he says. "You have nothing to be ashamed about. You have to understand this. Horrible things happened to you. It's all out in the open now. You don't have anything to fear anymore. And without that fear, you'll be free to become the person you were meant to be. You'll be better than you ever thought. Not worse."

I hear Phil; I listen to his assurances. I want to grab onto them like the lifesavers they are. But the other voice is louder. And the other voice is right. Everything was and is all my fault, and for this I can never forgive myself. I deserve this agony. I don't feel at all relieved that my vulgar past has been force-revealed. I feel dirty. I am not suicidal as I huddle against this tender man I have been married to since I was nineteen. But I don't believe him, not really. And my new secret is — I would welcome death.

CHAPTER 18

Defeated

Not Kathy! Not Kathy! Phil says, telling me the response to what *she*—the second-generation predator—sent in a recent letter bragging about contacting all the relatives of mine she could find. *Her* relatives, she boasts. *They deserve to know me, and I deserve to know them.* "Not Kathy. Not Kathy"—the shocked outcry of an unidentified older relative—I cannot bear to know who it is—to whom she blithely spilled my secret. Those words, phrased in brittle shock, echo my mother's wails the night she found out I was pregnant. The night my name became a keening howl of utter despair and sheer disbelief. *Not Kathleen. Not my daughter*—the cry I would have given anything not to have heard still slashes my heart with its blade-sharp spikes. Pain gnashes at my face; I can feel its pull and twist. Maybe I resemble a stroke victim, her features a great mar of loosened, misplaced muscles that are suddenly frozen into frightening grimaces.

The biting sting of helpless envy for those who had a choice to end their torment before it gained footing is like the relentless smack of a plastic belt against my bare skin. Each invisible welt is an abscess of jealousy for those girls—girls who took charge and had their secret misery scraped clean from their wombs. With their pasts erased by the fling of a scalpel or the hum of a vacuum, they never had their agonies obliterated, upgraded, and disguised as a mom-and-apple-pie tale, smeared with that degrading, lying term *birth mother.* Girls who are not forced to fear the mail or the phone, or the State. Girls, now grown, some old, who never have to worry about being hunted down and stalked. The abortion girls whose sins remain private, not resurrected and made public. Girls who are free, their names safely buried in dusty files where they will remain. Free. The vision of that is beyond my grasp.

It has been months since the original explosion. And it does not end. *She* continues contact — pleading, coy, angry — employing whatever emotions consume her as she flops down with a ballpoint and paper to once again crusade for her self-proclaimed entitlements. Each communication is an ambush that Phil now intercepts and conveys to me tentatively, tempering *her* remarks. And each ambush, no matter how delicately expressed, drags with it a flashback. The smell. The filth. The sights. Whatever is next in line for a viewing. Whether I am at the doctor's office, at the drugstore, or sleeping, it is merciless. And I am exhausted from crying, from the fear of being pursued and trapped once again beneath the rapist. From the badgering, screeching voices dripping ridicule, relentlessly proclaiming me guilty — guilty of all that was done to me. Worn down from the overwhelming loathing of myself. Of this person who will not stop her cruelty, her brutal mission to incite my attention and flaunt my shame.

But it's not all her, is it? *She* is only carrying on what the rapist began. If there were no rapist, there would be no *her*. And I do not dare visualize how the rapist inflated his chest and crowed of his conquest. What's the use of ruining someone if you don't parade the human wreckage down Main Street? After which *he* likely posed as a victim. A ditched Mr. Nice Fellow weeping enough crocodile tears to wring pity from his next victim. As he did me.

Phil tries to be gentle as he picks his way across this minefield — another of the dozens he's already shepherded me across — quietly telling me that my secret probably never was as secret as I need to believe. Clear. Thought out. Logical. And, of course, correct. And he'd better be damn careful, because right now I just might decide to hate him like I hate the rest of the world. But Phil is a truth-seeker, a truth-teller, except the truth, at this moment when the sole freedom I have rests within my illusions, is my sworn enemy, as it has been for generations of my family. Maybe I'll just slap my hands over my ears and trill several rounds of *tra la las* so I don't have to hear any more, so I can drown out all the stunned cries of *Not Kathy! Not Kathy!* echoing in my head. Public exposure is a gangrenous disease decaying me from the inside out, trouncing my chest with the weight of its wet rot, crushing knobs of shame and manic phobia that strangle all breath.

So it is a monumental effort keep from screaming at Phil, *That's not true! That's not true! Nobody knew anything. I hid in my coat! My own parents didn't know. Nobody knew!* I need to pummel him with my self-deception until he believes it just like I do. Facts will crush me as easily as falling boulders. Crunch. Splat. Gone. Can't I keep something, anything, for myself, even if it's sleight-of-hand deception? To fathom that my condition was common knowledge is to admit that my disgrace was obvious — that I was a shuffling billboard broadcasting my own scandal, my ballooning middle bragging rights for the rapist. And since truth is always relentless in its challenges, there's more to face than reliving the scorching humiliation from the scorn targeted at me.

All along Phil's been asking me, "Where was your mother when you were hiding in your coat? When you came home with a busted lip? Where was your father? Where was anybody?" In an era when no questions are considered stupid, these are. Just stupid questions with no answers — that is, until the slow-rising chill, the frigid weave of comprehension, begins to awaken me and I start to confront the brutality calling to be exhumed. That all the people about me — parents, relatives, neighbors, classmates, teachers, clergy, churchgoers — witnesses to my very evident decline, either blissfully ignored the reality, condemned me for it, or contentedly licked their lips and fabricated scathing gossip. Not. One. Person. Reached out. And to admit this truth is to accept the inconceivable: that there were people laughing and attacking me while I was drowning.

And now the State of New Jersey threatens to open sealed adoption records — to disclose names, dates, all the particulars. As if birthing a rapist's spawn is not enough. The State now vows to extort from me the personal privacies trolling my blood, to wrest away the privileged mysteries of my ancestors, calling for an official confession every five years. How can it be possible that for the rest of my life, through official, hand-delivered certified letters or a posse of State workers pounding on our door, the rapist will visit me on a carefully orchestrated schedule? A scheme that will resurrect his smirk, revive his snarl. Through the demands of what *he* implanted in my womb, sanctioned by the government, he will again and again remind me of the knife he longed to shove up my vagina — *cunt*, as he called it — even as I am eighty years old and all about me is withered and shriveled. Even then, with skin as fragile as parchment, I still will be smothered by his stink, as rank as if it is he with his own grease-inked fingers who hands over the notification that I am to once again give report.

But still there is more dread looming over the assault of flashbacks. Beyond the ghostly replay of my mother's cries, a bonus danger lurks above the horror of the State probing my genitals. A deathly fear that coils inside me like soured fumes: that one day I will be forced to encounter this second-generation predator. And there *he* will be. And in a final evil mockery, a fatal toxin designed by nature itself, there I will be, trapped inside his descendent body, forever fused to the rapist. My likeness abducted, intertwined with *his* in an imposed union, a sinister marriage of malice and pilfered parts. My features, phantoms fleshing out *her* face. My eyes stolen. My smile, once so stiff with emotionless compliance, ripped from me, reassigned and re-created in final, complete surrender to him. And I, and all those dear to me, will never ever be free of him or of his spawn. It seems a retaliation handed down by God, who picks and chooses His favorites, among whom I don't qualify — the smug teacher's-pet types who incessantly brag that God never hands us more than we can handle as they count their lottery winnings. Any unpleasantness regarding a car running inside a closed garage, misuse of razor blades, and/or a fitting stash of Valium conveniently excluded, of course.

What I know at this moment is that this seething pain, so frantic for the relief of revenge, could, given an opportunity and a small shift in the alignment of the planets, turn me into Lizzie Borden, reincarnated complete with ax. The grip of this blaze of temper, the devil storm of vengeance, is so fierce I believe I could commit mass carnage and not blink an eye. A revisit to the heydays of my father, John J. Allen, and brother Jackie, both masters at provoking thundering rage, who then broke into laughter when it exploded. Those glory days of blinding hate, where failed strength and not moral capacity kept me from killing my brother. Now I know better. I can employ restraint. Instead of focusing this anger-turned-lethal outward, I can aim it all at myself. Except what kind of person leaves behind her slashed carcass for her loved ones to discover? That's no option. But how am

I ever going to manage dragging this amassing tonnage of rage and despair across endless days?

The family room where Phil and I sit is spicy with the scent of cinnamon and apple, surrounded by pictures of our family — our daughters as toddlers, their wedding photos, our grandbabies. Antiques. Folk art. Wreathes I have crafted from stalks and pods and tied with gingham ribbon. And if you peek at our CD collection, surely you will find an Elvis or two. All assembled over a lifetime. And at this moment, I wish it all away. I need to curl up on the floor and slip into the darkness as easily as a dying shadow. Phil is looking at me, unaware of the wound he has just wrenched open. He does not deserve a bleeding, broken wife, unable to heal.

"This has beaten me," I whisper. "It's beaten me."

Phil rushes over and gathers my hands in his. I look up at him, at the sadness and worry worn into his face like too much time.

"I'm sorry. I'm sorry," I cry. "I can't bear this shame anymore. I can't."

"You don't have anything to be ashamed of. You were a victim. You were a victim."

"I'm sorry. I'm sorry for all this." It's all I can say, the same sentence over and over, a wordsmith with no good words.

"You have nothing to be sorry for. *They* do. Look at me," he says. "You're stronger than this. I know you. This is not going to beat you. I won't let it. We're going to fight. We're going to stand up and fight *her*. The State. Whatever it takes. We're going to fight. We might not win, but we're going to fight."

~ ~ ~

And so we do. Rather, Phil does, while I hide behind the curtain, too cowered to peek out. We engage an attorney who writes *her* a stern letter, stating terms: stop all contact with the Foleys; cease contacting the relatives of Mrs. Foley. The correspondence falls on raging ears, and she fires back with a pages-long, irate epistle of accusations and attacks and ceaseless lamenting over the pain and heartache she has suffered. "I don't know how to respond to this," our attorney says of the jumble of howling, petulant tantrums. But he does, in clear and concise easy-to-understand-English: no further contact. Grudgingly she agrees to stop contacting me — a promise she won't keep — but furiously maintains she will find and contact every one of my relatives she can, claiming them for her own.

I understand rage. I understand hate. What I don't understand is malicious spite, acid thrown into the face of a stranger. It is the helplessness, the utter hopelessness of her assault, that drains my spirit. And I am struggling to hold on to my dignity that she rips away in handfuls. Trying to halt the public display of my private parts. Trying to stop her from erecting billboards all over the place, touting my humiliation. This is a gross, irrational fear — that one day Phil and I will be tooling down the highway and I will see my name and all the specifics of my past painted in nine-foot letters adjoining an ad for a used-car dealership. I call this fear irrational only because that is how a regular person would describe it and, of course, I want to appear normal. But really? From my view, I believe that at any moment a construction worker will grab his nail gun and pail of paste and there I'll be, planted high above the weeds, right along Route 206 on the way to Atlantic City, near the old Two Guys where John J. Allen bought me my bargain-basement prom dress, sharing space with shots of rattletrap junkers fancied up with a fluorescent powder coat. Trauma is very creative.

So it is that this second-generation predator has carved out my options. And they are limited, just as they were by the rapist all those years ago, when he threatened, *Either you're going to tell your parents or I will.* Either I can let her slur my name all over my extended family or I am going to have to find the courage to reveal my shame myself. It is a colossal effort to collect bits and pieces of nerve and glue them together into a shaky semblance of guts that has more to do with abject fear than courageousness. She is not going to go away. All I can hope for is damage control, the retention of at least a speck of my dignity.

So I write a letter to my three surviving brothers. And say all the words. All the degrading, humiliating details of my shame. While I am at it, I decide to tell them that I am half adopted. That I was abused by John J. Allen and I know they were, too. Then I apologize for hurting them. For whipping them with a belt. And the ache of knowing what I did to them as little boys buffets me with brooding pain and regret that feels too hollow to ever be filled with the solace of forgiveness, though forgiveness is what I ask for. Before I close, I mention that I was molested in my bed over several nights just before I married. Most likely it was Jackie, I say, by way of reassurance. But I can't admit the haunting truth: that I am not convinced it was him.

Then, because I am so scared of their reactions, I tell my brothers — now my newly acknowledged half brothers — that they do not have to worry about responding to me. Acting as if I don't care whether they reach out to me or not makes it seem like it could be true. Or that I could make it true if only I could erase certain agonies from my head. But I offered the escape, and all of them scurried through that crack in the wall. Not one phones. Or writes. Or sends a message via skywriting over the vast pine barrens where I hide. I never hear a word from any of my brothers ever again. Guess they're gone.

Not that I expected to be coddled with benevolence or touched with the generosity of their compassion. From the beginning, my situation has been met with contention and bitter disgust. And why should my brothers forgive me for beating them? They have no obligations to me. We are, after all, not a family any longer. Even when we were, empathy and forgiveness were no more than words listed in a dictionary. So, my initial sense of empowerment and freedom at revealing the truth of my ordeal quickly fades beneath the weight of my brothers' silence, and I am swallowed, once again, by shame so intense my face feels permanently stained from the dirt I have ground into it.

Phil begins to knock on doors: assemblymen, senators, the chairman of the Health and Human Services Committee. He reveals our story. The devastation it has caused me. Our family. The fear and shame that cripple me. He begs for compassion. "My wife is being stalked by an adoptee. Don't expose other women to this," he pleads. "Don't open adoption records to strangers; understand that the adoptees are strangers to these women in hiding."

"Tsk, tsk," the smiling politicians say, and shake his hand. "Thank you for coming. It's a sad story," they add, and do nothing. Not for us, anyhow.

They rally to the side of the adoptees, who are angry and boisterous and who argue their cases with medical and psychological statistics and demands. The adoptees are lost ships with no beginnings. I am a stalked animal with no escape. Whose pain is greater? There are more mangled bodies strewn along this highway than can be counted. Everyone suffers and no one wins. Everyone is damaged. We all rage and sob at life's unfairness. But there is nothing that anyone, including the politicians, can do. No one can change the truth. The adoptees cannot undo the circumstances surrounding their births — adoption is their story. I cannot undo my story of rapes and a despised pregnancy. There seems to be no freedom in truth.

A newspaper wants Phil and me to tell our story and promises to print every word unedited. In a fleeting instant of fatal courage, I agree. Assuming anonymity, I compose the piece, revealing what I have never publicly admitted — my own adoption, abuse, sexual assault that ended in pregnancy, and stalking by the adoptee. I ask for compassion for myself and for other women who are terrified of being exposed. I ask that mutual consent for contact be required. Within the cloak of namelessness, I feel safe. Not fearless, but safe enough to speak. I ignore the buzz of vertigo that makes me feel as if I'm teetering on the edge of a crevasse with an avalanche rumbling toward me.

When the editor informs Phil that he won't run our piece unless we agree to include our names and town where we live, I know the icy onslaught is about to overtake me, but I say, "Well, OK," and think that I have completely lost my mind. If I want to torture myself, why don't I make it easy and simply jump headfirst into the ravine instead of waiting to be pushed? Or avoid all broken bones and opt for delicacy and lace my iced tea with ground-up glass and gulp it down?

I am still heart-stung by the silence from my brothers; the embarrassment of such indecent exposure clings to me like a coat of sticky goo that will not dissolve. The indignity of what I revealed and the sensation of dangling in the spotlight of condemnation throbs with such pain that it seems a mass wedged up against logic, and I am convinced that I can never show my face again at any extended family function, including funerals. My disclosure has shoved me beyond my ability to pretend, to make nice for the occasion.

What would I say? *Oh, hi. How are you? By the way, did you ever get my letter? You know, the one where I confessed to the misdeeds between my legs?*

How do I make the disgrace of rape and the resulting pregnancy palatable? Do I…ahem, ahem…make a little joke? Downplay it? Ignore the letter flapping between us like a bloodied flag? Crumple into a heap at their feet — pathetic and ashamed — and beg for their…what? Forgiveness? Mercy? Understanding? Plead with them to restore my dignity? What the hell would Miss Manners advise me to do? Put on a smile and nibble watercress sandwiches? Slit a main artery as proof of my disabling humiliation? None of the above? All of the above? And just before I slink away, do I mention the small matter of the indecencies committed against me during early-morning blackness in my bedroom and ask their opinion of the culprit?

So I ask myself, *Are you crazy?* Writing an article for a newspaper, then signing your real name? And your address? Do you understand how dangerous this is? Do you realize you're planting your own billboard along the freeway? *Don't do this,* I warn myself over and over. How are you going to lug around more of what you can't already carry? But there is a voice, as small as a vanished sigh, nudging me into the sunlight. I want to say, *No, I can't do this,* then run and hide beneath a thicket of brambles, a rabbit scared of its cottontail. Instead, I gulp down an oversized breath, ignore the arched brow of common sense and the teachings of my experience, and push send.

I am unprepared for the backlash. Instantaneous and lethal. All the responses are from women. It is how women kill women — by gouging out a living heart. One is civil. She writes, "I'm sorry Mrs. Foley was raped, but…" before she unleashes. I am no match for this scorned female wrath, and I wilt beneath the tirades. I berate myself for being so stupid, for stepping into the middle of their battlefield armed with only *pleases*. And there is more. *She*, the second-generation predator, has read the article and launches her attack. "Mrs. Foley is a liar," she states, bragging that she is the one who knows the truth. "Mrs. Foley is imprisoned by her husband," she claims, "and because she is so afraid of him, she has to lie about the past. Mrs. Foley was not raped. It was a love story." Her parents forced Mrs. Foley to give her up. Everyone she's contacted says so. *It wasn't rape. It was love. It was a love story.*

There is no more I can do except sink further and further into a hazy mire of helplessness and rage. Speaking out solves nothing; it simply raises the ire of the angry and scares away the uninterested, leaving me shriveled inside my own skin. I can't live like this. So I disappear inside the tight cocoon of my family. Forever. Forever. But forever doesn't last as long as I had planned. It lasts only until I hear from my brother. The dead one.

You remember Jackie — the kid with the big ears and lazy eye who goaded me into sweaty fistfights? The hated kid in the family who grew up to be a drug addict and a loathsome criminal? The one who died in squalor? That one. But it wasn't like when we were kids. This time he comes to me with a request. He asks nicely. I am not kidding here, or exaggerating. Outside of prayers, I don't talk to the dead. Not that I wouldn't like to, but it's never happened. Until Jackie. And his request.

And this bizarre turn of events will have Phil asking, "Why is it that the only one of your brothers who talks to you is the dead one?"

CHAPTER 19

The Dead Brother Returns

It's June 15, 2007.

Phil hands me an office-sized manila envelope, the kind used for memos in the old days before e-mail. "You don't have to open it," he says, being protective, offering me escape. He knows I don't want to, not really. Knows I'm scared of what's inside, of what I'll see. But I unravel the red string anyway and pull out my brother Jackie's picture — his mug shot, actually. I'm startled that despite the drugs slackening his eyelids, he's good-looking. I've forgotten that — or maybe I've just always refused to concede even this one, lonely point, rejecting anything about him that might lessen my hatred. But now I see — in his fine bone structure; his chin sculpted and bearing a slight hint of John J. Allen's cleft; his eyes, blue, as I recall, that would be piercing were they not hazy with drugs; his dark, wavy hair curling down his neck — what legions of girls coveted when he was just mildly dangerous, before he leaped full-time into hell.

Jackie has done terrible things. I stare into that groggy face, looking for something. The lost spirit concealed beneath the resignation plating his eyes? I don't know. It is so difficult to gaze into such raw pain. Maybe I am trying to understand all that was destroyed inside him, where the parts that defined the best of who he was went after he abandoned himself. After we abandoned him. In some ways I think that I am trying to comprehend the strange and odd energy that existed between us, beyond my hate and his antagonism, remembering now the visit to the Annandale Detention Center, where I shuddered at the muted undertone rumbling in the space between us. Through his grim image, is Jackie trying to tell me something now that I am not hearing? Or am I just an overenthusiastic believer of mumbo jumbo?

My eyes slide down the photo to the caption. Hamilton Township Police Department, Mercer County, New Jersey. Next reads the date. June 15. It is today's date. Thirty-six years prior, but the exact same day. June 15.

Jackie's been coming to me for nearly a year now.

Psychic. I just love that concept. Slap on a bright silky turban, lots of silver crosses and ropes of beading, and divine the mysteries of the dead. I want to do that. Stare intensely through the smokescreen of filterless cigarettes and reveal secrets of those passed on to the hopeful living. I could sit in a dim tent pitched on the Atlantic City Boardwalk and charge a buck a reading. And write how-to books. Too bad my only brushes with the mystical have been always brief and personal. Significant to me, suspect to all others. But this experience with Jackie has been different—long term. Sporadic, but intense. Spooky. And unmistakable.

When a spirit is close by, I've discovered, there is a pressure. A sense of someone lingering in your personal space. A physical body peering closely over your shoulder. Just the opposite of the dreamy states of imagination and wishful thinking. The sensation of moist breath against your skin draws your own clamminess to the surface—a fine skim of perspiration accompanied by a certain jellying of the knees. Menopause symptoms? Maybe. Except for the nudge of absolute presence and the sense of a powerful, extraordinary encounter. Menopause craziness leaves you exhausted, heading for a down pillow and a plush throw. A spiritual contact is electrifying. A transfusion of pure caffeine.

Jackie first comes to me through his own favored medium: drawing. I've recently taken it up because I am sick of writing novels that do no more than incubate dust mites in the shady corners of my closet. Drawing is a last-ditch effort to quell the persistent, maddening sense that's been haunting me for years—a prod and pull toward something I am to do. But of course, I have no inkling of what that something may be. Or of how to get to where I don't know I'm supposed to go.

Obviously, writing is not it. So I decide to try drawing and order dozens of art books and get down to the business of teaching myself the mysteries of lines and shadows, shapes, contours, shading, and all the rest of it. And soon enough, I take up the challenge of portrait rendering. I am no fine artist, but I can capture a likeness. And as each likeness evolves beneath my hand, a miracle occurs: suddenly the spirit appears and the subject glows from the inside out. And every time this occurs, it just about blows me out of my chair. It is always astounding. And always scary.

I don't know whether to fear this phenomenon or rejoice in its presence. Don't know if this happens to real artists or if it is just a novice apparition akin to beginner's luck that vanishes eventually beneath the cloak of hard-edged cynicism. Either way, I start thinking that maybe, just maybe, this is the answer to my search; this is my higher purpose. My calling.

And so, Jackie begins to reveal himself. Slowly. Unknowingly. In sketches of gaunt young males, slumped over in anguish that I draw feverishly, filling page after page with these penciled figures in differing poses. Hundreds of them. Obsessively working the angles of the shoulders, the droop of the head, the wash of hair over the face. Until I say, *Whoa, what am I doing here? What's going on?* Then begins the slow-yielding lift of realization, and in those sunken figures I see the eternally unredeemed. The permanently unforgiven. And I recognize my own self, naked and enfolded, skin against bone, never forgiven for my fall from grace.

But it's not me I'm looking at. It's someone else. A boy. A young man. But who? I flip back through the pages, then flicker them from beginning to end, making the sad figures squirm like dejected cartoons come half alive. And sink into a chair, my breath an audible sissing in the quiet. It's my brother. I've been sketching my brother, Jackie.

How many years has it been since I've even thought of him? Banished from all things Allen. Never ever a mention of him. That he even existed. Sometimes, sure. Between Phil and me, there were brief comments — a word here, a word there. I told Phil of the beatings, how Jackie was the hated one. Hardly any details, though, unless you count my reenactment of John J. Allen hurling crazily down the road, one hand on the steering wheel while the other swatted at the bodies crowded in the backseat, where Jackie usually caught the harshest blows.

I squint now into these simple graphic shapes, no more than pencil lines on paper, that somehow have accessed a mystery that does not retain its roots in dirt or in definable, explainable molecules. A mystical connection not called forth by devout prayer or the begging longings of the pious. What, then, does a middle-aged woman who favors sprigs of mint with her iced tea do when she believes that her long-dead brother — unforgiven and all but forgotten — is trying to contact her? What else? She laughs and shakes her head and says out loud again and again, *WOW! WOW!*

Even for me with my off-kilter sense of spirituality, this little event is so creepy, so eerily weird, that I don't mention it to Phil. But not because it's so wacky. I could easily say to Phil, *Hey, remember Jackie? Well, he's been nosing around in my sketchbooks.* And we'd have a big laugh. But this feels different, serious. Not geared for horseplay. I sense that I need to be respectful, quiet. Allow whatever is happening to unfold. But I need to be certain. If this experience is real, it must be treated with reverence. If it's just a screwy figment of my imagination, well then, the joke's on me. Truthfully? I *know* it's Jackie; the sensation of his presence settled already into my bones. But I believe that if I chase him, overwhelm him with my enthusiasm, or reveal his manifestation too soon, it all might fade away back into the world of the unknown. So I decide to wait. Listen. See what, if anything, develops.

And it does. How can it be that when I slide in a CD I have never listened to — one that was cut over a decade ago — a song swells and sweeps across the room in a ghostly romp? An achingly sweet tenor curls his bell-clear voice around his sorrow for his brother, a man who self-destructed in the flames of such acute emotional pain that there never could have been any other outcome but death? Days later, I slip a new DVD into the player to watch an innocuous concert and there is the same artist, performing that same song — the words, the notes, like outstretched arms straining, reaching for something. But what? What? Then again, when I am flipping through programming on television, there he is once more, the singer touching through this song his own grief — and now mine, as well, which is beginning to stir. Through that pure, clean voice that speaks of the pain only his brother could know, I begin to see something I have never before been aware of. Not the pain of the injured. But the pain of one who injures.

Some time ago, I began creating a piece of art I call *14 Beaumont Road.* Outside, the illustration is of a lovely suburban split-level framed in climbing roses. Inside reveals the images of a naked girl trapped between two looming male figures. The subject matter is aggravating and repulsive, and I don't understand why, when I'm left to my own undisciplined devices without the structure of negative spaces and precise measurements of portraiture, I create such stuff. *Dark art,* I call it. For no reason I can fathom, today I am inspired to revisit Beaumont Road. Called by impulse to furnish it with the proper dignity of completion, even though it lives out of sight, stuffed beneath a guest bed.

Only minor details are left to be added, and I am dabbling with my colored pencils when I am struck by an overwhelming sense of urgency that seems a response to a frantic call for help. Of course it is impossible, and you will have to call me batty, but I actually hear the phantom little-boy screams of my brothers from nearly fifty years ago. Intense screams, pitiful crescendos of fright and pain echoing from their bedroom just above mine. Cries fleeing down the stairs like flames, rushing beneath my door, bolting through the house, all the way down to my mother in the rec room as she smokes cigarettes and watches Milton Berle on television, then back upstairs again. Begging, pleading cries. Surging and gushing and finally exploding out the windows into the night. Shattering the summer music. Crickets. Tadpoles. The lonely call of the whippoorwill. Songs all quelled by four little boys and a man with a belt. The screams that on Beaumont Road embarrassed me but now chill me to aching.

And so the brothers who do not speak to me cry out in a way I don't even bother to question. Because really, what's the use of arguing? My art has tapped an extraordinary channel of the inexplicable; now I just shrug my shoulders and allow my hands to be guided. So I validate the abuse my brothers suffered. Instead of the few final flourishes I was planning, sealing all with my initials and the date, I insert a window in the upper level — a portal to my brothers' childhood bedroom — and surround it with tiny photos of the four boys. Within that window, I place the silhouettes of a man swinging a belt at a terrified little guy, not much older than our grandson. Seven? Eight? This idea brings such pain that I can barely finish.

If you have never communed with a spirit, I will tell you that it is exhilarating, challenging, all carried out on an emotional, intuitive level. And it leaves me exhausted. Excited exhausted. Unnerved exhausted.

Humbly exhausted. Jackie needs something from me — I am sure of this now — but I do not know what that is.

Running through the woods by our house many nights, I hear the beagle. In the pines, nights are pin-drop quiet; all noises from this theater of silence ricochet amplified. The beagle circles the woods endlessly, all night, barking five, six times successively; then there is a lull when I imagine him sniffing, nose to the trail, tracking what he is searching for. Then another sequence of barks. Then the lull. This goes on for hours — barking, sniffing, running in circles, searching for the prize he never finds.

I place on this little creature the human emotion of frustration. My frustration. Knowing I'm on the right trail but not knowing exactly what I'm looking for — only that I need to find it. And even more exasperating: what am I supposed to do if I actually happen to stumble across what it is I'm looking for? Will I even recognize it? It's not like it will be toting a sandwich board with the big announcement — *Here IT is! YOU'VE FOUND IT!!!* And OK, say I do find IT and say I even recognize IT. What then am I supposed to do if I don't want to do IT? Or can't?

I don't do things that get my hands or feet unnecessarily wet. No clay work of any kind. I will not submerge my fingers in cold, oozy slip and create a defining shape on a potter's wheel. No earth toil, either. I will not plant a tree or a bush for Jackie or maintain a memorial garden. Too many bugs. I will give no dirt the opportunity to burrow beneath my nails. My family labels me finicky for a reason. This would not come as a surprise to Jackie, who himself kept his massive collection of comic books in perfectly ordered piles. He tried for symmetry even in the rear of the '57 station wagon as John J. Allen two-tired the curves on the hot, spongy roads to the shore, all the windows rolled down to the sap-scented blasts that rifled the pages where cartoon heroes, Jackie's supermen, saved kids from the tyrants of the world, one whimsical feat at a time.

So yes, even a ghost must allow for my persnickety nature. But in spite of everything, assuming I do manage to crack the ghost code and decipher what Jackie is trying to tell me — or ask me — I may not have the ability or knowledge, or whatever the dead who chat with the living need, to be able to do anything for him anyway. As much as I don't like comparing myself to that dopey beagle incessantly chasing his instinct, that's what I feel like. Only my ears aren't floppy; they're perked. And I do my circle running in the daylight.

On my lap is the day's newspaper. Most times I bypass the dreadful and flip straight to the gossip — lightweight fluff that does not unsettle the dinner I've just enjoyed. Does the page just fall open? Or do I nonchalantly breeze through sections I never read, my eyes accidentally landing on the exact right spot? I can't say which, but my gaze falls upon a sketch of a man slumped inside a cardboard box. With the courtship of that grieving-heart ballad, I know by now that I am not experiencing coincidences. This figure uncannily resembles my images, only more fleshed out. "The true story of a much-maligned kin reveals a war hero," the headline reads. "Clearing Cousin Clifford" is the title of the article.

I sink into the piece and let the words swim about me like the familiar, unsettling waters of Gropp's Lake, a distressing site from my past that I have no wish to revisit but would recognize instantly if I were to go there. It is the same now. I recognize my brother in this story of parallel tragedy. Two men, not much more than boys when they fell off the path, forever lost, made kin by the same life truths. Both discarded. Addicted. Years spent stumbling in the gutter. Both men, decades apart, died destitute and alone — their funerals, cold governmental tasks. Cousin Clifford, too, died as Jackie did, in the bleakest of all places, unredeemed. There's a photo of Cousin Clifford, so sad in its short-lived image — a scrawny kid clutching two giant fishing poles. The writer wants us to see the teenage Clifford, the boy about to set out for an afternoon of barefoot pleasure in the days before he became consumed by forces he had no strength to fight. The time of *before* — a time, perhaps, when Cousin Clifford had dreams, as Jackie did. The once-upon-a-time that still held hope.

The writer, a distant cousin of Clifford's, searches, and in the end uncovers stunning bombshells about Clifford and gives him an amazing gift. She makes a splendid public announcement of Clifford's World War II heroism. Around here, the *Philadelphia Inquirer* is as big as it gets. And so Clifford, long dead and hopelessly disgraced, is miraculously redeemed. I stare into the text, each word a singular petition knit together to form a plea.

A personal love note written for Clifford that has somehow made it, this night, to my lap.

Via what? Did it float down from a cloud and land on top of all other newspapers at WaWa just before Phil made his selection? Why the *Inquirer* today instead of the other paper he often buys? Dumb luck? A thunderbolt to the senses that shouted, *Hey buddy, over here. Buy me! Buy me!* Who knows? Life doesn't get any loonier than when you're two-stepping with a ghost. There are no rational explanations. They've become unimportant, anyway.

Because now I know. Now I understand what I am being asked to do. Everyone needs someone's prayers, someone's good thoughts. Everyone, even the most wretched among us, needs some kindness. This is what Jackie is asking of me. Unlike the author of the story, I know I will find no surprises about Jackie. Well, not good ones, anyway. Still, through this series of strange occurrences — the only way, I suppose, that a departed soul is able to communicate — he is asking me to send him light. Finally, I get it. Finally. Light. Jackie, who lived his life in such tormented darkness, is pleading for light.

This revelation, this unmistakable linkage to the mystical, seems sacred. Reverent. A time for *ahhhhs* and whispers. I should lean back in my chair right now, fold my hands, and offer up a prayer. But come on, it's also nutty. Ridiculous. And I could rip this entire tale to shreds with quick, biting sarcasm. Oddly enough, though, it wouldn't matter. Because I've learned that spirits, including God, have a grand sense of humor. No smart-ass retort I could come up with would deter them anyhow. Besides, I am relieved that I can do what he's asked without getting my hands wet.

I play a little guessing game with Phil. "Guess who's going to be on our Christmas card this year?" This is the third year I've illustrated our card. It's always some kind of family thing. He knows I am planning to draw our four grandchildren. That's what he guesses; of course, he's wrong. He keeps at it a little while, until I say, "*Jackie.*" Outside of the orchestrated facial contortions of a comedian, have you ever seen anybody's jaw actually drop? This is the only time I've seen it in person. It's really funny. I mean, his whole face melted down on itself. Picture ice cream sliding off the cone. When he regains his voice, Phil asks, "Your brother *Jackie?*"

So I tell of the sketches, the song that steals through time and space and breathes into me something astonishing: compassion for my brother. My art piece, now not only a witness to my own girlhood agony but also permanent visual testimony of the trials of my brothers, who have never in my presence even hinted at the sins committed against them. And now the article of redemption—the guy depicted living in a cardboard box so similar to my own drawings barely cold on the paper.

"Jackie's asking me to send him light," I explain, as if this should be obvious. "So I'll draw his picture for the card, and maybe when people get it, they'll smile at his portrait and there'll go the light, straight up! Phil, come on now, don't you get it?" I'm insisting more than asking. "Jackie asked me to." It's not every day I speak of pleadings from the deceased; I understand this kind of thing takes some getting used to. All Phil says is, "Why is it that the only one of your brothers who talks to you is the dead one?"

Since I am keeper of all the old Allen photos, I rustle through the disintegrating pages of moldy albums—all the photos, fading now, affixed with tiny black triangles—searching for the Jackie of *before*. Before he became what was done to him. Before he jumped and condemned himself to a darkness the likes of which I cannot imagine. There's nothing great, but I settle on a fuzzy print of him in his Confirmation regalia and a baby picture where he's posed on a rocking horse, laughing as if all about him is there simply for his enjoyment. He's twelve in the one photo, right on the cusp of his fateful course. And the sadness in his eyes is oppressive and transparent and taps the soft core of the nurturer within me, and I question how a parent could ever look into those eyes and not ask why.

So I begin with a fresh sheet of hot-pressed paper and an array of pencils—graphite and charcoal, Bs and Hs, and a collection of blending stumps. I am wading into my brother's artistic territory, though he would have never had an assortment of creative tools at his fingertips. As his pubescent face emerges from the lines, I experience his presence so intensely that I can feel his tears drop onto the back of my neck and slide down my spine. It is as if I am giving water to one gasping with thirst. And I am embarrassed at the modesty of this gift that is no more than marks on paper but feels somehow graced with significance far beyond its worth. A simple offering of light that seems weighted with rescue.

Never would I be able to call to mind the minor details of Jackie's face, but as I render them — the smallness of his nose, the slight cross of one eye, one ear protruding more than the other — they are so intimately recognizable that I am astonished that these memories are stored and ready for recall. And many times I become so overtaken by his dispirited presence that only a few minutes of effort is possible. But I finish, and on the drawing above Jackie's picture, I ask, *What Is the Meaning of Christmas?* The verse on the inside is lighthearted and airy; my prayer is that people will greet this effort with a smile and that in some mysterious way Jackie will receive their smiles as the blessing of light.

Right here, right now, I want to interject levity, shrug this spiritual encounter off as dalliances of a menopausal mind. That's what a logical person would do. That's why I can't. Because there is more — a subtle but monumental shift of personal bearing for both Phil and me, as the exquisite and baffling converge to chart a new direction.

I'm biting into homemade pizza and silently musing about what to do with the Christmas cards lingering around. It's already January, but before I can decide their fate, I need to take the time to reread them in case one requires a response. Jackie's card is on top of the pile, and I wonder if anyone took the time to send him a blessing when Phil says, "I want to publish your book." As usual, I roll my eyes, but now I hesitate before telling him no for the thousandth time. He is talking about the novel I've written — *In the Clutches of the Beast* — that is currently taking up space in a plastic box in my closet.

It's a neat and tidy, cleaned-up version of my past. I like it because, besides being well written, in the end our heroine kills herself. It is her personal act of vengeance over her circumstances; the only solution to her despair; the way she finally succeeds in having her voice heard. Of course the ending is extreme, but where I come from, suicide and homicide are considered viable options to an unhappy life. And if you've ever written a novel, you know that your characters take over and tell you what to do anyway.

Suicide is what my character insisted upon; I simply indulged her.

Phil wants to self-publish. What else is there? My manuscript was rejected so many times that I decided I alone could save a forest if I would just stop wasting the paper it consumed to submit it. This was before the advent of e-mail submissions, where you could save trees and be rejected all within the same day. "It's time to tell your story," he says. "If only so we can pass it on to our children. To the grandkids."

Isn't this some kind of psychological hierarchy-of-needs thing where we oldsters take inventory and prepare to impart our wisdom to the young whippersnappers who have relegated us to the land of the permanently befuddled? Tell them stuff only we know, like how to use the sunset to predict the weather or determine when a cake is done just by the smell? *Philllll*, I say, planning to decline loudly, dramatically. But I stop myself mid-thought. As annoying as a mosquito buzzing beside my ear is that voice that likes to whisper truths. Truths I do not want to hear. And in the irritating manner of all good truth-tellers, the voice calmly reminds me that my story is already being told. And not by me.

This is not news. Yet the merest suggestion of this injustice stings me in all my unprotected places, landing low blows that instantly wrench from me all dignity and thrust me directly into a rage that I struggle to control. The adoptee, the second-generation predator's revised and polished version of the agony of my girlhood ordeal and declaration of it as a love story, continues its rounds to anyone who will listen, including my family members, where she casts me as a worldly, popular teenager in love with my heart's desire. And to her proclamation she has added the brutal strike that, as I think of it now, leaves me shivering and sick to my stomach. This adoptee asserts that I was well aware that *he* —the rapist she has molded into a genteel knight—was sexually active, saying not only that I am a liar, but that I am to blame and deserved whatever happened to me anyway. She has been wreaking this havoc for nine years. Nine years. Suddenly, the pizza staring back at me looks congealed and oily, unfit for consumption.

There is a hate that lives beyond forgiveness. Forgiveness has assigned to it activity, fervor. That hate seeks revenge, retribution, and ultimately, healing. This hate, the kind I've known since childhood—reserved first for John J. Allen, then for the rapist, and now for the second-generation predator — is colorless, frigid, settled into tissue and fiber like an inherited trait, as innocent as a dozing rattler. Should you ask, I might say, *I don't hate these people, these demons who have with such casualness devastated my life.* I'd say this only because I don't normally feel its blister, its furious call to action. I'd say this because this cold, detached loathing is so much a part of me that I live with it as I do my blood.

This, I think, might be the most dangerous kind of hate. It is a perfect wound. Untreatable. Never to be healed. It lies in wait. Impassive. Patient. Forever watching. Always at the ready of a whistle to sink its teeth into a pulsing jugular.

So I believe it must be this polar hatred that nudges me now to look up at Phil, and in the muted, slow voice of silence first budding into speech, I say, "Maybe." Not because I ever want to even consider the formal laying down of my story; I don't. It's ugly. Ugly. I say *maybe* because I'm trembling anew with anger as I do each time I am reminded of the wall that I have been pushed up against by the second-generation predator with her merciless, despicable lies. And the fear those lies generate: fear beyond the normal, expected fears — those of sickness, unexpected deaths of our beloved whose names we offer perpetually in prayer. Human, commonplace fears.

This fear, though, my fear of slander, moves into the territory of phobia. Except it is not irrational. Slander has proven itself to be an effective assassin. It has destroyed large parts of me. And since this blight has crashed into our lives, I agonize obsessively that *her* lies will creep inside the protective inner circle of our family and the poisonous gas of her malicious invention will be lethal and unstoppable, seeping far into the future to come to the attention of destiny and become twisted, accepted facts. And all that I have worked so honorably to build, the love and respect that lives inside our private boundaries, will be flattened beneath her lies. And the feeble cries of my truth will be completely smothered. Just like back then.

So I listen to Phil as he makes his appeal once more — an appeal that I am coming to sense is driven by something other than his determination with its rough edges and hardy stance. His appeal feels purposely, firmly motivated by...all right, I'll say it...grace. An amazing, powerful grace.

Grace as in sacred. As in spiritual. Grace as in spooky. Scary spooky.

At this moment, between us, corralled on our kitchen table, I feel the strong press of the words I do not want to say. Words, as solid as objects you could handle or cut through with a blade, all straining against their forced confinement. Words craving the form and structure of sentences, paragraphs, punctuation. Words craving life. Words I dare not speak, shouting now, *Come on. Come on.* These words pressuring me are not of the prose written in my novel—lovely turns and sanitized truths created to spare the reader and shield myself. Oh, I edge to the cliff. But I don't look over. And I certainly don't jump.

No. The words beckoning me now, offering their challenge, are horrible. Treacherous. Words capable of mining pain and despair. Unvarnished. Inelegant. Crude. Gutter crude. Words of truth that, of course, I do not have the courage to say. Because to speak fully of my past is to return to its bowels. It is to touch and smell its stink; suffer the yellowed sweat of fear; feel the boundless expanse of a hopelessness no different from imprisonment. I imagine my former self a specimen caged inside a bell jar. On display. Stripped of all protection—clothing, dignity. Publicly degraded for the sexual gratification of a vermin. Passersby laughing, whacking the thick glass with sticks. Me properly vanquished, staring downward, forever voiceless.

How dare these words—no, how dare the spirit—implore me? As if all I have to do is open my mouth and casually enunciate. As if these words did not drag with them the scorching blaze of humiliation, the anguish of betrayal. The unspeakable agony of my own self-betrayal. No, no, no. The spirit is powerful. But not powerful enough to move me.

Until I look at Phil and I am somehow reminded that for these lasts months we have been experiencing miracles. Not spectacle miracles, where broken bodies are restored by the sight of a holy icon, but small, personal miracles. When I tell you that my brother Jackie was hated, I am not exaggerating. How is it then that we have come to love him? How is that after a lifetime, we have come to comprehend, even honor, his humanity, after all he has done? I am such a sucker for a good psychic phenomenon saga. And this tale, I have to admit, has hocus-pocus written all over it.

So, maybe the spirit does move me. Let's say it shifts me. A little. "Look," I say to Phil, "we both know that *The Clutches* isn't really my whole story. There's a lot more. A lot. I'd have to write something else. Another book or something." He looks at me and doesn't say a word. Maybe he's scared that if he does, I'll growl at him and tell him that this whole thing is stupid. There are times when Phil knows to stay very quiet. "I'm telling you, Phil, my story isn't something anybody will want to read. It's ugly. And people don't like ugly."

I am completely and utterly convinced of this. My story is too ugly for the light. Phil needs to hear what I am saying. He needs to listen to reason. He needs to ditch this idea permanently and worry about routing the bats from the attic. But all he says is, "It deserves to be told. It needs to be heard." He says these things, I might add, very softly.

But there is this reality, a barrier that gates me inside its walls, a barrier I am completely incapable of breaking through. Literally, I am a woman in hiding, under deep cover, running always from my past. Crippled with so much shame that I still awake nights weighted with disbelief, shuddering, hating myself for being that girl, despising that ever-identifying slur, that despicable stain still being smeared all over me — *birth mother; Kathy Allen, unwed mother* — a looping, stabbing curse; slimy ejaculate that never washes off my skin. Identified forever by the come the rapist drilled inside me.

Birth mother, unwed mother, biological mother, I am called. Yes, even today, over forty years past, I am manacled, soldered to the rapist, to the eternal flame of his engorged penis. And I cannot bear this ignorance of civility, of the common courtesy denied me because of what happened between my legs. I have rejected my past. With huge shears I have cut out a gaping hole from the center of my life. Years exterminated, never brought to mind, all because of abuse, its stigma, its humiliation. Degradation made sport.

And yet it is a past that will not, despite my very best efforts, disappear. It has been resurrected again and again, by the second-generation predator — goading me for what? Nonexistent love? Entitlement? Revenge? It has been recalled from the ashes by newspapers and magazines with their sentimental "reunion" stories of love lost, love restored, those rosy articles that encourage and tutor the lost to hunt down the hiding. And it is also recalled in all those dusty governmental files, where my past is permanently romanticized, officially designating me as a mom in an apron waiting to serve up apple pie warm from the oven.

I have a record, the same as a felon: I will be forced by the State, should the whining adoptees have their way, to register my whereabouts, to disclose what marrow fleshes my bones. This record will never be expunged, no matter how much time I have served; no matter how much good behavior I have exhibited. I am legally documented as *Mother* in the files of Catholic Charities, in sealed State adoption records, and termed so by the State of New Jersey as it freely argues my fate. Relentlessly referred to as *biological mother, birth mother*—as if rape were my pleasure and what grew inside of me its honored gift. It reminds me over and over that I am forever the whore—a whore whose future was sealed on those filthy mattresses, obligated to the growth jammed inside me, duty-bound to graciously accept the permanent consequence of assault, under penalty of public contempt. Under penalty of law.

Sitting across from Phil in our hushed kitchen, I am squelching the urge to shriek; I feel its boil inside my skin, bingeing on my anger. The hidden abscess of my perfect wound unearthed and salted. *Rape isn't making love,* I say. My tone is a low, scornful snarl that shadows his eyes with pain—the pain, I think, of any husband who doesn't have the power to heal his wife's anguish. "Nobody ever calls a woman who had an abortion *mother,*" I say. I spit out these words, these truths. I embody anger.

At this moment in time, I am in unholy communion with the darkest souls who snap. Just snap. But it's never *just*. It cannot be *just*. Those souls turned monsters, whose storm of wrath manifests pure destruction, don't *just* snap. They seethe, I believe, for a very long time. How can I be this? How is it on this January evening as iced-over pine boughs crackle beneath the might of winter outside our door, and pizza sits in a puddle of grease on my plate before me, that I am empathizing with the ones who, with total composure, clear their pathways of tormentors?

I do not dare even call their names to mind. Lists of the country's infamous. Blood avengers. Are they me, except once removed? Do they battle this identical free-floating, powerless rage that has nowhere to land?

Until they make it so? Might my rage embolden me if I were born of a touchy temperament and driven hostile? This rage that now circles and circles, a vulture trussed to a tree by a certain length of rope, kept always mere inches from its strike. A voiceless, futile wrath endlessly searching for a place to spend itself. It is unsightly and frightening, my rage. And what if someday it explodes? Outward?

My thoughts spin now to all those certified, validated records poised to be thrown open by overfed minions fawning for votes who refuse to hear the cries of the silent. The cronies who nod their heads, feign sympathy, and do what they were planning to do anyhow — appease the big mouths. I want to rip into those official records, gouge away all evidence of that intolerable slur, and in thick black letters, scrawl a description of my own choice: cunt. A vulgar label. Capitalized. C-U-N-T. What I was reduced to by the rapist. A cunt. Out of which burst *his* full-blown seed. BIRTH CUNT. The accuracy of this term, its vileness that lumps in my gut, stalls in my throat and finally grates across my tongue, thrills me with its precision. Its truth. *Biological Cunt.* With it comes no confusion. You would never expect apple pie from a woman labeled *cunt.*

But my anger, however deeply rooted its ravenous appetite for revenge, wilts beside my fear. Yes, my secret is out, freed into the world beyond my hiding place, but I live tethered to its darkness, terrified of it always. What does it matter that the events of my past were forced upon me? Do you think shame cares? Do you think shame's finger points to the guilty? Shame *owns* the victim. Always. No truth-telling can ever set me free. I am bound in fear by the living descendent of the rapist, of her torments, of her clawing at the flesh that remains on my bones, of her raiding our family. Pillaging loyalties. Robbing what I cherish. I imagine her sidling up to our children and grandchildren, casting herself as victim, reeling in my loved ones with her sobs and pathos and cunning fictions.

"Who the hell would want to hear my story?" I ask Phil now. "It needs to be told," he repeats. His words are solemn, issuing from a place I don't understand. What I do know is that whatever is inspiring him to coax my story out into the light is crazy. Phil's crazy. The spirit is crazy. Amazing grace is crazy. It's all nuts, and it's all ganging up on me with one huge *please.*

Maybe I should wag my finger at Phil from my chair across the table, waving it high above my cold pizza. It would be a great, dramatic flourish of anger, of pending surrender to some damn thing that feels larger than me. Some God or Jesus thing that is growing bigger than both of us, growing larger even than my fear.

Instead, I forgo the drama and just shrug — a wimpy nod to possibility. An unconvincing yield to my daily prayer for the highest possible good. It's something that I say every day, maybe ten times a day or more — *may the highest possible good be served.* But I never expect to actually have to submit to it. That's God's work, not mine. What do I know about the highest possible good? Unless it kicks me in the butt, as it seems to be doing now. So yes, I shrug and say, "I guess. I guess I'll try." And in my best cynical voice, I warn, "I can't promise anything. I don't think I can say the words. I'll do whatever. Whatever." Then I toss Phil a dirty look and slide the pizza into the trash.

I mess around for months making notes about my grandmother, aunts and uncles, about John J. Allen, my mother, my brothers — especially Jackie. Sherwood Avenue. Beaumont Road. And I stay away from the really bad stuff, the stuff with the power to kill. I fill journals and transcribe them onto the computer, pages and pages of words. Mostly, I fool around with my art. I order lots of supplies: books, paper, pencils, paints. Gel mediums for the neat, funky papers I am collecting, planning to create collages. I write and illustrate a couple of books for our grandchildren. I am having a great time. I dance around the perimeter of my story, a happy little butterfly flitting among words I love.

Until today, June 15, and Jackie's mug shot with today's date, minus the lapsed years. And this heavy, nagging sense of commune I cannot figure out. I stare into my brother's image. "I've already done his portrait," I muse out loud to Phil by way of picking through this unnerving sensation of unseen presence. "What else could he want?" We are quiet, sitting on our porch, rocking, listening to the newborn chickadees peeping for food, the squawk of the Eastern Phoebe who has made her nest just above the screened door. What is this struggle between Jackie and me that does not end? This sense of forward motion that feels stuck? What does he want? Phil takes a sip of coffee and looks over at me. "Maybe," he says, "now Jackie wants to help you."

June 15: the day I get hit between the eyes with a brick. And it hits the spot it was aiming for. I only guess this because a sudden light flicks on inside my head, kind of like in the old days when a good swat to the side of the television set was the only thing that brought up the picture. I know now that my answer has to be yes. *Yes* to ditching the attitude. *Yes* to getting down to writing my story in earnest, using the words — all those damn words that have been hounding me. *Yes* to crawling back down that path to darkness. I don't know why I'm saying *yes*. I do not understand what kind of good it will serve. I only know that the nagging sense of restlessness is vanished with this decision to become a storyteller in a family of secret keepers.

Staring into Jackie's face, I take in the clarity of his defeat, of his hopelessness that is a silhouette inked upon the arc of a bright sun. And I know his story did not have to be. And I also know that it is buried back there deep in the dark, somewhere near mine. Two kids, trying, but failing miserably. So I will write the story. Our story. Maybe Phil does know what he is talking about. Maybe somewhere along the way it will catch the sleepy eye of a wayward miracle and some benefit will arise from its dreary truth.

The truth. There is no freedom in it as the faithful claim. Not for me. Since the truth of my past has been revealed, I am only more of its prisoner, growing smaller and smaller inside the hiding place it has erected for me. How can I even consider tattling about what I know of my parents? Of describing John J. Allen's cruelty, when he prided himself on his public appearance, on his hair sprayed into a stiff wave, his bowties, his freshly ironed shirts? All delivered with an easygoing smile, a joke always at the ready? How can I write of my mother's nonchalance as the screams of her children settled like welts at her feet, while her immaculate beauty flourished beneath the poetry of John J. Allen's devotion? Of both of them, in their parenthood, readily allowing me to carry the burden of malevolence, NO QUESTIONS ASKED?

What is the value of exhuming truth if it will tarnish the image that this couple, so in love, worked to create and keep? What of my own past, infested with my failures? Why should I display once perfectly good flesh, now infected with pathogens that continue their creep? I willingly accept the bitter price of a secret's protection and gladly ingest the poison that leisurely eats away my insides but leaves my facade intact. Don't you remember? *It's better to look good than feel good?* The truth, I believe, will lead to nothing but complete destruction, my own included. Nothing else is possible.

How then, as I place my entire body on this path I am about to walk, could I ever imagine truth's strength? Not as a trite saying, but as bedrock from where a life can be reborn? How can a girl who was born into a family where secrets consume entire lives, who grew into a woman frozen inside her own darkness, possibly comprehend its enormous power? Even as it encases the ugliest words fathomable, dripping its offal and contamination across memories, well into the present? How can I possibly foresee its power to build when I only know its penchant to destroy?

On this day I am bruised with doubt and fear. As I look down at Jackie's mug shot, then over at Phil, I have no idea that there will come an afternoon when I will stand on the ugly, unshakable ground of my darkest truth and launch myself into a freedom I never knew existed.

Today is June 15, 2007, the day I think I am nothing short of insane. The day I say yes.

CHAPTER 20

Ten Years of Torment

"She wants your medical information," Phil says to me, from where else—across our kitchen table, where these bombs are always dropped. There's no pizza lazing in grease this time, only the detritus of a crock pot stew of some mystery meat I don't remember because I only eat the potatoes anyhow. But I level a stare at him that rises instantly from the sharp freeze laying waste to a certain portion of my heart. That swath of hatred that I have always known could make me an executioner of high regard, enabling me to flip the switch, tighten the noose, inject the poison, and simply turn and stroll right back to my magazine and Tastykakes.

It is the same hate that wished John J. Allen would gag and fall dead at my feet. The same collected loathing that had me gouging Jackie, trying to kill him until I ran out of little-girl muscle. And the same covert rage I was too frightened to expend at the rapist. It is glacier and absolute and deadly in its desire to destroy. And it is daggering its ice as I glower now at Phil.

"She's got some medical issue. A lump or something," he explains in his best soothing tone. Phil always tenderfoots these advances, hoping to avoid upsetting me. It never works. "I don't give a shit," I reply with such contempt that it drips off my tongue like sludge.

"George thinks it would be in our best interest to give in to her." George is our attorney, George whom we've known for over thirty years; he's on *her* side now. I've known this for a long time. I don't know when she flipped him, but sometime over these ten years it happened. Not that he would admit it—he doesn't have to. It's all there, the ghostwriting between the lines. His friendliness toward her; referring to her by her first name. Seeing what he can do to encourage Kathleen to be reasonable. Little inside jokes have crept into their communications, a flirtation of sorts, a familiarity that has turned into a backdoor betrayal. A vague shift of loyalties that hints at misconduct, so easily ignored, dismissed as imagination or misconception, even paranoia.

Because he's just being nice. What's the harm in being nice? And that is what George wants of me. Niceness. Acquiescence. It is Phil who must correct George's tenor in the communications to the adoptee, eradicating the hopefulness George weaves between his words, the promising under-speak of softening — my softening. This casual arrogance, of the unraped, the untraumatized, spiked with such cruelty, stuns me every time. Since the days of John J. Allen. Bighearted misdeeds window-dressed for the sly debauching of young, juicy meat. Injustice pimped as virtue. It is the loft from where the shockingly ignorant portray themselves as noble; from where they hurl righteous misconceptions and stinging declarations, to betray one in the service of indulging another.

It is from this swagger of exquisite blindness that George does not hear my *nos*, however loud, however forceful. What he hears is *maybe*. And those *maybes* leak into the fantasies of the second-generation predator, bolstering her resolve, her belief of "one day." So with this mom-and-apple-pie sentiment, George does not protect me from her intrusions, her behavior that borders on criminal. Maybe her attention, as she turns to him with her neediness, flatters him — the involuntary flush that warms all our lonely spots when we believe we are genuinely called upon to minister, when we cannot see the deception smirking beneath the phony tears. Or maybe she pierces within him the soft raw longing of paternity, and he must help heal this very troubled woman. He coddles the adoptee stalker and loiters in the cunning of his grand delusion lapping up her slobber and sucking up our money while laying fresh nicks into that ancient wound of mine that never heals.

And I give in. Goddamn it, I give in. Even though I know I am being bullied. I have felt its low punches enough times, camouflaged blows to the plump swell of my belly just beneath the ribs that knock out my wind and leave in its stead singe and scorch racing for victory. I am not supposed to notice that George coerces me — that he believes that if I would just give her what she cries for, she will be happy. With such a storybook ending where the princess wins over the wicked witch, George will be the hero.

And all will smile. Except for me. But I will come around eventually anyway, so George thinks.

For now I am to see only reasonable action. Understand that I am merely submitting to a simple invasion of my privacy. Just a minor listing of, you know, all that I tell my doctor in private. What I am to see very clearly, however, is the warning that dangles like a two-ton boulder over my head: if I don't comply now, later I could be forced. By the State. By a judge, should some type of legal action be instituted. And how unreasonable would my refusal appear then? Why, there's no telling what some future judge could accuse me of. Contempt? *I confess.* Willful concealment? *I confess.*

Chills whisk unseen across body angles and crescents. My gut spins acid. My brow draws into tight, dark furrows. All my bulk and senses converge and blast their warnings, igniting the frayed edges of my nerves. *Don't give in to her. This is just another ploy. She is a stalker. Giving in to a stalker is a personal invitation for more nonsense. It is the way of bullies, of predators. You know this. Stand your ground.* I reel as all this thunder and sizzle roils against my bones. And I whack it away. Once. Twice. A hundred times. And give in. I goddamn give in. And I goddamn resent myself for it.

Yes, I give in. And worse, I surrender with dignity and grace, when I ought to seek my revenge. Invent lists of dreaded diseases. Strike fear, create disorder and chaos as has been done to me. But I don't. I surrender without a fight. And ask of myself integrity.

As always, as I have done since John J. Allen, I condemn myself with congeniality, so as not to offend, so as to do the right thing as defined by the good Catholics, the etiquette police, and strangers on the street. It is a sacrifice I begrudge. I can barely tolerate my obedience, my serene acquiescence, as I list the maladies of my family and go further—I write a letter to the predator. A lovely one. Sending wishes of peace to this woman of pathetic woes. *Yes, you were conceived in rape,* I say. *But that does not define who you are...* I reiterate my firm refusal of contact; the same words I have been stating over and over for years: contact is impossible; it is never going to happen. I don't rant. I don't vent. I do not say what I really want to say: *Leave me the hell alone.*

There is a price to pay for what I have done, this personal abandonment of self. And it is anger that sags into the sputters and pauses of fear.

Phil commends my acquiescence as courage. Grace under pressure. He is wrong. I am just disabled somewhere in the center of my spirit. A huge chunk of me is missing in action — destroyed in battle, maybe. Too frightened to stand up and say NO. *Damn it, NO.* Because of what might happen. Someday.

So Phil gives my family medical history to George, along with my typed letter, for forwarding to the adoptee. And George does what every person does when he thinks he has won. He smiles. "I see Kathleen's letter as a breakthrough," he says. "A real possibility for a reunion, as hope for a happy ending." I look at Phil, stare at him as he relays this, and just shake my head, close to tears. Close to exploding. Close to disintegrating, while what holds me together sifts outward like dust through riddled cloth. George and his gallant vision of a reunion. Of Kathleen. And the rapist's spawn.

"I'm so pissed," I say to Phil, "I don't even have words." I swallow. Hard. Call for my composure. "Reunion? Reunion?" I finally manage. But I am stuttering, my speech a bounce of flames and bullets. "What the hell is it with this reunion shit? There is no reunion. I have never met this fucking woman. OK? Never. Met. Her. Why does no one get that?" I suck up air, hold it, release it slowly to the count of five. But my heart is thrashing as if I've just sprinted the three miles to town and back.

"I get it," Phil says. "I get it."

I think George has never been raped. I think George has never been forced to breed. I decide I hate George.

~ ~ ~

Ten years. God, it has been ten years since that day in Kelly's kitchen and that drive to pick up Phil from work. And the fear in his eyes. The terror in my own. Confessing. And all the rest of it. Ten years of torment. Am I to be grateful that I have not been, for instance, battling cancer for all this time? Thankful that things aren't worse? My body could be putrefying, right now as I speak. I could be no more than a stump wheeled about on a gurney. Do you know of that woman on the Atlantic City boardwalk? No arms? No legs? Lying there on a stretcher? Playing "Amazing Grace" on her keyboard? With her tongue? That could be me.

In fact, that darn well might be me if I don't start falling down in gratitude for this blessing of torment—because it could be worse. Once when I complained to my mother about my fat thighs, she said, "Would you rather be your grandmother with gangrene rotting your legs?" Give me a minute to think: a decaying old lady fighting off flies or a girl with fat legs? Ouch. Look, I grew up Catholic, and there are codes and certainties. Even if I am a lapsed Catholic, I take the trials-and-tribulations principle very seriously. Even though I am failing, you can see that.

I never give thanks for the rapist, the adoptee, John J. Allen, all the Georges of the world, and all their life lessons that I could just as easily learn without their benefit. No. I damn them. I resent them. I stop just short of wishing them dead, though two of them are. This is sinful, of course. As is my refusal to keep turning the other cheek, my unwillingness to be generous of spirit. Not smiling in the face of adversity. It is all spitting directly in God's eye. And this can cause a lot of aggravation. For me. And for you. Because in the Catholic code, pious suffering and godly sacrifice help save the world. And there are consequences for offending this religious policy.

Such as becoming a stump. Or causing someone to become a stump. Though I'm not quite sure how all this works. Believe me, only a nun with a pointer and a chalkboard could explain it. But I know it is all tied up with starving children in Africa and eating everything on your plate, and Italian women in black stockings crawling up mountains on their knees. And fax machines. Because nobody knows how they work, either.

So here I am, an ingrate, quite possibly risking my husband's arms and legs that could, at this very minute, decay and fall off. And that would show me, wouldn't it? Me and my lousy attitude. How would I like changing size-large diapers and stinky bandages on Phil's stump of a body? Listening to everybody whispering, *I knew him when he was a cop. He was so strong. Now look at him—no more than a stump.* That would teach me to be grateful for abuse and rape all right, and for the predator adoptee. Because what if I didn't even have a vagina to be raped in the first place? Then what would I do? I'm telling you, there is logic here somewhere.

OK. OK. So I heed the fire-and-brimstone mind lectures and decide I can do gratitude. It is simply a matter of gritting my teeth and tolerating the vise crushing my skull. And ignoring the devious part of me that scorns, *You are such a damn wimp.*

So I send mental blessings. Pleasant prayers of peace and prosperity to those on my shit list. Yes. Fine blessings. Every time I feel anger begin its climb and all I want to do is beat my fists against concrete, I stop, take a breath, and repeat my soothing mantra of bountiful blessings. This lasts about as long as it takes to spell *R-E-A-L-I-T-Y.* Because in this pursuit of holiness, real life intrudes and there is this other maxim Phil reminds me of that I have forgotten to consider: *Things always get worse before they get better.*

CHAPTER 21

Out of Hiding

For ten years, Phil hounds New Jersey legislators. And they give him assurances. They will call and invite him to testify before the Senate Human Services Committee when they begin their public debate about unsealing adoption records. Yes, they surely will. And no, they don't. Not one. Is it because he represents me and I am hideous — the hag with the warts kept locked up in the attic who has escaped? and now chances to mess up everybody's orderly notions? Because I am not supposed to exist. A girl. A woman. With a name. And with a story that might scar the tidiness of the committee's fantasy ethics.

Our legislators have their stand now. It is deemed that the adoptees shall have their way; sealed birth records will go the route of transistor radios and saddle shoes. And back-alley abortions. All this decision needs is official sanction. What it does not want is the messy story of a girl who was raped into pregnancy and then tormented by the adoptee. And what about the promises that pregnant girls and women were made when they signed the adoption forms — the guarantees of confidentiality and anonymity? The promises that gave a girl her life back? Oh, well. You never see the blood when you stab a woman in the dark.

We, of course, are losing the fight to keep the records sealed, to keep women safe inside the lives they have created. No terrified woman ever comes forward to testify. To what? Face the hordes of angry adoptees packing the room? Who glare and whisper snide comments at testimony that dares breach the sanctity of their personal suffering? *What about the baaaaaaaaaaby?*, one adoptee will whine. And the reporters who treat us as if we sold the kids to drug lords and now live fat off the gains? The senators who do not see they are strapping us into stirrups while giving the public dirty speculums to dig into our vaginas? Then, of course, there is the one senator who bears the attitude that, well, women have already been found, despite the sealed documents. What's the big deal? As if keeping the door locked after your mother has been raped is useless, even though your wife and daughter live in the same house. It is a world spun and capsized for those of us who believed promises.

A few women in hiding send letters to the senators. I read them. They are anonymous and sad. And these faceless women always apologize. For the unwanted pregnancy. For the circumstances that led to the adoption. And they beg to keep their anonymity, to be protected from those wanting to hunt them down. From those determined to reveal their secrets. From those who demand their secrets. In all the letters these are proper women, benevolent and virtuous, who speak of what was best for the child. They plead only that they be given the same consideration now, all these years later. They appear pleasant, courteous women who do not complain of what they have endured — even the ones who were raped. They ask only that their secrets be kept. There are no raves of anger, only sorrow and fear. We are women who beg.

Phil is the face of women in hiding. Only professionals — coalitions with specific agendas — step up to speak. The ACLU, the Catholic Conference, the New Jersey Bar Association: all fine organizations fighting for the common cause of rights to personal privacy. Each has its own sterile purposes, all so easily dismissed. None of them speak from the hidden bleeding ghetto of wounded girl parts.

Phil slips in to give testimony by way of the ACLU — a pairing as odd as, well, a cop teaming up with a liberal defense attorney. "Two and a half, three minutes," the area director of the ACLU warns him. That's all anybody gets. Phil is worried about what he might not get to say. About how he will represent me — all the women in hiding — honorably. His is the only first-person testimony ever given before the committee. Finally, our voice will be heard. I write a statement for Phil to read. Though it is like every letter of every woman in hiding — expressing sorrow for everyone's pain, pleading for understanding and compassion. But I tell my story of rape and stalking. Somehow I am fighting for my life, though I cannot explain this.

What I do not do is allude to my fury. This I keep politely hidden, never hinting at what festers deep in the perfect wound ripped open ten years previous. A wound that is now loose and unwieldy. Ceaselessly furious. Never do I mention that a *fuck you* is in order to what feasted uninvited on my flesh and now lunges for more. Nor pronounce my unrepentance for wanting to dig out of my uterus what was growing there. Or apologize for the belief that what slid from the low regions of my girl body is solely of the rapist. Or express my anger at abortion denied me. I am polite to a fault and never demand what I am entitled to in this society that changes its agreements: a legal, retroactive paper abortion, certified official. All contents sliced and diced and dumped into a virtual bucket. So that at long last I am freed. The committee owes me this as price for the promises it intends to smash.

Phil is not an angry man. He is cranky on occasion, and frustrated more than he'd like, but not angry. Though I cannot prove this from the way he storms into the kitchen. "I thought I was going to see breasts flashing," he fumes. "It was disgusting. I really thought one of the senators was going to flash her breasts."

Uh-oh. The Human Services Committee hearing obviously didn't go so well. "Our government in action," he continues. "It was like a damn rap concert, and every senator there was caught up in the big party. You should've seen them; they were like groupies." A celebrity showed up to give testimony—a celebrity who also happens to be adopted. A famous adoptee with a poignant story.

Run DMC captivates the senators and spectators with his artistic persona, his notoriety. The glow and buzz surrounding him makes it easy to yield to his story presented as stage entertainment. Run DMC goes far, far beyond the allotted three-minute limit. He captivates and performs dramatically. And one senator, a former local celebrity herself, so utterly enamored, calls for an immediate unanimous vote to pass the bill out of committee—refusing all others the opportunity to speak.

"It made me sick to my stomach," Phil says.

"Didn't you get to testify?" I am not sure I want to hear the answer.

"I testified," Phil says. "For three minutes. But at least twenty others didn't get a chance. There was one senator who really listened. At least there was one."

Not that it mattered. The committee voted unanimously to pass the bill. It does not take long—a few days, a week: word of Phil's testimony before the Human Services Committee must race on all pumping fours around the militant adoptee community. Our lawyer, King George the Delusional, forwards e-mails from the predator.

"Look," Phil cautions, "I don't want you to get upset about this. You need to be angry." I hold my breath against the roller coaster my body insists it is riding. "She's spreading our address around the Internet, apparently asking every low life she knows to send us some kind of evil. And she's e-mailed out a rant trying to dig up one of her adoptee buddies to get me to shut up." He shrugs, unfazed. "And listen to this: she told George to warn me not to show up at the next hearing. 'Tell him I don't want to see him there,' she said."

Fear settles over me in a cumbersome, weighted lethargy. I struggle to keep my eyes open. They burn with…what? Unspent tears? Strain? The need to just close them and give myself over to the pull of numbing sleep? In a bizarre trickery of emotional time travel, I am once again fifteen years old. Trapped in a commotion of threats, sinking somewhere far out of sight. Into hiding. Into safety. I know this is not so. I am here, feet planted on our kitchen floor. On the porcelain tile that is of the gentlest green, it reminds me of fresh, even with its scuffmarks and water stains. One hand is resting atop the day's mail that Phil has deposited on the center island, though it is not an island at all. It is more a sideboard of rough pine that is stained pale mustard, a color I love. My right hand presses against my chest, which feels bony and underfed, rushed there in the automatic way of persons who have just received news. Disturbing news.

I know I am not now fifteen years old, wavering at the bottom of a dark set of stairs with its curtain of swamp odors, gamy sweat rising sour from damp wood, the stench of an unflushed toilet drifting downward as I am being steered upward. Plump meat. Up the stairs, holding my breath through the stink, my clean white sneakers touching, touching the human slough and peelings colonized along the risers beside moldering leavings and something sticky that latches on to the rubber sole of my shoe. Juicy meat. In the slow-motion climb that is too quick. Rushed into the bedroom. Tender meat. To the mattress with its contagions and broad stains of secreted waste. All for the price of a few threats. Tendons and flesh ripped from defeated prey. Chewed. Swallowed. A gluttonous binge of torn labia. The feast so moist. So succulent. An intoxicatingly tight squeeze for a vulture plundering fresh meat. My girl body silently ravaged, my entire life quietly marauded for the price of a few threats. My entire life raped. Because I believed as gospel *his* threats, even those held only in *his* eyes — the same eyes as John J. Allen's — full of glaring malice. And now *her* threats crawling over me. Warning me of what *she* is attempting to destroy.

I am not that young girl. I am not back there. I am here in this kitchen, standing on this floor, staring at Phil. But the threats feel like the warning of spittle on my face, of her vow to continue her torment. Because she enjoys pleasuring herself with my agony, doesn't she? She's already stripped me in front of my family, forced them to run their eyes up and down my naked, swollen body. Paraded my shame out onto the street, dragged it behind her as some prize, preening herself as she went — didn't she? When she promised she would not take no for an answer, she told the truth. And despite wanting to employ some common sense, I am, once again, that cowering young girl wishing only escape, the blunt drag of sleep. Shrunken into a far corner. Listening from this vanishing point as Phil pleads, "Get angry, not upset."

Maybe that is what a regular woman would do — handle this rationally. Point to this adoptee predator as a crackpot, a pathetic lunatic. Brush off her threats as the ravings of a mind unhinged. But I am not regular. I am frightened of shadows portending evil, the evil I know personally. Over and over again Phil repeats, "Stop giving her so much power. She has no power over you." But I believe she does. In the way of evil. How it curls unnoticed like thin milky smoke beneath closed doors and poisons all it touches.

Assessing threats. It is the oddity of this, the absolute bizarre nature of even considering that we need to think of weighing and evaluating options. It transports me into a vague, embarrassing sense of grabbing jugs of purified water and dry matches and scurrying to the bomb shelter because the

Russians are coming, the Russians are coming. But the only ones who show up are the Boy Scouts. But what if the Boy Scouts are Russians trained by men in face scarves and saggy loincloths? It is humiliating to be taunted, to have a complete stranger clamp on to your life and shake. And shake until the surface where you stand is no longer solid, but a swaying, lurching sieve of twigs.

Is this adoptee-turned-predator dangerous? A permanent, menacing creature skulking the perimeter of our lives, lobbing ever-bigger grenades at will? Whenever she gets pissed at her kids? Or starts foaming at the mouth because the bank is threatening foreclosure on her two rooms and a bath? Or gets depressed over scoffing down an entire gallon of Ben and Jerry's and decides that yelling *GERONIMO!* and chucking a Molotov cocktail through our living-room window is easier than hitting the treadmill to relieve the *I can't believe I ate the whole thing* angst? Or does she screw up her medication schedule and become snared in the wild current of her mental fireworks and go haywire? And figure, what the hell, and aim her double barrels at us? Is she simply a sad, lonely woman, an alien to her real life, wandering about constructing a fantasy world to brag about? Harmless as a bag lady sporting layers of rags, spouting nonsense? Her cruelest deeds behind her? Or is she malicious, wanting and willing to destroy more and more of what she cannot have, as she has demonstrated?

I do not know the answer. I only know what stands directly before me. And she rallies her cohorts against us — to create more chaos, more damage. Are those cohorts other militant adoptees whose Web site reads as a war zone? I do not know how to frame any of this other than through my experience. Or construct as meaningless this echo from my past when it all feels so evil.

How much time passes, I don't remember, but it could easily be counted without the aid of a calculator. Twelve days? Two weeks? It is long enough for a lull to begin its gentle lapping and comfort me with the thought that just maybe she has finally run herself ragged and her tormenting days are over.

To date, no storm trooper adoptees have parachuted onto our property demanding a kidney as reparation for my offense of being rescued by the adoption process and wanting to keep it private. Though I think these antagonists will have their way, sooner or later. Women in hiding shall be found. As for the deceased secret keepers? It'll be up to their kin to sort it out. Dead women? Living women? Seriously, is that important? Whatever it is that we women in hiding clutch so tightly against our sagging breasts is what the adoptees covet. But it does stink of sweat and desperation, that scratching and grasping to be counted as a member of some ragtag collection of strangers that could draw its legacy, as my family does, from pornography, rape, child abuse, and an assortment of addictions and mental disorders too long to list.

But maybe what I'm really smelling is the bitter tang of retribution not easily masked by cheap perfume. I see what you do not see. All predators wear polished masks and cry on cue. Perhaps credit should go to my father, who hid cruelty behind his bow ties and smiles. Or the rapist who wept and lured from his poor-me con game. Maybe I'm twisted, made hyper-vigilant by those malicious characters rooted in my dark years, vermin that still live back there crawling around like lice.

But I know how pretty can curl its way around mean and make you believe it's savoring fine wine when what it's doing is chewing on mucus too thick to swallow. Predators have a certain cunning for the art of public boohooing. Who wouldn't feel for a cancer-ridden, asthmatic orphan with a limp? Look, I would. At first. But mean always gives itself away. And the predator adoptees' mission of sneaking up behind old ladies and yanking down their underpants has nothing to do with pretty.

But here's the good thing: with fewer kids available to be adopted, legalized abortions, and open adoptions where everybody is one big, happy family, militant adoptees are a dying breed. Who needs guerilla fighters when the village has already been plundered? After all we old-timey ladies have been stripped of our old-timey secrets, what's left?

The maternity homes we once holed up in as frightened girls are gone now, replaced by a new world order of proud ingénues flaunting their baby bellies. Planned Parenthood peddles reproductive services in the finest newspapers, promising sterile environments where mistakes and catastrophes can be discreetly and confidentially washed away. Right-wing screeching and hysteria aside, abortion is legal—for now, at least. So far removed from...*before*.

Today there are options even for the unrescued girls among us whose spirits have been fatally wounded. Whose souls and wombs rupture and spill blood and agony. Girls, stifling cries, who give birth in secret. In a public toilet. Or a dark closet. Alone. With terror. And shame. Alone with *it*. Girls who know what no other human can possibly comprehend or accept as real — the flash flood of panic that whips her into mania or stuns her into gluey lethargy. Of fumbling hands swaddling her shame in a ragged towel. And wobbly legs that *must* rush. Because she must...she has to...get *it* away from her.

These days a desperate girl can bypass the Dumpster and take it to a Safe Haven. A firehouse. A hospital. And walk away, unidentified. She'll be branded despicable, a monster, or a would-be baby killer by vultures on the local news. But her leaking body won't be chased by bloodhounds. And the kid will live. Who that kid will clobber when she grows up and rages over this injustice, I don't know. But it won't be the woman in hiding.

So militant adoptees' days are numbered. And short of harnessing herself into a chute and belly flopping onto our front lawn, and barring the passing of any brilliant laws calling for the forced surrender of DNA samples and living body parts, what else can this individual predator adoptee do to me?

She's heralded her lies through villages and town squares, inserted herself as family with those of my relatives willing to humor her. Gotten me to fork over medical information. Plus for good measure, flexed her muscle with a few unsettling threats, though I am coming to believe these are perhaps more wishful than physically dangerous. And so far she hasn't issued any further warnings for Phil to shut his mouth. All small signs of hope as spring approaches and green begins to poke through the crisped brown piney grass. February slides easily into March, the month of crocuses and forsythia. And this year, Easter. It seems a perfect time for new beginnings. Not a forecast for a perfect storm.

After ten years I should not be surprised by sucker punches that hit low and mean and seize my breath with direct slams to the gut. But I am. Maybe it's because I am always otherwise engaged. Looking the other way. Or just too dense to have learned needed lessons. I never see the shot heading for my solar plexus, and always, before I know it, I'm hammered.

Too startled to react. Confused. Punch-drunk. Staggering like some damn old boxer too weak to stand, too feeble to strike back. It is what I pay for relaxing my guard and convincing myself that finally the predator adoptee has tired of her spite and decided to leave me be. But it does not happen. Ever. It has been ten years, and still she straight-shoots acid into a wound that never heals.

It is my mother who seeds this last great flourish of agony, a mushroom cloud that will balloon and drift its way forward through the years, all the way to today, to unleash its toxin. My mother has no understanding of this as she sits before Sister Social Worker in that spare, bitter office at Catholic Charities. While temporarily banished, I am sitting somewhere outside its closed door, slumped inside my black raincoat, my pallor surely as ashen as the walls and floors scummed gray, trying to shield my face from a boy I know from school who sits with his own mother just a few chairs down. And, oh God, what if he knows what I am hiding?

My mother in the office. Does she hold her head in her hands and cry? Before she betrays me, does she glance up at the crucifix that is always in these drab ecclesiastical tombs, golden and ornate with a finely sculpted corpus? There is our dear, dead Jesus, fully human — except for his…um… erections, which we fanatically believe never occurred — who weeps at our frailties. Jesus fully divine, who scares the hell out of us as he condemns us for those same frailties. So that we hide and don't seek the truth. Because any messy talk about genitals, Jesus' or anyone else's, is strictly forbidden. And if it happens to be your genitals in question, you must accept facts: the what, how, or why is always unimportant. Your genitals, your fault. Indisputable. No one — not your mother, not even Jesus, who is rumored not to have had a penis anyway — wants to know what happened in the sinister regions of your body.

So there is my mother in my belief, positioned before church authority and the penis-less Jesus himself. Does she draw a pained, ragged breath before she abandons me? Hardly. It is not the way of her family. Her betrayal glides out smoothly, easily, oiled with relief, saving her own vagina from scrutiny. Her own wretched secrets protected, she can shove me off the ledge and remain Catholic. She can burden me with sin and stay virtuous;

display her wounds — the injuries inflicted by a wayward daughter — and be embraced as a martyr. And there is Sister, her own self, purity in motion. Unsullied by the sins of the wanton, above reproach, she hides nothing dark and shameful beneath her black habit — nothing she would admit to, anyway, least of all to the sinner crying in front of her desk. The pious nun sits in judgment and my mother knows this; my mother has to save face. This is an inherited maneuver, instinctive and polished as any sacramental ceremony. Open your mouth and betray. Open your mouth and lie. It is my family's chosen method for personal preservation.

But I long now to reach back to my mother sitting on the edge of the raggedy vinyl chair before Sister Social Worker. Lay my hand on her leathered, sun-freckled forearm, and by the warmth of my blood radiating into hers, melt her terror of the truth, persuade her of its powers of restoration. Of its promise of wholeness. Convince her that it is not truth that destroys life, as her family has taught, but the other way around: it is the lies and secrets that sicken and mutilate. I want to rewrite history, somehow instill my mother with courage, show her how to straighten her shoulders and stare unflinching into Sister Social Worker's scolding eyes, defying Sister's assumption about me. About her. I want to shake my mother out of her submissiveness, chase away the fear that cripples her, as it does me. Wake her from her oblivion.

Think, Mom, think! I want to scream, rousing her from her self-pity. I want to kneel before her, beg her to see the potential that lives inside me — potential that stands to whither under the burden of her guilty verdict. I need her to stand up and protect me. Protect me, not herself this time. *Mom,* I want to say to her now, *look at me. Look at me. Help me, please. Mom, help me.* I want to lean into her sad, beautiful face and warn her how the opinion she is about to deliver will boil and fester, and forty years hence explode into my life in an attack so unexpected, so brutal, that it will leave me reeling and demolish all that is left of my dignity.

I am not asking you to confess your sins, I would tell her. *Just don't condemn me.* Even if all she can give is a half truth, at the very least she could admit that she does not know the answer to Sister Social Worker's question. *Mom,* I want to plead now, *you've never even talked to me about all this. Just tell*

Sister you don't know the answer. Because you don't. And that is the honest-to-God-truth. At least half of it. My mother does not know the truth. The other half is that my mother does not want to know.

But of course, the past is committed. No one changes it. So to appease Sister Social Worker and absolve herself, my mother answers yes. *Yes. Yes, my daughter is partially responsible for what happened to her.* And in the quarter rests between her words, my mother paints joy on my face as I ride up the escalator at the World's Fair as grease-stained fingers dig into the bare flesh of my exposed backside. With her betrayal, my mother pulls from me lustful, sexy moans while I drown in despair on mattresses teeming with crud. And Sister takes detailed notes, in ink, on her official forms. In that stark office, cooperating with Sister Social Worker as Jesus looks down from His sacred perch, my mother links invisible hands with the rapist and says yes. *Yes, my daughter is partially responsible for what happened to her.* And sacrifices me. And saves herself.

I am folding towels in the laundry room — in half, then in thirds — and plunking them on top of the dryer when Phil sticks his head in. "She's at it again," he says. I don't need to ask who. "We just got a bunch of e-mails from George." I stop, look at him, then return to folding. In half. Then in thirds. "Do you want to know or not?" No, I do not want to know. I want to bury my head far into the sand. I want to run as fast as I can into the woods out back, my hands slammed against my ears, and keep running and running. I do not ever want to hear from that lunatic again. Ever. But first I have to fold these towels. And yes, I have to hear.

"Do you want to sit down somewhere?" Phil asks. "No," I say. "Just tell me." I stop folding and turn toward him.

"It's about your mother. Somehow the predator got hold of information from your file at Catholic Charities. Evidently, your mother said you were partially responsible for what happened to you. And the predator is circulating this all around the Internet as proof that you weren't raped."

I start folding again, ignoring the rush of heat to my face, the numbness sponging up my knees. "Is that it?" I ask. "Why don't we go sit down," Phil suggests.

Is it more comfortable being butchered on a downy sofa than in a laundry room? Since there aren't any beef cattle lolling around to consult, I make my own decision and stay put.

"I didn't know you wrote a thank-you note to Sister Social Worker," Phil says.

My body falls into a slow melt toward the floor, but of course I remain upright in that old amazing way of crumpling while appearing impeccably composed.

"She has a note you wrote to the nun where you thanked her for all her help. It was in the file, and somehow she got it. Or a copy of it. Or something. Anyway, she's circulating that around, too. Calling it proof that you were in love. Saying you're a liar. That the note proves you were never raped like you say."

This room is too tight, too stuffy, too sweet with Tide and mountain breeze-scented fabric softener. My heart is too noisy knocking around in my chest. Phil is too calm as he looks at me. Something, anything, needs to explode. Maybe the dryer. Its gas line is inches from my face. I need it to rupture, burst into flames so hot, so bright, that I am incinerated on the spot. Instantly. Because I can't, I can't bear defending myself anymore against this woman's hiss and strike. Hiss, strike. Plunge fangs. Hiss, strike. Into the fevered, abscessed wound.

My mind scrambles in a mad dash back to…back to…when? Sitting by myself on my bed at lunch break at the hospital? Yes. My feet throbbing from standing all morning on a cement floor, my body fattened with its shame. Scribbling my anguish onto paper. Then sealing those open wounds into an envelope addressed to my parents only to have them tossed back to me swabbed with John J. Allen's mockery. Shouldn't I have understood by then that John J. Allen, his casual cruelty, lives in everyone? But that had to be exactly what I understood. Terror is the only reason I would have licked Sister Social Worker's dirty boots with thick syrupy gratitude. Terror that she would break her promises to me would have reduced me to belly crawling on fresh stationery in flowing, slanted script. I have no memory of writing this thank-you note. But of course, I did. I don't remember eating Sister's boots, either, though I would have done that, as well. Asked, I would have even turned my beloved mother over to the Communists. Short of rendezvousing with the rapist, there was nothing I wouldn't have done to get my freedom back.

"There's more," Phil warns. "She's really been digging around in your past. Evidently she located some of your old friends. They told her that you were in love with this guy. They called him a real catch. They told her the pregnancy was common knowledge. And that you even named her after your best friend. Did you do that?"

Phil asks this by way of curiosity, I think, though I feel accused. Rounded up in a sting, hauled before a judge. Pronounced guilty by the authority of doubt. If only I would give up the rape bullshit, admit to the love story theory, we could all go about our happy little lives. This is what I hear in Phil's question. Accusation. Suspicion. What, in fact, I hear in anyone's questioning or ignorant comments about my dying time.

I struggle to inhale, but my breath stays shallow, swallowed by heat and burn and the bitter taste of bile that bolts from my throat to the bottom of my gut. "I would have sliced her out of my body if I could have," I say to Phil in a clipped, savage tone that could easily sever a man in half. "I never named her. Tiny Sister told me the damn nuns named her. And I hated that bitch for telling me. I didn't give a shit what they did with the kid. I never met her. I wanted nothing to do with her. I want nothing to do with her. I have told you everything. There is nothing else."

Phil knows he has just stepped on a landmine. And now half his foot is missing. Ask me if I care. I don't. Trauma leaves one nasty boot print, and rage is it. And this rage does not fake nice. My rage takes names, records every insult, and will glare you down and snarl, *Jesus forgives. I don't.* It is my gangrenous leg; my humped back. It gives no apologies and offers no compassion. And no amount of meditation, Valium, or therapy will ever erase it. It just is. Postscript damage. Blatant. Livid. Easily riled. And the best I can do is manage it. At this moment, I am not doing a very good job.

"I'm on your side," Phil whispers.

I suck in what air I can, compel myself to breathe even as I surge toward eruption. Suddenly I despise all those idiot gurus who call for inner peace and absolute serenity in the face of nuclear anger. Right now I'd like to string them all up by their gonads. But the rational, undamaged part of me, the part trying now to get my attention, knows Phil would hack off his own foot if it would help me. And he knows that no less than a blood apology will ever lure me back into reason. An offer of penance as big as my pain. And I'm going to be waiting for that foot. The left one will do.

I cannot choke down dinner. Or fall asleep in the grip of this woman's malice. Or pull my mind away from the girl I was at the hands of the rapist. Then, living under the threat of Sister Social Worker, who had the power to restore my freedom or withdraw its promise at the stroke of a whim. Over and over my mother's words taunt me, chanted in verse by a circlet of sadistic little girls in ruffled dresses, skipping to its cadence — *yes…it's my daughter's fault…yes…it's my daughter's fault.* Maggots and vermin infest my dreams when finally sleep seizes me.

The dreams last only for minutes though, because my eyes flash open to the sound of the phone. Except there is no ringing — only the peal of rage thickening the blood in my ears. It pounds louder and louder as I imagine Saint Nancy, the Social Worker at Catholic Charities responsible for rooting out all sins of the flesh, ransacking my confidential file, stealing its contents: Sister Social Worker's intake entries, my mother's accusation, my groveling self-betrayal written in my own hand — all the damning, intimate minutiae. Couldn't Sister have at least politely averted her eyes instead of feverishly logging the agonizing details of me whimpering, clinging to my mother? Details, among all her other noted details, that would forty years hence be perverted and used to reignite the blaze of vicious gossip? In the approaching months, I will come to know just how unconcerned Saint Nancy the Social Worker is as she pores over my records and swipes from its pages echoes of indescribable pain and awards it all to a grinning stranger. Saint Nancy will bat her eyelashes at me as she defends her good works and softly praises herself for the empathy she feels for the old women she's bullied into confessing. And will remain unfazed by her betrayal that has brought me to this day — a lying slut of a whore, held by the scruff of the neck, marched around the virtual public square of cyber space by a gloating victor.

The unholy ghost that prowls the night shackles me and hauls me back to the past, back to the girls who once ripped me apart piece by gory piece with their gossip. Now they've escaped the glossy pages of the 1965 Hamilton High School West yearbook and, talons splayed, pounced on top of me here in my bed. Aged girls still lusting after a good smear campaign, even if it has to be sprung from the grave and fed rotten meat. I feel their dancing feet stomping, stomping on my chest. Can hear the cluck, cluck of their tongues against their lies. Those lies flocking and gouging my skin, crowing at the spurts of blood, cawing for a free-for-all binge. Those familiar, savvy lies that know how to bite and squeeze, and elbow their way past the truth, and burrow deep to sow their poison.

Whether these girls — crones now — stagger around trying to look sober with flasks concealed in the folds of their housecoats or zip about in electric wheelchairs racing between nickel slots and all-you-can-eat buffets is anybody's guess. But I do not think that many beady eyes are peeking at *their* shriveling vaginas, speculating aloud about *their* ancient breeding grounds: have the old gals' privates fallen into disrepair? Found new life as for-rent sex widgets servicing horny geezers in the same apartment complex?

What I know as true is that these women have voracious appetites and a taste for roadkill. Though I shouldn't be, I am amazed that strangers peeled from the dirty undersides of my past are brazen enough to be so open about their identities. Flick on the lights and guttersnipes always scurry for cover. Not these ladies. There they are, strutting proud on our e-mail, name tags and all, waving from the garbage pit.

None of it matters, though, in the middle of the night when pull-out-my-hair madness washes over me. I can go out to the street and run eight miles but cannot find the strength to fight lowlife biddies with chin whiskers and hormonal mustaches. My last prayer just as the birds begin waking the world with their gentle songs is for the savagery to commit sweeping, cold-blooded acts of revenge.

Whether I dream this or it arrives via a flight of fancy I can't say, but I am running. Swift tracks across nowhere, to anywhere away. Running. Ducking. Hands over my head. Legs, arms pumping. Faster, faster. Then I stop. Just stop. For a few seconds I stand rigid. Breathing very slowly.

Then raise one eyebrow on my face grown just this moment cold and hardened, and calmly turn around, my eyes leveled in a fixed, dead stare. I see this image as clearly as if I am watching it on a large screen, and I know I am done. I'm done.

It's just past seven thirty, and Phil left for work only minutes ago. The scent of coffee still lingers as I walk down the stairs and into the kitchen. His chair is slightly askew, the cushion probably still warmed. In this weird state of absolute composure, I pick up the phone and call him. "I'm done," I say. He's not sure what I mean. "I'm done running. I'm finished. It's over. She's pushed me as far as I'm going to go. I'm not running anymore, Phil. I'm not hiding anymore. I'm done. She can call me slut and whore. Keep calling me a liar. She can dig that rapist up out of the dirt and put him in Superman tights and call him a hero. I don't care anymore. I'm done running. I'm done hiding."

I put the phone in the cradle and head back up the stairs. I must be rabid with anger. Or drunk with fatigue. Or just plain whipped from the ten-year chase, all sense gone. I don't know. But all of a sudden it occurs to me that I possess a vagina of public interest. How many women can claim that? How many women can brag that their vaginas and all their goings-on are on the most wanted list?

I am caught in a Vagina Vortex. The adoptee wants my vagina. Catholic Charities raided my vagina. Over forty years past and my vagina's still discussed in the tract houses and cul-de-sacs where I grew up. Then there's the State of New Jersey not only laying claim to my vagina, but wanting to make official announcements about it. I think I have missed something very important in all my years. They all must be right: I must have a wonderful vagina. I start laughing — not the laugh of a woman driven insane, but the laugh of someone who's just heard a hilarious, demented joke. *Help! I'm being swallowed alive by my own vagina. I can't get out of its way. QUICK! Call 911! Forget about the terrorists. Worry about my vagina. It's got the power....oh, Jesus...*

Shortly past noon, Phil calls. How I'm doing is not his only question. The *Philadelphia Inquirer* is putting together a piece on the New Jersey adoption records controversy and wants to interview us. Interview *me*. Am I interested? "Why me?" I ask. "Because no other woman will come forward. It's your voice or none," Phil answers.

It's been but a few hours since I've stopped running and hiding. Hours. Not weeks of pondering and analyzing: hours. I'm still swirling about in the Vagina Vortex. I haven't had a chance to tiptoe to the ledge or peek around scary corners yet. "When?" I ask, thinking next week might be good. Two weeks even better. "This afternoon," Phil says. "Three o'clock."

The reporter shows up at our door with the air of a spring bouquet. Sweet, delicate, looking freshly plucked from journalism class. The shine on her silky black tresses has surely been coaxed by expensive silicone products bought in a high-end salon where stylists sport orange hair and rivets in their tongues. Her almond eyes are black and intense. And yes, kind.

Not once as I tell my story do I notice the razor hidden behind her shy, accommodating smile. "I'm talking too much," I say to the reporter. "No. No. Please. Go on." So, I do — unveiling my pain, revealing my wounds, giving her all she needs and more. I am a pitifully easy catch. "Good-bye," we say, waving. "Thank you for coming. Thank you for giving us the opportunity to speak." The reporter smiles and waves back. And dives in for the kill.

I don't feel the knife until Phil hands me the morning paper. We're on the front page. Oh. Here right in front of my eyes. Look. She's quoted me exactly. Oh. Ooooh. I get it. I get it now. The reporter yanks a quote: *All I wanted to do was get rid of it.* And wedges it next to her comment: *Mrs. Foley said, speaking of the infant.* So it reads, "All I wanted to do was get rid of it," Mrs. Foley, said speaking of the infant. And on it goes, my hard, unflinching statements snatched away from their explanations and shoved up against loving family scenes and the ever-so-unimposing snarky comments from the reporter, in an article cluttered with standard loss and longing, aching-arms sagas.

There in newsprint for all eyes to read, she strangles me with the wire noose of sappy, contrived family ties. Any mention of rape and stalking are dubious afterthoughts. So I get it. I am not included in this article to offer differing experience, an opposing perspective. I am simply an example of the self-indulgent, promiscuous bitches withholding the human rights of adoptees — a would-be baby killer, eager to do anything to get rid of the kid so she can continue living in greedy, wanton splendor while the poor adoptee sobs away her miserable life. Boy, do I get it.

When the *Bergen Record* calls, we are down the shore burning up the road — me in my supremely-engineered running shoes, Phil in his two-for-one bargain sneakers. Before we left home, I threw the *Inquirer* in the trash. I am trying to hold on to that anger, not let it burn down to the pinch and swell of emptiness, where hopelessness is just waiting to fatten itself on my stupid candor. Where it will waste no time working itself into a frenzy, pointing its finger, indicting me for damaging the cause of women in hiding who have no voice as it is, and damn little support. And who the hell do I think I am, spouting my dark truths, fucking everything up worse?

So I need to stay mad. Like Phil. Keep my fists balled and jabbing. Keep that damn despair on the run. Phil's anger more pulses than shivers, and it shows up in long, quick strides, in the whomp, whomp, whomp of his size twelves punishing the road. I can hardly keep up. At the other end of the cell, the North Jersey reporter asks for a phone interview. Before I can stop it, my anger slithers away and defeat slips easily into the void. And I shake my head no. Honestly, what is the point? Just to have my remarks twisted and distorted, used against me? Generating hate mail?

But Phil talks. Well, he does more than talk. OK, he explodes. I can't believe the reporter doesn't hang up. Phil fires off words like *vultures, corrupt, setup*. She does not even yell back. God, I can't believe she's letting him go on unchallenged. The shore is deserted on this drizzly March day, and after Phil hangs up, the beat of waves on the sand is the only recognizable sound.

We are silent for a few blocks. "There has to be a place for this truth," I finally say. "I know it's dastardly ugly, but there has to be a place for it."

Why do I say this when just twenty-five miles away buried in our garbage is black-and-white, front-page evidence of the hostility I invite by speaking? I must be certifiable, because I continue, "I just…I just feel like we need to keep talking. We have to keep saying the words. No matter how ugly they are. We have to say the truth."

Phil just shakes his head. "You're sounding like me now."

He calls the newspaper back and apologizes to the reporter, who is gracious and understanding, and in the end, writes her article without sawing off all my toes.

We log eight miles through the salt air and eat our packed lunch overlooking the bay that smells of brine and is shrouded in thick, gray mist. A seagull screeches at us for the entire thirty minutes, demanding whatever it is we are eating and not sharing. Phil gives in and throws it pieces of apple. Not me. Sorry, buddy, all crumbs are mine.

Just as we reach the bay bridge on our way home, Phil's cell phone rings. It's a woman from the Catholic Coalition, which along with the ACLU and other organizations is fighting the legislation seeking to unseal adoption records. She is responding to the complaint Phil lodged about Catholic Charities compromising my personal file. And she wants to talk to me. Ugh.

I take the phone. Syrup drips from her voice. She's chatty and friendly. *Oh, the silly things kids do, blah, blah, blah.* I don't know what she's talking about, so of course I chuckle and answer, *Yes, they sure do.* But there is no bridge from light to dark, and when she asks me what happened and I tell her about how Catholic Charities released my note and my mother's exact words and my crippling embarrassment at all of it being paraded around the Internet by the adoptee, she treats it like a slightly humorous anecdote.

"Well, I don't think there is much we can do about this," she says, and instantly switches the subject to adoption and tells me how I did the right thing.

"It was rape," I say. But I really want to shout away that buoyancy in her tone. I want to tell her I had no choice. I wanted an abortion. And no, I did not do the right thing for me. But she is Catholic, and I can't be disrespectful. "Well, you still did the right thing," she insists. And the perk in her voice is a burr grinding into my patience.

"She laughed at me," I tell Phil, handing back the phone. "She laughed at me."

I can't stand any more looking at the bay shore through this drizzle. I want warm and sunny, not damp and dreary. I want to smell roses, not seaweed and decaying fish. I don't want to see abandoned shacks and weathered, broken hulls plunked in the middle of marsh. I want colors, damn it — red, yellow, pink. Purple. I want to blow up.

"There's got to be a lawsuit here somewhere," I am nearly shouting.

"Who would we sue?" Phil asks.

"Cool and rational is not working for me right now," I snap.

"I'm just asking," he replies.

But he's right. Sue who? An attitude? Mrs. Happy Catholic? *Your Honor, she giggled about rape.* Sue a charity that believes bullying and betraying are God's work? An unstable adoptee with mental-health issues who would pounce at the chance for face-to-face combat?

"And how do we prove damage?" Phil asks.

"Phil, stop it!" I hate that he's being logical. OK, OK. So I'm not a corpse with slashed wrists. And so what if no shrink has declared me stark-raving mad? I glare out the window at all the ugly flying by, and grit my teeth with each tar bump the car takes like a pothole. They have it all wrong, the engineers and scientists toiling over the energy crisis. Just hire a few really pissed-off people and plug in. My anger alone would power the whole of New Jersey.

I NEED MY VAGINA BACK. I WANT MY VAGINA BACK. I could punch fists through the window and screech into the fog and flats of salt water until I'm hoarse. Shout myself crazy about vaginas and freedom, shriek righteous savage screams. Rant about who stole my vagina. And who's holding it hostage. Swear to God to do no more pleading. No more playing nice. From now on — demands. That's it. That's what I need to do: demand exclusive rights to my own vagina.

Oh, but there's little pleasure in imagined fury. No relieving climax. So the knotted ball of it just bumbles to my feet while I wait to disintegrate inside its mania.

Until a muscled, beefy gladiator of a thought springs from the gloom. "I want my note back," I say to Phil without thinking. The potency of this tiny statement rips through me with the buzz of a caffeine jolt. "I want Catholic Charities to give me my note back."

Am I serious? Get a bureaucracy to flex?

"They've abused it, Phil. They don't deserve to have it." Then I take a deep breath for this bald-faced fantasy: "And I want Catholic Charities to amend my file. I want it to tell the truth. I want it to say rape."

I will have my way. Somehow, I will get my way.

No matter how brave, how committed, however determined I am during the day, the middle of the night always returns. My maiden name riding on the whispers of guilt wakens me tonight. *Kathy Allen, Birth Mother. Kathy Allen, Unwed Mother.* A thick swamp of anguish presses into my chest and I think that I could steal into the darkened underworld if only I would just let go. In a display of victory, shame breathes in the shadows that dance and weave about the room, while its long, delicate fingers pick at my day's triumphs. It is a midnight juror and is here to remind me what I so carelessly ignore in the daylight: that I deserve all the punishment I am getting—for what I did and for what I did not do.

Father in heaven, please forgive me for what I have done and what I have failed to do. But God does not listen to that prayer, does He? Not in the dark, anyway. *I did not fight. I did not stand up for myself against the rapist.* And for this sin, the night crawler snorts, I am not a victim. I am a whore. And I can never be free.

It is not because I am ashamed that I rarely speak to our daughters about the particulars of this casualty in my life, and now in Phil's life. It is because I do not want them tainted by unnecessary evil looking always to lay down more roots. Vile details can rob thoughts and dreams. Our girls have lovely families and beautiful homes. They don't need to be cuffed with swill from the gutter. They have their own life's work to accomplish. Immersing them in mine would be beyond selfish; it would be immoral.

But Kristi has read the newspaper articles, and today as we are chatting on the phone, she asks me how I am doing. And there goes my willpower, bolting for the woods. And all that is tangled begins to untie. "It's just...it's just that she's taken everything from me, you know? My dignity. She's got mom-mom's actual words betraying me. She's taken that innocent note I wrote and used it against me. The whole Internet thing. The lies she's spread to who-knows-what relatives. Digging up old classmates, starting all that shit gossip again."

I know I am whining, that thread lines of pain are squeaking past my good-manners filter. And I want to stop, I do. But I don't. Or can't. "The only damn thing she hasn't stolen from me is my face." Suddenly I am crying unexpectedly, as if I just walked to the sink and tapped the spigot. *Stop*, I warn myself. *Don't say it. Don't say about the haunting, in the dark by the greensick light from the bedside clock, when the only sounds are soft snores and that dumb hound barking, chasing ghosts. And the pressing on my chest — down, down, to where I really live. Where I hide my corpse with the slashed wrists.* " I didn't fight," I whisper-cry to Kristi. "I didn't fight him. And I can never forgive myself."

Thirty-one miles separate us. Yet a flower as sweet as March waiting to bloom tends the spanning distance. Birthed from the frightening, tender secret of womanhood, bequeathed to every female, it is what girls come to understand when breasts bud and wiry hair sprouts in unseemly places. It is a special knowing. About the dark, wet place on her body from which she is born. The heart of pleasure, the root of love — or rescue. But with chilling, primal comprehension, she can point to that very spot — the extraordinary essence of her femininity — where she is most likely to be destroyed. Where I was destroyed. With an easy threat of a blade taken to moist skin. My moist skin. Plunged deep into hidden recesses. Where I cowered.

It is what Kristi understands as in the half-breathing moments of my low cries, she ushers in to my sadness a blossom of light I have been unable to see. "Mom, you have to ask yourself, would fighting have made any difference?" How is it that inside such a simple question, the soft gentle words of one woman to another, lives the mystery of healing? How can so few words radiate such glow into a hidden grave?

Would my fight have changed anything? Silently I shift back to *then*. What would have changed? Would I be standing in this room of brick and windows, looking out as March sways the pine trees in the last of winter's scrimmages? Deeply inhaling the intermingled scents of fruits and spices? Tooling about in size-two jeans? If instead I had taken *his* knife? In the murmurs between Kristi and me over the phone lines — which are no longer really lines but now signals, I suppose, while in the background thirty-some miles south, my little granddaughter shouts her demands — I hear the last door to hell slide shut.

It's been only hours since I talked to Kristi, and I'm floating around as if I've bathed in the waters of Fatima or Lourdes. Sites where the afflicted get...*poof!*...healed. Phil calls. What? Did I hear him say CBS news? Local from New York? Wants an interview? With me? And all that has been these last ten years sweeps to a gracious halt with a simple, crystallized question. *Do I speak? Yes or no?* It is Alice's dilemma at the crossroads in Wonderland: *Which way?* License plates that tell us *Do or die.* The rites that warn *Speak now or...*or what? Or keep your mouth shut and stop whining. Forever. Because this precise intersecting, this exact alignment of pain and repair, occurs once. One time. Get it? Once the opportunity passes, it does not return — not like this, wrapped in sheer perfection.

I may be damaged, but I'm not stupid. "Are you up to it?" Phil asks. "They'll film you in shadow." I let no daylight pass between his concern and my response. "Forget it," I tell him. "Let them film my damn face."

Monday, March 10, 2008: another day I say *yes*.

~ ~ ~

Tuesday, March 11, 2008. I am sobbing, sobbing, in such anguish that I am convulsing. Because of what happened yesterday. What I did yesterday. I call Phil because I don't know what to do with this sobbing. It won't stop. "Should I come home? Should I come home?" he asks. There is a tightness, the cop restraint in his voice that he uses only occasionally when something is in danger of spinning out of control. Like me. Right now.

I know he thinks I am sorry. That I am sobbing because I am sick that I plastered all of my shame, everything that I have clawed to keep hidden for over forty years, all over the place, worse than erecting a billboard along Route 206. But no, no. That's not it. I am sobbing so deeply, surely he cannot understand what I am saying. I can't catch my breath. What I say over and over again is, "I can't believe I'm free. I can't believe I'm free."

~ ~ ~

But today is Monday. I know nothing of tomorrow while we wait for the crew, the TV people coming to film me and my dirty story. Phil and I are looking out the window, watching. Can they find our house? When they turn onto our road, will they think, *Oh God, what if these people have chickens running around their kitchen?* They're New York City folks. What do they know about shacks camouflaged with rope netting and of Rottweilers roaming loose, looking for trouble? If they are relieved when they arrive, neither Kristine, the TV reporter, nor her cameraman shows it. But I bet they're glad they don't spot any chickens.

Kristine is barely finished shaking our hands and is removing her coat when I blurt, "Do not call me Birth Mother, Biological Mother, or anything to do with mother. And do not refer to the adoptee in any terms other than *adoptee.* Do you understand that? No familial terms. None."

What I learned from the *Philadelphia Inquirer* has stuck. I leave no terminology to chance. I will not permit anyone to degrade me with those slurs. Not ever again—not if I can help it.

"What shall we use?" she asks.

I want to demand that she refer to me as Biological Cunt. Do-you-hear-me? Let me spell it out. B-i-o-l-o-g-i-c-a-l C-u-n-t. Then I want her to jerk her head around to glance at the man behind her—his skin, burnt caramel; his eyes, friendly, the hue of deep earth—and ask her, just ask, "Would you call him a…a….?" But I can't summon forth that offense that's been stricken, erased from the mouths and wits of decent people.

Kristine seems kind of shocked already, so I say, "You can refer to me as just a woman. A rape victim. If you must, Biological Source, female, Biological Carrier—whatever. But not, under any circumstances, Birth Mother or Biological Mother. And do not dare use the term *daughter* anywhere in your report."

And my anger that seems to be from out of nowhere but is always from the same somewhere pulses raw in my veins like a thriving, living beast, and now I want to shriek, *You don't force motherhood on a girl who was raped. Why can't anyone understand this?*

And oh, how I want to turn to the camera and shout at that damn lunatic adoptee as she stares into the screen. That woman of vain sorrows as she sucks in minute details of the only thing she has not managed to steal: my face, the face she has been stalking for ten years. I want to shout at her as she scrutinizes every wrinkle, records each feature — nose, eyes, lips, *mmmmm*, hair color from a bottle, huh — and compares all against herself, her kids, as she balances and contrasts the entirety of me and extorts from these few seconds of television broadcast every distorted wonder she has been searching for. Slurping in the final prize that she believes will finally make her life whole and complete. Because without me as her trophy, apparently she is nobody.

I want to bellow into the frightening vastness where life begins and ends, where all of us are born or murdered. Or healed. Bellow until my head explodes into ragged fragments of pain and blood-splattered exhaustion. *I'm not your goddamn mother! I'm just a girl who was raped.* Then take a breath. And try again. Civilly. *Just a girl who was raped.*

We chitchat for a few moments, Phil and Kristine and I. About scents, the cinnamon and apple that wafts through this room of windows and brick. What I don't mention is how far removed this sweet-spiced fragrance is from the soured tang of sweat in dank, unholy places. Kristine marvels at the expanse that looks out into the woods, our woods. Am I afraid to be here alone? she asks. No, I answer, thinking that what I should be afraid of is what I am about to do.

Why am I not? Why? But I'm not. The cameraman clips a battery pack and a tiny microphone on me. I should be afraid. Where's my fear? He fusses for a second or two and seats me on our sofa. I insist Phil sit next to me. And he does, sliding his hand into mine, quietly. Kristine sits in a dining-room chair across from us, a handsome black-painted Windsor pulled around for just the occasion of my debut. But I am not a debutante, and there is nothing elegant about this dive I am about to make into the blackest part of my past.

Kristine fluffs her hair, then looks at me. Phil squeezes my hand, lightly. And I know he is breathing with me, for me. Pacing me up the mountain. Calmly. Kristine signals the cameraman, and he flicks on instant garish light, artificial sunshine manufactured right here in our living room. It is bright enough to bare the gray grabbing at my roots, to flaunt every misstroke of lipstick. A riot of light exposing me. In all my shame. And failures.

Kristine says, "Tell me your story." Phil's hand is warm, covering mine. The light is brilliant, shining in my eyes. I look up at Kristine. I begin to weep. So softly it is as if silk petals slide down my cheeks.

~ ~ ~

Tuesday. I sit down to e-mail our daughters. I just hung up with Phil, and my voice is gagged still, low in my throat. It promises no more than the guttural cries of a tortured animal, should I try to speak. But I want them to know I am OK; I know they will worry. So I begin typing: *Hi. I'm fine.* When suddenly I erupt into sobs so fierce that I double over in spasms until I think I am going to tumble onto the floor. Oh my God, I can't stop sobbing. I'm breaking apart, cracking wide open. Going insane.

I bolt from the chair and into the room of brick and windows. I try to yank myself back into sense, grasping at the pieces ripping away. My arms, tight around my waist, clutch at imaginary seams. Willing myself back together, I stare into the trees, trying, trying to inhale their peaceful sway against the March winds. *Look at the clouds. What are they, cumulus? Bumbling along like that, there through the sky, pearly white framed in blue. The brightest blue. Look how beautiful.*

But I can't pull myself away from these great sobs. They are heavings from a ruptured, barren landscape. Then, with no warning, my legs cave and I topple down in a disarray of bones and limp, spongy flesh. Whispering thuds and thumps onto the gold, sculpted carpet. In a muffled collapse of aging female. To the floor.

I am seized by a keening. A wailing heard only at the funerals of… children. It is so violent that it wrenches every pinch of breath from my lungs and boomerangs in this huge space like brays echoing from a madhouse. I hear then high-pitched squeals. Keening as I have heard only once before — a lone figure huddled on the charred wasteland of lost — as my mother stands miles away, demanding my confession. How many times did I fuck? *How many?* A naked girl wailing from far, far away. From her hiding place. In the dark.

I am on the floor, wailing, wailing, and I don't know what is happening. All this howling. Of a child. Of a woman shattering. I have to stop this. Right now. Or I will be carted off. Injected with drugs. Medically rearranged until I am but an imitation of my former self. Because by the time Phil gets home and shuttles me off to the asylum, only unrecognizable bits and pieces will be left. Too small to reassemble in any kind of proper order. Destroyed beyond repair.

But this anguished howling, somehow unleashed, will not cease. Maybe I am destined to spend the rest of my life cinched tight inside a straightjacket because nothing else will hold me together. This is what it is like to fall off the cliff and smash into the rocks. But…but…I realize I am not falling down. No. While churning inside this maelstrom of noise and insanity, I am jetting upward, my loosed pieces shooting into the light. Rising, unfolding, twinkling in the radiance.

Me. The little girl, the shy teenager, the frightened woman, screaming from the agony of running. Constant running and hiding, racing a lifetime through the dark, with footsteps chasing so close that the clicks echo in the hollowness left by fear. And in the distance, the faint slap, slap of hardened leather in relentless pursuit. Then the stall of all sound. Forbidding and unnatural. Pausing. Waiting. Me straining. Listening. Because *it* is always nearby, ready to pounce, to rage from the dark. Always.

Keep running! Hide! Hide! Go! Go!

Then yesterday. Unchained by the might of my own hands. Me, buoyant, floating into the light. Such sweet, glistening light.

But here, now, this delirium of wheezing and bawling. And a phantom clawing at my insides, clinging, begging. I hear its screams within my own: *Don't let me go. Don't send me back into the dark.* I am trembling with dread; so petrified of it; to look at it. It is so vile, so filthy. I cringe and recoil; shame and revulsion thrash somewhere deep inside to rise like vomit. *Go away!* I want to scream. *Don't make me look!*

Despite my hysteria, beneath my skin, suddenly I freeze. It is not an *it*. It is a *her. And I see her.* I cannot breathe. I cannot breathe. Yet I am sobbing.

Panting. A dead woman gawking into the waters that are keeping her afloat. *I see her. Oh Jesus, I see her.* But she's just a young girl. Stricken with panic. And grief. And abject terror.

And I realize, *Oh my God, it's me.* It *is* me. The annihilated me. It is Kathy Allen. Through this apparition that seems both mystical and invented, I force myself to stare at Kathy Allen. Kathy Allen, the girl I despise. I am sobbing as I gape at her nakedness, at the raw shame that has scalded her tender skin red with its merciless, unrelenting slapping, has shackled her wrists to her ankles. Kathy Allen trying to save herself with a smile. I do not know now whether I am sobbing in fear or sorrow. For my entire life, I believed Kathy Allen was the villain. An unforgivable sinner. A pig. An easy lay. Swirling in the gutter when other girls — good, pretty girls — wore strands of pearls and patent-leather shoes. And studied ballet.

But what I am staring at is not a dirty whore. She is merely a child. So broken. Kathy Allen looking up at me, pleading. And I can hardly bear her anguish. And my own. Because in her eyes, I see the kindness of our daughters. The innocence of our granddaughters. In her eyes, I finally see what was done to her.

I am hunched over on the floor and cannot tell whether my eyes are propped open with fear or swollen shut from crying. I cannot describe the light I see. Or don't see. Can only tell what it seems. Maybe I am having a hallucination or am daydreaming. Or creating something spiritual with the powers of my bold imagination. I have no answers as I watch from my post curled up within this volcano of the extraordinary.

Do you know of the times when light slumbers overhead, suspended horizon to horizon, and lazes there just for the pleasure of glowing? When even moist, rich soil tilled fresh for the garden looks bleached under the afternoon's brilliance? And all sounds halt, awaiting exhale?

I watch her running through this dream of glow and silence. Unsure whether she is a frightened child or a panicked woman. Faltering, striding down the path spilling out far ahead of her. Perhaps she's both in her unending, lickety-split rush to escape what chases her. Yes, I think now she is both.

I swear I do not construct in my mind the sharp left that the path takes so abruptly. I only follow her startled gaze as she shifts her attention away from her noiseless footfalls angling the corner. In an instant, I see what has caught her eyes. At the path's end, a figure waits. I can tell you right away, it's not Jesus. Or God. Then again, maybe I'm wrong. Maybe it is. I simply see, as she must, an outline. An impression of a man, the slant of the light lending a broadness to his silhouette. He is straining, reaching, seems desperate to leap onto the path, to dash forward, but seems to know he cannot; he must not. I watch him gesturing, calling for her, mouthing encouragement, willing her forward. Words she seems to hear as she races faster, running now toward instead of away. When she gropes for his outstretched hands and he lunges forward to catch her, the silence breathes and I hear him whisper, *You're safe. You're safe now.*

~ ~ ~

It is Monday, March 10, 2008. I know this because I looked at the calendar earlier when Phil called and asked if I would be up to an interview with the news station. I don't know why I was gazing at the calendar when I said yes. But I know this day, March 10. Kristine is looking at me, waiting. I take a breath. Glance quickly out the window and back to her. I am nervous, but I am not afraid. Phil sits so quietly next to me. Patient. Holding my hand. My heart slams inside my chest, pumping, pumping. And then I speak into the microphone, clearly. I speak louder than my fear.

"I thought I could help him," I begin. "He raped me on mattresses you would not let a dog sleep on."

I say this into the light. And suddenly, miraculously, I am free.

~ THE END ~

VISUAL NARRATIVES

14 BEAUMONT ROAD

Kathleen Hoy Foley
Colored Pencil Drawing w/ Mixed Media Collage
20" x 30"

JACKIE

Kathleen Hoy Foley
Pencil Drawing and Collage
15" x 22"

‽

RAPE – A LIFE SENTENCE

‽

Kathleen Hoy Foley
Mixed Media Collage
21" x 32

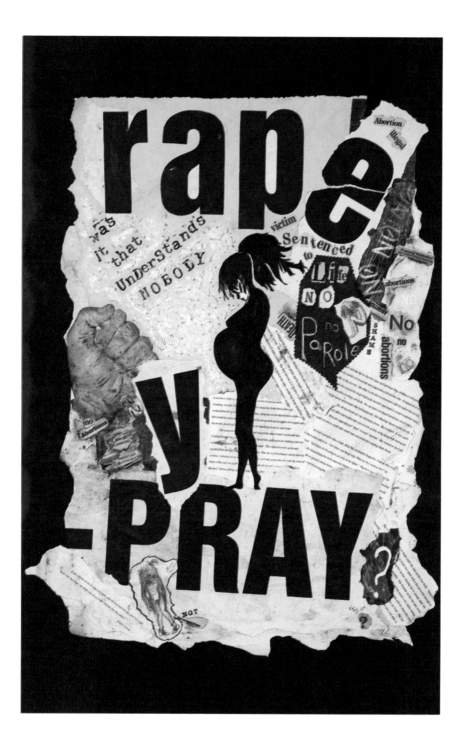

ANIMUS FORWARD

Kathleen Hoy Foley
Mixed Media Drawing and Collage
11" x 14"

FORCED TO BREED

Kathleen Hoy Foley
Mixed Media Collage w/ Found Papers and Found Objects
30" x 40"

BLOOD & BARBED WIRE

Kathleen Hoy Foley
Mixed Media Collage w/ Found Papers and Found Objects
36" x 48"

LAST WORDS

CRAVEN FAIREST

by Kathleen Hoy Foley

Craven Fairest trumpets: *she's just not over it........yet*

from her perch upon the dead body of her christ.

Celebrates every rape

that begets honor to her god.

Pillages from every butchered girl. Every mutilated woman.

ANGER.

RAGE.

Casts off all bloodied females. young. old.

Ridicules torn she-spirits

that dare curse

the sanctity of feminine rupture.

Craven Fairest,

with her pretty white legs

steps over the conquered graves of silent cunts.

Her own fairest cunt glorified. Consecrated. by her god.

And chants her myth: *she's just not over it.....yet.*

Then grins. And eagerly awaits

obedient smiles from executed women.

ACKNOWLEDGEMENTS

There's nothing else like a good old fashioned, socially unacceptable plight for revealing the truth living in a person's heart. I am intensely grateful for all the hearts of courage that have reached out to Phil and me.

I could never have withstood this ordeal without my husband, Phil's, unwavering love and unflinching support and his junkyard dog determination to get this story told. His belief in the truth and his ability to embrace it — even in all its ugliness, with all its brutal ways of expression — has shown me God.

The loyalty of our daughters, Kelly and Kristi, and the grace and dignity they have shown since that devastating invasion into our family have given me enormous comfort and the self-assurance to continue being *just Mom*.

It takes a mystical alignment of events that I don't understand for a dead brother to come calling and linger about until his voice is heard loud and clear. I am astonished and humbled that my brother Jackie's broken spirit found a way to create miracles.

Dr. Gayle Wurst's enthusiasm to lend her literary credentials to champion the merits of my manuscript, her protective sensitivity and unfailing conviction that my tale — deemed too unfit for telling in proper circles — needed to be told, opened a possibility in my life I never believed available to me. Since the moment I first clutched a No. 2 pencil in my fist and scratched bold letters onto yellow lined paper, I have longed to be a real and true writer. Gayle pronounced me...me!...a writer. How do you thank someone for that?

I am in awe of my first readers, Rebecca and Sue, women I do not even know personally but who responded to my story with deep compassion and support and many, many acts of unexpected thoughtfulness.

I am deeply grateful to our Web designer, Mark; our printer Michael who went far beyond professional expectations and supported us publicly; our book designers, Liz and Bob; Dina, our copy editor; our photographer, Bryan. Their willingness to work their specialized magic despite the explicit